Bikepacking South East Gravel

The Cantii Way and 11 long-weekend bikepacking adventures

By Ed Hunton

JUNIPER HOUSE, MURLEY MOSS,
OXENHOLME ROAD, KENDAL, CUMBRIA LA9 7RL
www.cicerone.co.uk

© Ed Hunton 2025
First edition 2025
ISBN: 978 1 78631 237 2
eISBN: 978 1 78765 166 1

Printed in the UK by 4edge using responsibly sourced paper.
A catalogue record for this book is available from the British Library.
All photographs are by the author unless otherwise stated.

 Route mapping by Lovell Johns www.lovelljohns.com

© Crown copyright 2025 OS AC0000810376. NASA relief data courtesy of ESRI

The Cantii Way © 2025 Cyclists Touring Club trading as Cycling UK™. All rights reserved

Cicerone's EU representative for GPSR compliance is Easy Access System Europe, Mustamäe tee 50, 10621 Tallinn, Estonia. Email gpsr.requests@easproject.com.

For John Spurr

Updates to this guide

While every effort is made by our authors to ensure the accuracy of guidebooks as they go to print, changes can occur during the lifetime of an edition. Any updates that we know of for this guide will be on the Cicerone website (www.cicerone.co.uk/1237/updates), so please check before planning your trip. We also advise that you check information about such things as transport, accommodation and shops locally. Even rights of way can be altered over time. We are always grateful for information about any discrepancies between a guidebook and the facts on the ground, sent by email to updates@cicerone.co.uk.

Register your book: To sign up to receive free updates, special offers and GPX files where available, create a Cicerone account and register your purchase via the 'My Account' tab at www.cicerone.co.uk.

Front cover: Heathland outside Dunwich (Route 11)

Contents

Map key 4
Route summary table 6

Introduction   9

What is bikepacking?. 9
Gravel riding 10
Getting there and around 10
Choosing a route 10
Rights of way 12
Navigation 12
Accommodation. 13
What to take 14
Fuel strategies. 14
Using this guide 15

The rides   19

Route 1   The New Forest: From the Forest to the Sea 20
Route 2   Isle of Wight: Ticket to Ryde 33
Route 3   Surrey Hills: A Tower, a Temple and a Punch Bowl. 49
Route 4   Chiltern Hills: The Chilterns Off-Road Cycleway . . 65
Route 5   Kent Downs: Come on Pilgrim 79
Route 6   East Sussex/Kent: High Weald Drifter 89
Route 7   Kent/Sussex Coast: Battle Cruiser 104
Route 8   Kent: The Cantii Way. 112
Route 9   London/Essex: The Only Way 134
Route 10 Essex/Suffolk: Stour Valley Villages 149
Route 11 Suffolk Coast: Three Ferries and a Power Station 162
Route 12 Norfolk: North Norfolk Ways. 175

Appendix A   Accommodation. 190
Appendix B   Bike shops 204
Appendix C   Recommended kit lists 210

Symbols used on route maps

~	route	—•—	station/railway line
---	off-road section	⚓	ferry
▶	route direction	▲	hostel
🚴	start point	Ⓐ	campsite
🚴	finish point	Ⓞ	self-catering/glamping
🚴	start/finish point	⊙	bike shop
🚴	alternative start point	ⓘ	refreshments available
🚴	alternative finish point	●	all amenities
🚴	alternative start/finish point	**18**	waypoint number
>	steep ascent	ⓜ	castle
>>	very steep ascent		

SCALE: 1:150,000

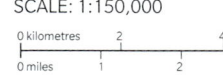

Contour lines are drawn at 50m intervals and labelled at 100m intervals. Route maps are drawn at 1:150,000 (1cm = 1.5km)

GPX files for all routes can be downloaded free at www.cicerone.co.uk/1237/GPX.

Features on the overview map

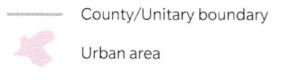
County/Unitary boundary

Urban area

National Park
eg **THE NEW FORESTT**

National Landscape
(formerly Area of Outstanding
Natural Beauty) eg *Norfolk Coast*

The prehistoric Icknield Way (Route 4)

Route summary table

	Route	Start/Finish	Time	Total distance
1	The New Forest – From the Forest to the Sea	Brockenhurst, Railway Station	2–3 days	167km (103.8 miles)
2	Isle of Wight – Ticket to Ryde	Ryde Pier, Ferry Terminus/ Railway Station	2–3 days	135km (84 miles)
3	Surrey Hills – A Tower, a Temple and a Punch Bowl	Godalming, Railway Station	2–3 days	132km (82 miles)
4	Chiltern Hills – The Chilterns Off-Road Cycleway	Wendover, Railway Station	2–3 days	133km (82.7 miles)
5	Kent Downs – Come on Pilgrim	Otford, Railway Station	1–2 days	76.2km (47.5 miles)
6	East Sussex/Kent – High Weald Drifter	Eridge, Railway Station	2–3 days	159km (99 miles)
7	Kent/Sussex Coast – Battle Cruiser	Battle, Railway Station	1–2 days	69.4km (43.3 miles)
8	Kent – The Cantii Way	Wye, Railway Station	2–5 days	249km (154.7 miles)
9	London/Essex – The Only Way	Chingford, Railway Station	2–3 days	148km (92 miles)
10	Essex/Suffolk – Stour Valley Villages	Manningtree, Railway Station	2–3 days	144km (89.5 miles)
11	Suffolk Coast – Three Ferries and a Power Station	Felixstowe, Railway Station / Beccles, Railway Station	2–3 days	109km (67.8 miles)
12	Norfolk – North Norfolk Ways	Diss, Railway Station / Sheringham, Railway Station	2–3 days	179km (111.2 miles)

Acknowledgements

A massive thank you goes to all the bikepackers who helped me research this guidebook: my partner Nicky Stoupe, Kieron Chissik, Norman Poole, Tim Brocklehurst, Nick Bowden, Clare Piconne and Marc Mathison. Special thanks to Luke Morris, who helped me design Route 9 and gave permission to use one of his great photos, and to Tim Wiggins, accomplished author, rider and trailfinder, for kindly donating Route 2.

Route summary table

Off-road distance	% off-road	Ascent/ Descent	Grade	Way type (singletrack, track, road)	Bike choice	Page
77.7km	46%	1220m	■/Easy	23%, 23%, 54%	Gravel	20
74.3km	55%	2090m	▲/Moderate	4%, 51%, 45%	Gravel	33
93.5km	71%	2050m	▲/Moderate	49%, 22%, 29%	Gravel/MTB	49
74.8km	56%	2210m	●/Difficult	39%, 17%, 44%	Gravel/MTB	65
28.9km	38%	1050m	▲/Moderate	23%, 15%, 62%	Gravel/MTB	79
69km	44%	2320m	▲/Moderate	21%, 23%, 56%	Gravel/MTB	89
29.2km	42%	730m	■/Easy	7%, 35%, 58%	Gravel/MTB	104
127.9km	51%	1400m	■/Easy	6%, 45%, 49%	Gravel/Hybrid	112
71km	48%	1020m	■/Easy	16%, 32%, 52%	Gravel	134
26.9km	19%	1040m	■/Easy	5%, 14%, 81%	Gravel	149
38.8km	36%	470m/480m	▲/Moderate	13%, 23%, 64%	Gravel	162
52.8km	30%	1190m/1200m	■/Easy	3%, 27%, 70%	Gravel	175

Safety and emergencies

Carry a charged mobile phone and backup power sources. In case of serious injury, call 999 with your location (grid reference or W3W) and phone number. Bring a spare head torch, and ensure your sleeping bag suits the overnight temperature. Don't rely solely on a single mobile phone; it can easily become the single point of failure.

A gentle section of the Greensand Way (Route 3)

Introduction

The start of a stunning descent on the Serpent Trail after leaving the Temple of the Winds (Route 3)

Long before the Roman invasion in AD43, England's most populous region, the south-east, was already a thriving hub for habitation, trade and industry. Although it may not be the first place you think of for bikepacking, it offers plenty of opportunities for adventurous riders within a short train ride from many urban centres. Bordered by two chalk uplands, it boasts three National Parks, seven National Landscapes (formerly Areas of Outstanding Natural Beauty, AONB) and over half a dozen Royal Forests, and is home to four of the UK's ten richest biodiversity areas.

This guide distils a decade of exploring the wildest places in the south-east in search of bikepacking adventures and epic gravel rides. For those short of time, some routes can be completed in a day or a day and a half, providing a wild adventure without taking up a whole weekend or cutting into your annual leave. If you only have a single day to play with, the Big Gravel Days are suggestions for a long day out on the bike: without the extra kit, you can travel light and bust out some miles in the wildest terrain in the south-east.

What is bikepacking?

Bikepacking, much like backpacking, involves multi-day journeys where you'll need to carry gear for comfort when you're off the bike (see

Refreshments at Orford (Route 11)

Appendix C for kit lists). Essential items include a tent or bivvy bag, a sleeping bag, and food – along with a way to prepare it, if needed.

Unlike cycle touring, which typically sticks to paved roads, bikepacking takes you off-road. While you might occasionally ride on roads or stay in a B&B or YHA, bikepacking is mainly about exploring wild places and camping along the way – on two wheels.

Gravel riding

Gravel is a style of riding that covers everything in between road cycling and mountain biking: farm tracks, bridleways, green lanes, gravel drives, canal paths, forest tracks and forgotten rights of way. The advantage is you are immersed in the landscape, away from the traffic and on your own peaceful journey into unfamiliar territory.

Getting there and around

This guide covers an area stretching from the New Forest in the west to the Kent coast in the east, and from the Norfolk Broads in the north to the Isle of Wight in the south. The guide emphasises using the area's extensive rail network, which offers a faster and more sustainable alternative to its often congested roads. If you only have 1 day of riding time the density of railway stations provides flexibility for where you start and finish the route. If travelling by train, some operators require advance bike reservations.

If driving to a circular route, try parking on a suburban street (respecting driveways and restrictions) or in a long-stay car park for affordability.

Choosing a route

The main factors influencing route choice are time, difficulty, weather

Choosing a route

and access to the start point. All the rides in this guide begin and end at railway stations or, in the case of Ticket to Ryde (Route 2), a ferry terminus, so journey time will affect your route choice. Except for the Cantii Way (Route 8), these routes are meant to be ridden over two to three days, although Battle Cruiser (Route 7) and Come on Pilgrim (Route 5) can be completed in a day.

When to go

The south-east generally has milder weather, even in winter, but seasonal timing still matters when choosing a route.

In summer and during school holidays, leisure infrastructure can be stretched, so book campsites in advance. Wild camping is an option, but choices can be limited and discretion is key. Spring and autumn offer mild weather and fewer crowds, making them ideal. Winter has its own charm, with quieter trails, although many trails will be churned up with mud and there's less daylight. Tighter planning is crucial, as longer rides may take more time than expected.

Choice of bike

The south-east is hilly but not mountainous. All routes are gravel-bike-friendly; while a mountain bike might be fun for some sections, it can be overkill and could slow you down. Check the information box at the start of each route for recommended bikes.

Regardless of your bike, ensure it has been recently serviced, and carry tools for basic repairs, inner tubes, lights and other essentials. Bike shops are listed in Appendix B.

Family bikepacking

Three routes in this guide are suitable for children aged 10 and up. Stour Valley Villages (Route 10) can be shortened, and closely follows

Follow the River Yar to the coast (Route 2)

Introduction

family-friendly campsites. The same applies to Three Ferries and a Power Station (Route 11). Although it's the longest ride in the guide, the Cantii Way (Route 8) predominantly follows the coast on esplanades and can be easily adapted for younger bikepackers.

Route challenges
All these routes are challenging. However, some are more suitable for beginners. If you are new to bikepacking, Three Ferries and a Power Station (Route 11) and Stour Valley Villages (Route 10) are good choices. Three Ferries, North Norfolk Ways (Route 12) and The Only Way (Route 9) are stunning but with limited climbing.

Rights of way
Riders are permitted to use bridleways, cycleways, green lanes and permissive bridleways. You are not permitted to ride on footpaths.

The National Cycle Network
Managed by Sustrans UK, this network of numbered routes (labelled 'NCN' in this book) is a great resource. The routes in this guide often take advantage of them to link sections of off-road cycling. They tend to be relatively quiet and are often picturesque.

Navigation
We provide GPX files for each route that can be loaded onto a bike computer or smartphone navigation apps.

However, don't rely solely on one device. GPS units can fail, especially in cold weather (keep them warm in a pocket, if necessary), and phones can run out of battery. Carry a power bank (or two), and consider a physical map and compass as backups.

A wild camp on Pitch Hill (Route 3)

Accommodation

Wild camping for the entire trip is an option, but it's not mandatory. The goal is to enjoy the routes, whether solo or with others. The south-east offers diverse accommodation: campsites, shepherds' huts, glamping pods, hostels, B&Bs and even luxury spa hotels. Your choice will depend on factors such as weather, your group's experience, budget and flexibility. If poor weather is expected, consider delaying, booking accommodation in advance or preparing accordingly. Mixing accommodation types can be a practical solution – wild-camp one night, stay in a B&B or campsite the next, or opt for a hotel to dry your gear and enjoy a hot meal.

Wild camping in the south-east

The south-east is busy in summer. It is also a densely populous area, with many people depending on it for their livelihoods and their leisure. When you intend to wild-camp here, plan your ride so that you will be in more remote locations as the day ends. One reliable strategy is to study the map beforehand, looking for bridleways that lead onto common land near where you expect to finish that day. Often, following these can lead you to good locations for a night's kip.

Wild camping

This is defined as camping anywhere that isn't a licensed campsite. Although technically illegal in much of England, it is widely tolerated on open access land, providing you adhere to the following rules and guidelines:

- Camp high and away from settlements. Where possible, head uphill, away from paths and buildings.
- Respect the privacy of others.
- Do not interfere with livestock.
- Camp late and leave early. As the day's riding comes to an end, begin keeping your eye out for good spots so that you can camp before it is dark. In the morning, pack up your tent or bivvy before breakfast and get back on the road straight away.
- To avoid disturbing the environment and your neighbours, only wild-camp solo or in small groups.
- Bury human waste at least 10 inches deep with your shovel. Do not pollute any water courses. Take toilet paper and wipes home.
- Leave no trace. Take all litter home.
- Do not light an open fire.

Introduction

What to take

There are a few factors affecting your choice of kit, not least the weather, where you plan to sleep and what you are going to do for food. See Appendix C for recommended essential and extended kit lists (the latter with additional items for out-of-season or fully self-supported trips).

Fast and light

All of these routes include off-road sections and some are hilly, and you'll be hauling your gear over rough terrain. Pack light, consider the conditions and allow a margin for error based on the weather forecast. Choose the lightest gear that suits the conditions – don't bring a summer sleeping bag if it's going to be minus 1°C, or a tarp if heavy rain is expected. The lighter your load, the more comfortable your ride. Evaluate each item for necessity, and opt for tried-and-tested gear.

A word on fabrics: if you are planning multiple nights' camping outside of the summer months, merino wool is a good choice for base layers as it is very warm, has great wicking properties and is relatively odourless. For shorter summer rides, you might prefer synthetic mesh materials for wicking and comfort.

Fuel strategies

Bikepacking is physically demanding, especially off-road for multiple

Coffee is served

days. Consider how self-supported you and your group will be. Ensure everyone agrees on food expectations or acknowledges differences before starting. Sometimes, choices may be limited.

Plan before setting out and give yourself options.

Bringing your own food

Weight and packability are crucial. Try to avoid 'cooking', especially complex meals such as fried breakfasts or stews. Opt for foods that don't need heating, such as oat cakes, cheese, chorizo and fruit. For reheating, consider boil-in-the-bag meals, canned beans or dehydrated foods. Dehydrated meals are lightweight, have a long shelf life and only require boiling water and some insulation (like a sleeping bag) to rehydrate. You can prepare these yourself or buy from speciality suppliers.

Rely on local infrastructure

A pub lunch is often well deserved, or plan to visit a Co-op near the end of your first day's ride to pick up supplies and lighten your load (a micro-rucksack is useful). You can also arrive at a pub before they stop serving (phone ahead and check), enjoy dinner and then bivvy under the stars.

Hybrid model

Mix it up by bringing your own breakfast, such as overnight oats or granola with milk powder, and a few portions of dehydrated food as a backup. Take advantage of opportunities to visit excellent country inns throughout the south-east.

Snacks

Dried fruit, nuts, cereal bars and protein bars are commercially available or can be made in advance.

Hydration

The importance of keeping hydrated cannot be understated. Take any opportunity to refill your water bottles. There is no need to carry large quantities of water as there are countless streams to refill from and you can use a water filter (eg Sawyer® Micro™). Consider adding electrolyte powder to improve hydration, but remember to keep some free of flavouring if you plan to use it to make coffee or hydrate food!

Using this guide

Approach these rides knowing your limits and decide when, or if, to push them. Consider difficulty, timing, weather and route conditions. Use the route profile for guidance on when to refuel or rest. Plan accommodation in advance or be prepared to adjust on the go (campsites and hostels are listed in Appendix A, along with recommended areas for wild camping).

We offer alternative schedules ranging from one to five days, depending on your pace and daily distance. Alternative start/finish points are provided as suggestions – adjust the schedule and sequence of waypoints

Introduction

accordingly if you choose to use them. The shortcuts and extensions should be treated in the same way.

Route components

Each route has the following components:

- **Information box**: the first place to look when choosing a route, providing details of start/finish, time, distance, ascent/descent, grade (based on the hardest stage), terrain and bike choice.

- **Introduction**: a brief description of the merits and features of the route.

- **Route options**: alternative start/finish options, shortcuts and extensions, Big Gravel Day suggestions.

- **Summary table**: key details of each numbered stage of the route, including distance, ascent/descent, surface and grade. The stages are logical blocks within a route, but are not necessarily equal in length – they correlate more closely to terrain or refuelling and rest options.

- **Profile**: useful for strategising, since it shows refuelling and camping opportunities, access points, railway stations, bike shops, and alternative schedules.

- **Turn-by-turn directions**: the main component of each route, which you can follow alongside the inline map if you need to rely on the guide rather than the GPX on a device. We suggest that you read these detailed directions before choosing a route, so that you are aware in advance of any shortcuts or challenges. Direction arrows indicate left (←), right (→) and straight ahead (↑).

Boarding the ferry from Felixstowe to Bawdsey (Route 11; photo: Luke Morris)

Heading toward Hastings from Battle (Route 7)

1 — 46% off road

Route 1 – The New Forest

From the Forest to the Sea

Start/Finish	Brockenhurst, Railway Station
Time	2–3 days
Total distance	167km (103.8 miles)
Off-road distance	77.7km
Percentage off-road	46%
Total ascent/descent	1220m
Grade	Easy ■
Terrain	Singletrack 23%, track 23%, road 54%
Bike choice	Gravel

The New Forest is a unique landscape, where huge tracts of heathland and deciduous and coniferous woodland are criss-crossed by cycle paths. The area teems with wildlife: at dusk, any of the park's five species of deer could be spotted within metres of the route, and in spring the air is filled with the call of cuckoos.

Forestry England maintains fantastic cycle paths, and the off-road riding is restricted to these. Stick to these designated cycle paths and the going is firm year-round. Outside of the central area, there are some great bridleways and byways, and this route also takes full advantage of these. If you have plenty in the tank, take on the loop east of Beaulieu, visiting Henry VIII's Calshot Castle and the beautiful Lepe Country Park. Don't forget to take a dip in the Solent at Tanners Lane.

Directions

1 ■ Turn → out of the ticket office along Station Approach and cross the level crossing onto Lymington Road. Turn ← onto Mill Lane. After 200m, on a left-hand bend, turn → onto a car-wide gravel track. On regaining the road,

From the Forest to the Sea

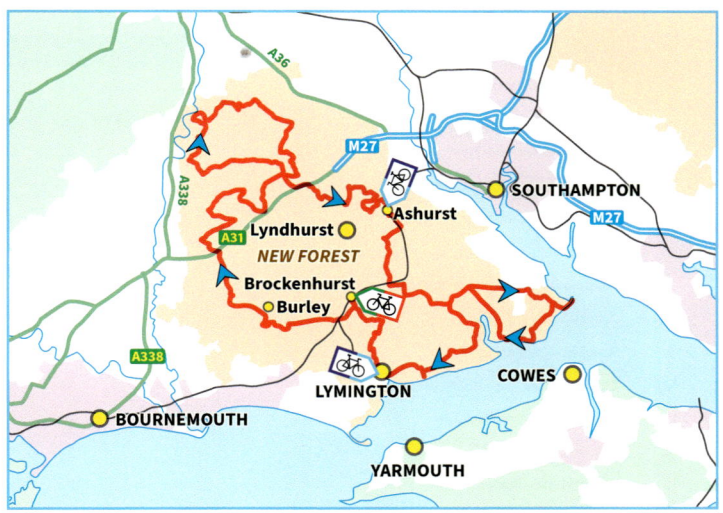

Route options

Alternative start/finish: You could start at Ashurst, two train stops before Brockenhurst: camp at the Ashurst Campsite the evening before and start at Stage 8. Lymington Station would also make a viable start/finish location, starting at Stage 14. Thanks to the gentle gradients, the route lends itself to being reversed.

Shortcuts and extensions: For a shorter version, remove either the northern or the eastern loop, or both. For example, ride Stages 1–3 and then Stages 7 and 8, then jump to Stage 13 and complete. The central circuit is 102km in length, the northern loop is 36km and the eastern one is 29km.

Big Gravel Days: With only a single day to play with, a great loop would be from Brockenhurst to Ashurst at 59km (Stages 1–3 plus Stage 7). Another great day ride, at around 70km, would involve following the B3055 to Beaulieu from Brockenhurst and riding Stages 9–14.

turn ← and bear → on Church Lane. Continue over the junction onto Tilebarn Lane. At the junction, turn →. After heading under the railway bridge, fork → onto a repurposed railway line, NWP 217 (Numbered Waymarker Post).

Route 1 – The New Forest

Summary table

Waypoint	Section	Distance (km)	Ascent (m)	Descent (m)
1	Brockenhurst Station – Burley	16.5	120	80
2	Burley – Linwood	12.7	150	140
3	Linwood – Janesmoor Plain	12	130	60
4	Janesmoor Plain – Woodgreen	15.7	130	200
5	Woodgreen – Nomansland	11.7	140	90
6	Nomansland – Janesmoor Plain	8.7	80	60
7	Janesmoor Plain – Ashurst Campsite	18	80	160
8	Ashurst Campsite – Beaulieu	15.6	90	120
9	Beaulieu – Calshot Castle	11.9	50	50
10	Calshot Castle – Lepe Country Park	6.8	30	30
11	Lepe Country Park – Beaulieu	10.5	60	70
12	Beaulieu – Tanners Lane	12.1	50	70
13	Tanners Lane – Boldre	8	40	30
14	Boldre – Brockenhurst Station	6.8	70	60

Continue for 4km before the track curves left to a road. Turn ←, and after 300m turn → onto a sand drive (NWP 181). Follow this good gravel path through the woods. After 1.5km, at a junction in the track, fork → and then continue to the perimeter of the wood. Walk your bike on a path for the final 100m to the road, turn → and descend for 600m. With a house on your left, turn ← onto the old railway line cycle path once more. Follow this for 3km to the road, turn → and head **towards Burley**. If you are camping at the YHA in Burley, continue into town, turn right at the Queens Head pub and follow signs from there.

2 ■ With a small green on your left, take a sharp ← onto Castle Hill Lane and follow it for 2km through the wood to the road. Take the second of the two lefts, signed 'Picket Post, Ringwood'. After 2km, fork → through the underpass beneath the busy A31. Bear ← and continue to the road; turn →. As the road bears left, fork → and make a shallow climb to the junction. Here, turn → and take NWP 71 for 3km before taking a sharp ← at NWP 61. When you reach the road, turn ← towards **Linwood**.

From the Forest to the Sea

Surface	Grade	Description
mixed	🟩	A short hop from the station onto a perfect cycleway
mixed	🟩	An easy climb through ancient woodland
mixed	🟩	A short off-road section leads to a minor road over open heath
mixed	🟩	Leave the heart of the heath on a good cycleway and head west
mixed	🔺	The landscape changes on bridleways through the woods
mixed	🔺	Head south on minor roads before returning to the forest
mixed	🟩	Fantastic sweeping forestry track
mixed	🟩	Woodland singletrack leads to a short section where walking is required
mixed	🟩	The most easterly point: Calshot Castle
mixed	🟩	Pretty back roads lead to a coastal gem
paved	n/a	Return to Beaulieu on quiet back roads
paved	n/a	Minor roads past historic naval hard and the chance to dip in the sea
mixed	🟩	Easy lanes and singletrack along the riverbank
mixed	🔺	The sting in the tail of an otherwise mellow tour!

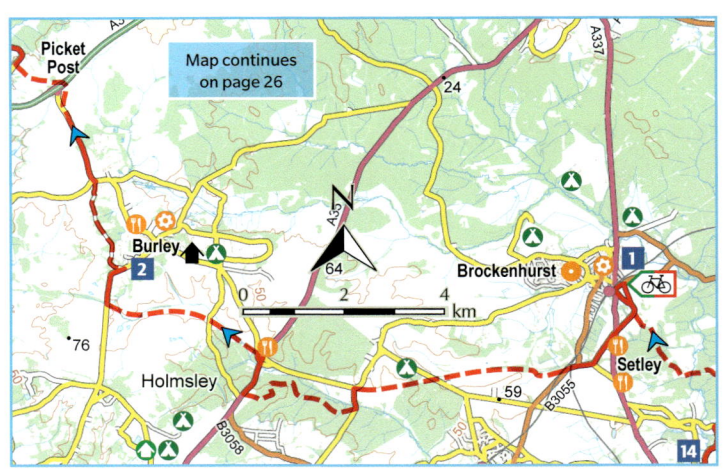

Route 1 – The New Forest

		Brockenhurst Station to Woodgreen
3 DAYS		*56.9km* *530m ascent*

		Brockenhurst Station to Ashurst Campsite
2 DAYS		*95.3km* *830m ascent*

A perfect YHA in Burley

From the Forest to the Sea

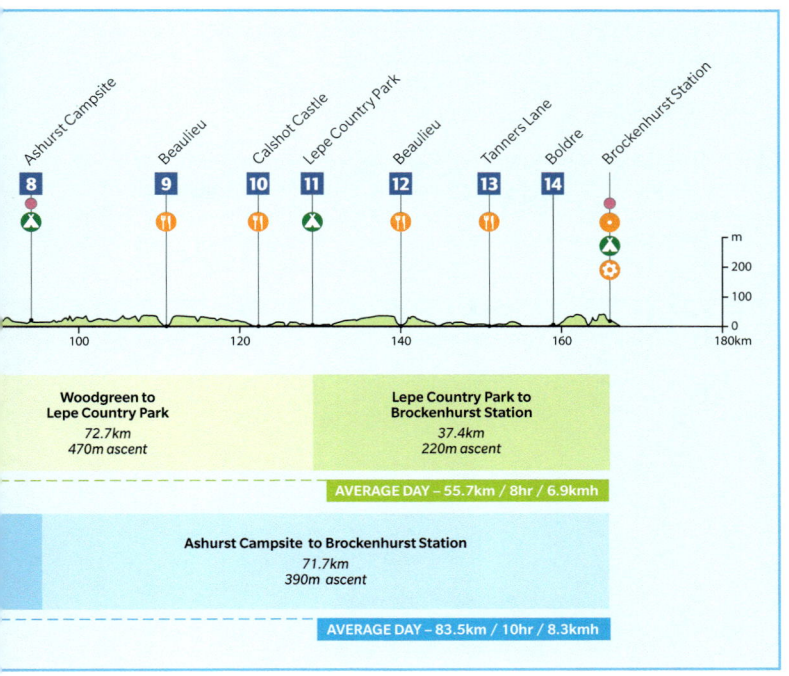

3 ■ Turn → by the postbox and head past the Red Shoot Inn and Camping Park, continue over the ford and bear → onto Toms Lane, the gravel NWP 41. Follow this for 2km, over a footbridge and into Broomy Inclosure. At NWP 36, fork → and continue to NWP 50; fork ← into Slufters Inclosure. After 2km you reach the road; turn → and continue for 2km to the junction on **Janesmoor Plain**. To shorten the route by 36km, turn right here and follow Stage 7 to jump to Stage 8.

4 ■ Turn ← onto Forest Road. After 800m, turn ← and head through **Fritham**. Continue beyond the Royal Oak and through a small car park. Take cycle path NWP 14 and continue on this for 5km to Abbots Well; turn →. Bear → at the next junction and continue for 400m to a crossroads; turn →, signed 'Brook'. Head to **Godshill**, and at the Fighting Cocks pub turn ←. Descend to a ford then climb to Godshill Farm and follow signs for Woodgreen. Top out onto a

Route 1 – The New Forest

long straight road, and after 100m turn ➔ onto cycle path NWP 3. Follow this to the road, turn ⬅ and descend into **Woodgreen**. Turn ➔ at the Horse and Groom pub. *At the apex of the route, the Horse and Groom pub comes recommended.*

5 ▲ Bear ➔ and climb on Hale Lane, bear ➔ signed 'Hale, Redlynch', fork ➔ and cross a red-brick bridge. Continue until the road runs out then turn ⬅ onto a byway, signed 'Higher End Farm'. After 200m, turn ⬅ onto a bridleway. Follow this north as the tree-lined rollercoaster hugs the shoulder of the Stricklands Plantation before finally delivering you back to a road 1km later; turn ⬅.

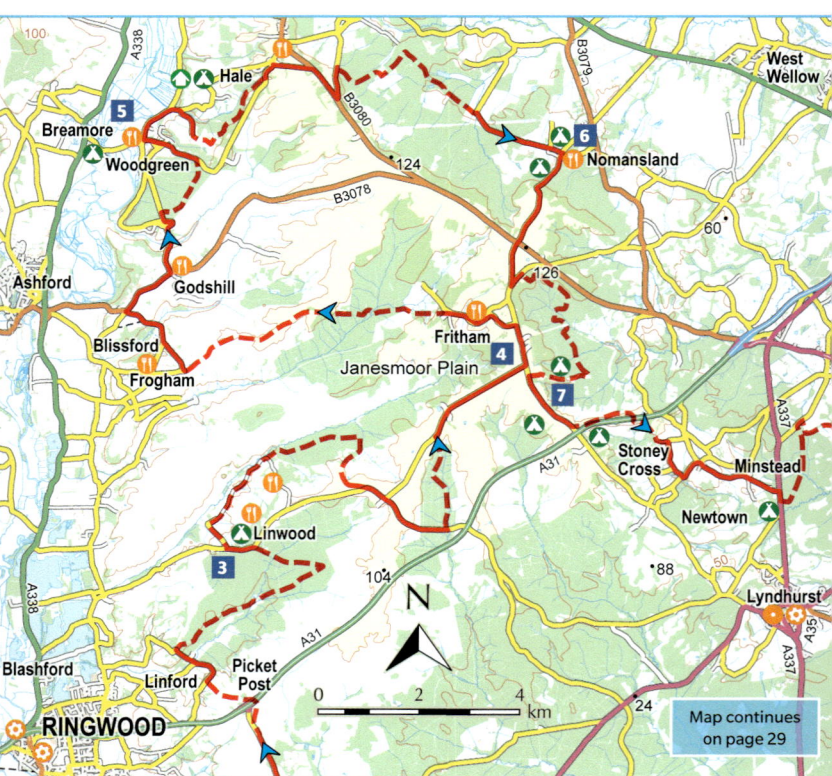

From the Forest to the Sea

One of the 5000 ponies that roam free in the New Forest

At the crossroads turn →. At the junction with Forest Road turn →, then after 400m take a sharp ←, signed 'Redlynch'. After 400m take a → onto a bridleway. After 300m take the ← fork. After 1km fork →, taking the byway. Follow this for 1.5km to the road before turning →, signposted 'Nomansland'. Continue to the junction in **Nomansland** and turn → past the Lamb Inn.

6 ▲ Continue for 2km on Forest Road, cross the B3078 and head over Longcross Plain. At the junction, take a sharp ← onto Furzley Lane, signed 'Bramshaw, Brook'. After 200m turn → onto cycle path NWP 20. After 100m, fork ← and follow the cycleway for 1km on outstanding gravel through the wood to a junction; turn ←, NWP 23, then fork ← at NWP 26. Follow this for 2km until it returns you to Forest Road and **Janesmoor Plain** once more; turn ←.

Route 1 – The New Forest

7 ■ Follow Forest Road south as it bears ←. Before it meets the **A31**, turn ← onto the cycle path that takes you through the underpass. On the south of the road, the bridleway meets a footpath; turn ← onto the footpath and walk your bike here for around 200m as it bears → then ← to meet the road. Turn →, continue south and bear ← as you head towards Minstead. Turn → at the phone box and continue through **Minstead**. The Trusty Servant at Minstead is a great pub, and stocks on the green add extra character.

> The following section takes you into **Rushpole Wood**, beginning on NWP 353. It then meets a bridleway via a 200m walk around Nicholas Corner, before taking you back into the woods to ride NWP 356. These dog-legs are necessary as other paths through the woods are restricted. It's great riding though, so worth it if you have time, but if you don't, continue along Woodlands Road to Ashurst and bear → onto Southampton Road.

Continue on the Minstead Road to the **A337**; turn →. After 100m, turn ← onto a cycle path (NWP 353) through Rushpole Wood. Head north to the road, turn →, and after 100m look for a footpath on your right. Dismount and follow this footpath for 200m until it joins the bridleway. Follow the road and turn →, continue to the next junction and turn →. After 400m turn → into the forest and join NWP 356. Continue on this through the forest until it returns you to Woodlands Road; turn → and bear → onto Southampton Road. After 100m, turn ← and ride into **Ashurst Campsite**.

The well-managed trails are rideable all year

From the Forest to the Sea

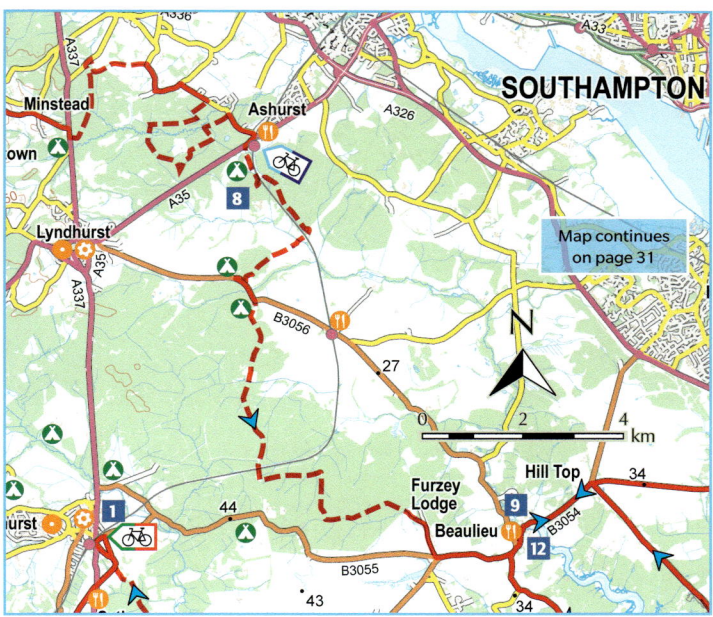

The next section, your last in land controlled by Forestry England, finishes with a short walk across **Matley Heath**. Despite being a popular route with riders and very atmospheric, cycling is restricted here.

8 ■ Head through the campsite and exit over a small footbridge into the wood. Bear → and turn ← at the junction. Head over a bridge crossing the railway line. Turn → and then fork → and continue for 1km south. The track forks → but is restricted for riders, so dismount and cross a second railway bridge, then head across Matley Heath and through the woods to the road. Turn ←, and after 300m turn → onto cycle path NWP 294. Beaulieu Road Station is 1.5km east of the route.

Follow NWP 294 for 4km past NWP 296, 301 and 324, cross the train line once more and then take the ← fork at NWP 326. Follow this to NWP 332 and fork ← and then ← again. Follow this to **Furzey Lodge** and then south to the B3055. Turn ← and head towards **Beaulieu**.

The coast near Lepe Country Park

> Stage 9 visits **Calshot Castle**, an imposing fort constructed in the reign of Henry VIII. If the weather is poor or time is tight and you choose to miss out on the loop around Calshot Castle and Lepe Country Park, follow Stage 12 from here to jump to Stage 13.

9 ■ Fork → and head through Beaulieu and over the bridge. Climb to the crossroads at the Royal Oak pub and turn →, signed 'Exbury, Holbury'. Continue for 3km through **Holbury** towards Fawley, ignoring possible right turns. At the staggered junction that meets the busier roads to Calshot, turn →. Head up Chapel Lane. At Blackbird Cottage, turn → on the bridleway. Continue on this good gravel track for 800m before turning ← onto the asphalt Badminston Drove. Turn ← when you meet Badminston Lane and continue to the fast B3053 once more; turn →. After 1km bear ←, and at the beach huts turn ← for **Calshot Castle**.

10 ■ Return to the B3053 towards Fawley. After 800m take a ← onto Stanswood Road and continue 2.5km to the next junction. Turn ← and descend to **Lepe Country Park**. Lepe Country Park is a stunning, isolated section of coastline.

11 Continue along the coast and stay on the road as it bears → and heads inland once more, following the course of the Beaulieu River. Head through **Exbury** before returning to the crossroads at the Royal Oak pub (Stage 9). Turn ← and descend to **Beaulieu** once more.

From the Forest to the Sea

You reach the sea at the end of Tanners Lane

In Stage 12, the tourist village of **Bucklers Hard** is a good stop for a cream tea. **Tanners Lane** is a short detour to a beach, where you can take a dip in the Solent.

12 Head through the town, back to the junction where you came in at the end of Stage 8. Turn ← and climb before forking ←, signposted 'Bucklers Hard'; follow this to **Bucklers Hard**. Continue on minor roads following the Solent Way. Fork ← onto Sowley Lane. After 3.5km the road bears sharply right, but here you can take a sharp ← onto **Tanners Lane** and continue for 800m to the sea.

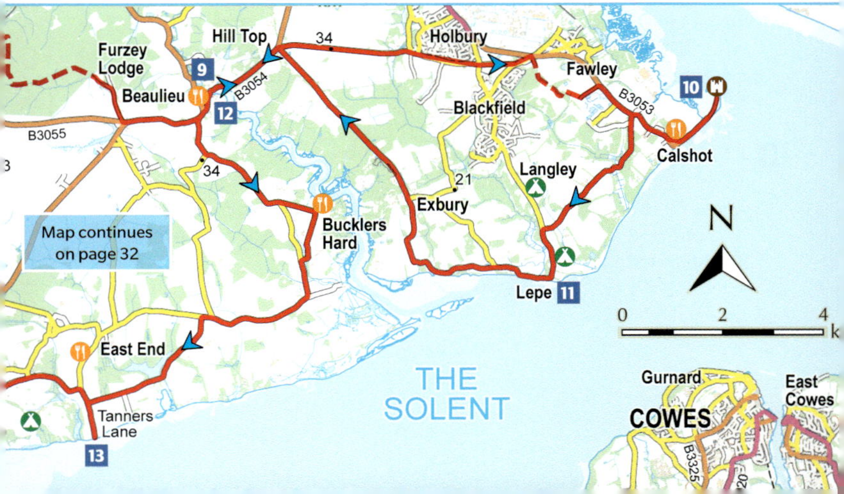

Route 1 – The New Forest

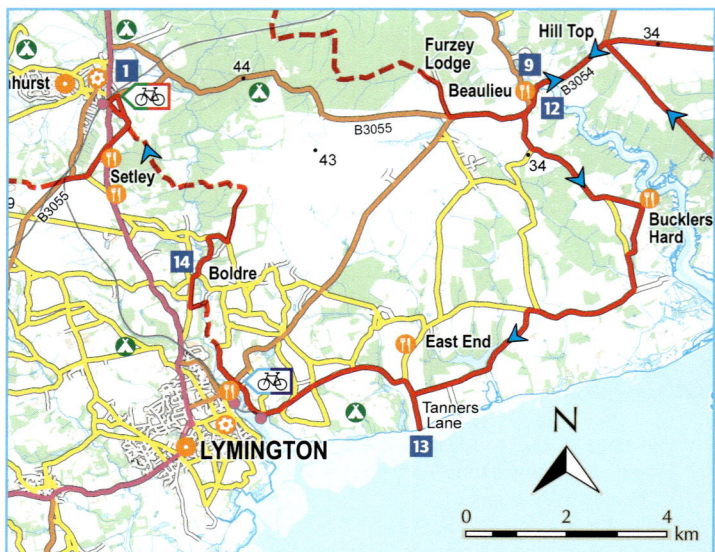

13 ■ Head back on Tanners Lane. At the next junction, turn ← and follow the road into the eastern side of **Lymington**. A train can be taken from Lymington Pier Station north to Brockenhurst. Follow the course of the river. Join a bridleway for 1km through Lymington Reedbeds Nature Reserve towards Boldre. If it's been raining, the bridleway could be muddy so follow the road to Boldre instead. When you meet the road, turn ← over a footbridge and continue to meet another road; turn →, head past the Red Lion pub in **Boldre**, turn → and descend to the bridge.

14 ▲ Turn ← after the bridge and climb to a junction. Turn → and head past the church. Turn ← onto a bridleway. Continue through Heywood Farm for 1km. When the bridleway splits, take the ← fork. Continue on this fantastic singletrack over a ford for 1.5km before forking → and continuing to **Brockenhurst**.

55% off road

2

Route 2 – Isle of Wight

Ticket to Ryde

Start/Finish	Ryde Pier, Ferry Terminus/Railway Station
Time	2–3 days
Total distance	135km (84 miles)
Off-road distance	74.3km
Percentage off-road	55%
Total ascent/descent	2090m
Grade	Moderate ▲
Terrain	Singletrack 4%, track 51%, road 45%
Bike choice	Gravel

Credit for Ticket to Ryde goes to Tim Wiggins, a native of the Isle of Wight. His route was spotted in *Cyclist* magazine and ridden shortly afterwards. After chatting to Tim, he was happy to donate this very special route for your enjoyment. His blog can be found at www.lifeinthesaddle.cc.

When you disembark from the ferry to start this route, perhaps hours after leaving London Waterloo on a Friday afternoon, it's really possible to feel like you have stepped back in time to the 1950s or are about to begin a foreign holiday. Don't take the gradients for granted here: it's hilly. However, this route delivers some of the most spectacular vistas to be had in the south-east of England.

Route options

These schedules assume you are setting out on Stage 1 from Ryde Pier, but this may not be the case if you are starting from London that morning or after work on a Friday. Take this into account when planning your trip. The Isle of Wight has many campsites and good potential for wild camping (see Appendix A). If following a two-day schedule and looking for a campsite, continue past Limerstone Down to Chale and Paradise Cottage Campsite. If riding over three days, good

Route 2 – Isle of Wight

Summary table

Waypoint	Section	Distance (km)	Ascent (m)	Descent (m)
1	Ryde Pier – The Old Mill Pond, Wootton	5.8	70	70
2	The Old Mill Pond, Wootton – Havenstreet Station (nr)	3.7	70	30
3	Havenstreet Station (nr) – Hare and Hounds, Downend	3.5	90	10
4	Hare and Hounds, Downend – Newport	5.6	60	130
5	Newport – Clatterford	3.4	60	50
6	Clatterford – Worsley Trail junction	7.2	170	20
7	Worsley Trail junction – Freshwater Bay	8.2	120	290
8	Freshwater Bay – The Needles	6	180	70
9	The Needles – Freshwater Causeway	5.2	40	140
10	Freshwater Causeway – Yarmouth (nr)	4	0	30
11	Yarmouth (nr) – Chessell Pottery Café, Shalcombe	6	90	20
12	Chessell Pottery Café, Shalcombe – Limerstone Down	7.4	180	70
13	Limerstone Down – Hoy's Monument	12.4	230	250
14	Hoy's Monument – Niton	2.9	10	90
15	Niton – Ventnor	5	30	90
16	Ventnor – Wroxall Down	4.1	250	30
17	Wroxall Down – Appuldurcombe House	10.2	120	240
18	Appuldurcombe House – Pedallers Café	2.8	0	80
19	Pedallers Café – Culver Down	15	170	150
20	Culver Down – Bembridge Harbour	8.5	90	170
21	Bembridge Harbour – Ryde Pier	8.1	60	60

options are Stoats Farm on the first night and a wild camp on Wroxall Down on the second night.

Alternative start/finish: If taking the ferry from Lymington to Yarmouth, start and finish there: begin the route at Stage 11 and ride Stages 1–10 after continuing through Ryde.

Shortcuts and extensions: You can slice 25km out of the southern section by continuing to Godshill after Chale Green, skipping from halfway through Stage

Surface	Grade	Description
mixed	🟩	Join the cycleway and head west into gentle landscape
mixed	🟩	Easy green lanes
off-road	🟩	Gentle climbing on good car-wide tracks
off-road	🔺	Meet the Bembridge Trail and drop into Newport
mixed	🔺	Leave the town and head to the start of the climb
off-road	🔴	A steep climb on singletrack to the ridge
off-road	🔺	Possibly the best views in the guide
paved	n/a	A popular tourist spot and the chance of an iconic view
paved	n/a	An easy roll into the town
mixed	🟩	Follow the east bank of the river to the outskirts of Yarmouth
paved	n/a	Quiet roads across the valley
off-road	🔺	Steep climbing through the woods
mixed	🔺	Stunning descents and tough climbs to a lonely monument
off-road	🔺	Drop into Niton
paved	n/a	Restricted coastal road into Ventnor
paved	n/a	Steep road climbing onto the wild downs
mixed	🟩	Blistering singletrack descent towards Shanklin
off-road	🟩	Easy descent to an unmissable cyclists' café
mixed	🟩	Road section to a headland detour with great views
paved	n/a	Through Bembridge to the harbour
mixed	🟩	Follow the minor road to the coast and then west to Ryde Pier

13 to Stage 18. The western sections could be removed by stopping at the end of Stage 6 and picking the route up again at Stage 13, saving yourself 37km and 610m of climbing.

Big Gravel Days: For a big adventure, travelling light with no camping equipment, why not access the island at Yarmouth and leave at Ryde? This is an 84km gravel ride that touches the majority of the most dramatic bits of landscape. Alternatively, for a 54km route, start at Ryde and leave the route at Yarmouth.

Route 2 – Isle of Wight

Directions

1 ■ Leave the ferry terminus and roll along the wooden pier to the junction right of the railway station. Turn ➔. As the road bears left, turn ➔ onto St Thomas Street. Climb gently for 100m before taking a ➔ onto Buckingham Road, signposted 'Coastal Path'. Bear ← with the road and climb to the junction with Spencer Road; turn ➔. Ignoring the dead-end signs, continue on this concrete drive until you approach a busy road. Look for a wooden gate on your right and a signpost for the coastal path, and turn ➔ here onto Ladies Walk. Continue on this concrete path, past the church, until you bear ← and rejoin the road. Take the ➔ and continue following signs for the coastal path. Leave Church Road and continue on the leafy path as it gets narrower. When you meet a track (Quarr Road), turn ➔. This good concrete path is yours until you reach the highway once more at **Fishbourne**, opposite the Fishbourne pub; turn ←. The Fishbourne pub is a potential lunch spot, if this suits timings.

Continue up the hill for 150m. Turn ➔ onto a well-signed bridleway. Descend and bear ← over a small bridge, climb Ashlake Copse Lane to the main road and turn ➔. Descend Kite Hill to the East Quay on your right and the Old Mill Pond in **Wootton** on your left. Cross the bridge and immediately turn ← onto NCN 22 (National Cycle Network).

2 ■ With the large Old Mill Pond on your left, ignore the first cycleway offered to you on the right and continue on the wide concrete drive until it turns into a car-wide track and continues through Hurst Copse. It first descends and then climbs as it crosses a succession of streams and takes you to a secluded level crossing. Cross with care and head through the farmyard. Continue to a junction where you meet a second bridleway; turn ←. Climb through Great Briddlesford Farm, bear → and continue over a stream to the road. Turn ←, then 100m before you reach **Havenstreet Station**, ignore the drive leading to

Cyclists are well catered for on the island

Route 2 – Isle of Wight

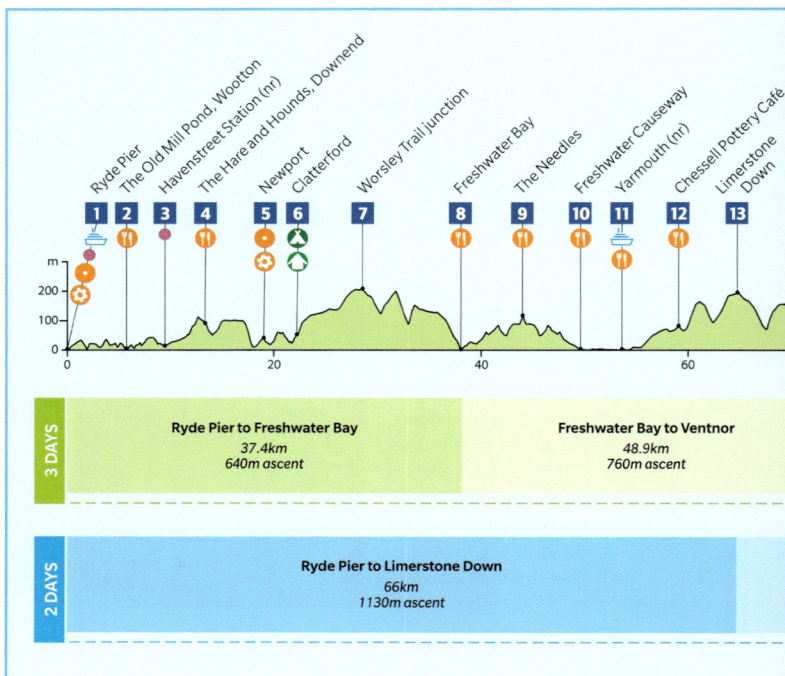

Havencroft Farm and turn ➔ onto public bridleway N18, signed 'Combley, Gallows Hill'. The Isle of Wight is criss-crossed by well-signposted bridleways and a series of trails named after famous local writers.

3 ■ Continue on this fantastic gravel track along the edge of the wood, over Deadman's Brook and on through Combley Farm. Climb steeply until you meet the Downs Road, turn ➔ and continue to **Downend** and the Hare and Hounds pub on your right.

4 ▲ Turn ← and continue on this busy road for 100m until the landscape opens up and you take the ➔ onto Burnt House Lane. You are greeted with magnificent views as you descend gently for 1km, before taking a tight ←

Ticket to Ryde

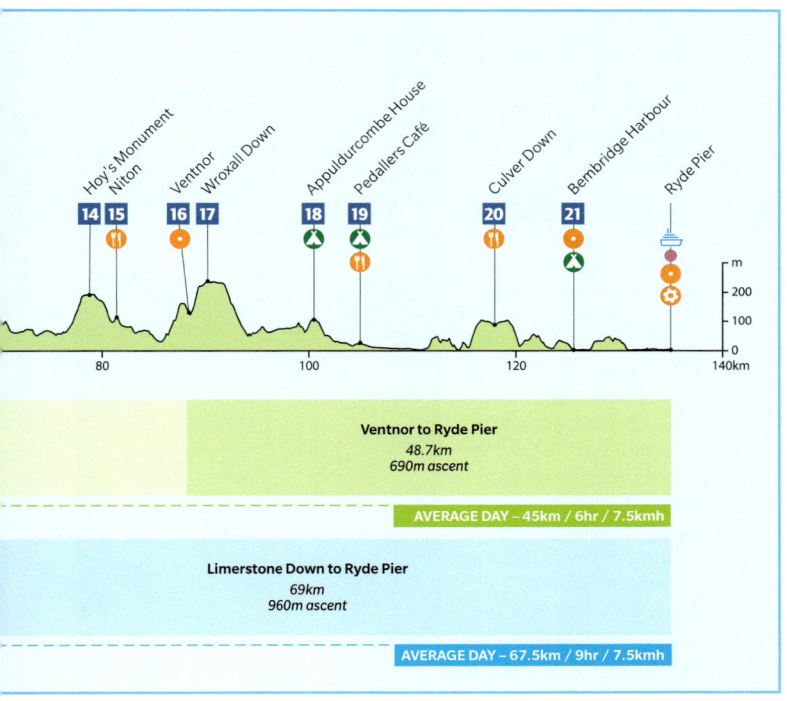

signposted as a dead end. Head through the idyllic Great East Standen Manor farmyard and climb steeply on the byway until you turn ➔ onto the Bembridge Trail. Maintain your direction for 2.5km, past the Newport Golf Club on your right, and descend on St George's Lane until you meet the busy A3020 on the outskirts of **Newport**. Continue to the road, cross via the pedestrian crossing and meet Shide Road opposite the red-and-yellow MOT Centre.

5 ▲ Climb to a mini-roundabout and take the first ⬅ onto Watergate Road. After 1km, turn ➔ by a red-brick house onto Nunnery Lane and continue for 1km, past Carisbrooke Priory to the busy Whitcombe Road; turn ⬅. After 200m, turn ➔ onto Froglands Lane. At the junction with Froglands Cottage turn ➔, signposted 'Ford'. The Windmill Campersite (Froglands Farm) is a good

Route 2 – Isle of Wight

candidate for a stopover before tackling the ridge the next day. Continue over the picturesque ford in Little Clatterford below **Carisbrooke Castle** and climb to the junction.

6 ● Turn →. After 50m, turn ← onto Nodgham Lane and climb on this to a group of detached houses. Take a steep, leafy singletrack signed 'no motor vehicles'. Now the fun begins. This steep, chalky restricted byway, the **Tennyson Trail**, takes you up onto the ridge, and you maintain this well-signposted cycleway for 6km, ignoring bridleways on your left and right. At the summit of **Brighstone Down** you reach a junction with the Worsley Trail, and the views towards the coast open up in front of you.

Crossing the ford below Carisbrooke Castle

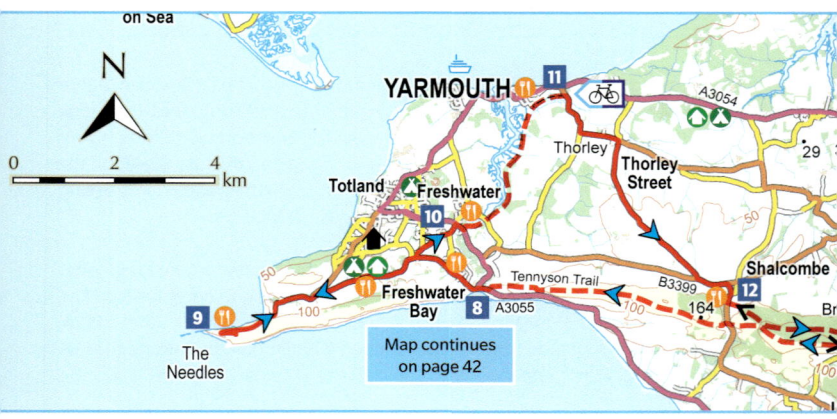

7 ▲ At the junction with the Worsley Trail, turn → and continue on the Tennyson Trail along Mottistone Down, following this sweeping gravel drive to Lynch Lane. Turn → and then immediately ← into a gravel car park. At the far end of the car park, a gate with a National Trust sign beckons you out onto open land, and you commit to the climb onto Brook Down and one of the most spectacular sections of riding in this guide. Continue over Compton Down along the spine of the ridge, through Freshwater Bay Golf Course, and descend to the A3055. On meeting the road, with the sea view ahead of you, turn → and drop into **Freshwater Bay**. The cycle-friendly Piano Café in Freshwater Bay is the perfect place for lunch.

8 After stopping for a well-deserved ice cream, climb up Gate Lane and head past St Agnes' Church onto Bedbury Lane. It's an easy-going 2km to the Highdown Inn, and you continue on the road as it bears ← before descending towards the Needles Park. Follow the road as it climbs past the tourist shops and bears →. Now it's 1km to the Old Battery and a steep 100m ascent to the Coastguard Cottages on the headland. The Needles are the white chalk outcrops that push west into the sea at the furthest westerly point on the Isle of Wight.

9 Retrace your steps to Middleton, en route to Freshwater Bay. Turn ← onto Queens Road. Head through the outskirts of **Freshwater** to a green with two benches, turn → onto Camp Road, signed 'Freshwater Bay'. Bear ← when this becomes Stroud Road and follow this for 1km to the A3055. With the Gulf

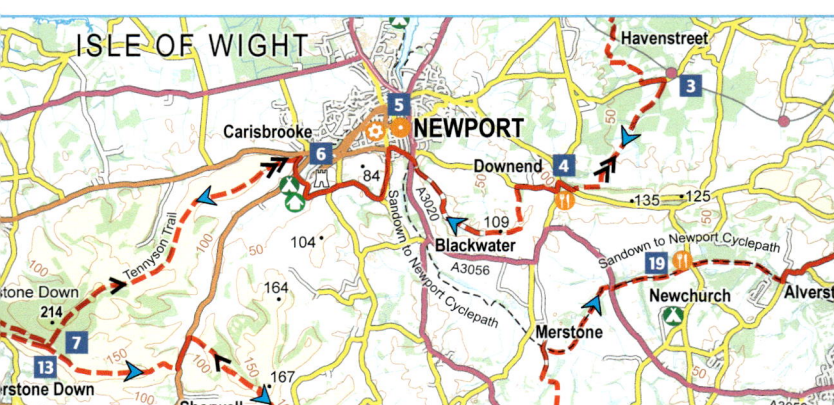

Route 2 – Isle of Wight

garage on your right, turn ➔ and continue past the End of the Line Café (a snack option) in the car park on the left. Turn ← onto public bridleway F61 at a signpost for the cycle route to Yarmouth (the Freshwater Causeway).

10 ■ Once on the Freshwater Causeway, it's a wonderful, flat, breezy 3km until the gravel track deposits you at the road near the seafront at **Yarmouth**.

11 Turn ➔ onto the B3401. After 800m on this fast road turn ← onto Thorley Street and head towards **Thorley**. After 500m turn ➔ onto Broad Lane. Continue uninterrupted across the valley floor for 3km to the B3399; turn ←. After 500m, turn ➔, signed 'Chessell Pottery Café'; the café is on your left, 100m later. Grab some refreshments at the bike-friendly Chessell Pottery Café.

12 ▲ A further 100m past the café, you reach the intersection with public bridleway B21 on your left; take this gravel trail and climb towards the wood. At the edge of the forest, fork ➔ and climb steeply through lush deciduous woodland onto Chessell Down. Bear ← at the next intersection with a bridleway and follow the good car-wide gravel track over Westover Down to Lynch Lane. Cross the road and take the adjacent gravel track. Ignore the path on the right and follow the track parallel to the road before bearing ← and beginning a steeper climb back onto **Brighstone Down**, where you eventually rejoin the Tennyson Trail on a familiar track that returns you to the junction you met at the end of Stage 6. This time you turn ← and continue for 500m to Limerstone Down.

Ticket to Ryde

13 ▲ Take 10min at the vantage point here to take in the views south before continuing on the stunning, open gravel track over Fore Down to Cheverton Shute. Turn ← and climb towards Cheverton Farm. Take the bridleway on your → and climb towards the television mast you can see in the distance. Fork → with the bridleway as it dips down steeply through a chute before bearing ← and delivering you to the road; turn → onto Berry Shute. After the crux of the climb, descend through Billingham before climbing to Beckfield Cross. Turn ← onto the byway, Ashbridge Lane. The asphalt gives way to a dirt track as you reach the top of the hill before a great descent to the sewage works.

Turn → and follow the bridleway back to the road. Turn ← onto Appleford Road and continue past South Side Farm to Appleford Lane; turn →. When the road bears left, you fork → onto Dolcoppice Lane, signed 'dead end'. Bear → when the road forks and take the route marked 'Private Road' (leading to the Hermitage). After 500m you leave the asphalt and head through a gate on the right to join an ill-defined bridleway, heading directly into a field and bearing ←. Push your bike towards the wood on your left. Head through a gate onto a tree-lined green chute and drag yourself up the gully to **Hoy's Monument**.

14 ▲ Continue south from the monument on a good track, in the only direction open to you. On meeting a second bridleway, turn ← at the foot of the imposing **St Catherine's Hill**. After 800m, turn → onto a bridleway (Bury Lane) and descend steeply. On meeting a concrete path, continue towards **Niton**.

Great views from Brook Down to the Needles

Route 2 – Isle of Wight

A fantastic gravel descent east from Brighstone Down

15 Turn ← at the junction. After 80m, turn → at the next junction. Head past the White Lion pub and continue along High Street. Make a shallow climb up Institute Hill. Bear ← on the A3055 and follow Undercliff Drive along the foot of the wooded coast road to **St Lawrence**, a suburb of Ventnor. Bear → and descend, with occasional gaps in the lush Victorian gardens affording a view to the sea below.

16 Continue to Inglewood Park Road and turn ←. Follow this through the suburbs for 300m until it begins to dip downhill to your left; here, you take a leafy track and follow this as it climbs to Whitwell Road. You emerge by a blue sign welcoming you to **Ventnor**. Here, take the bridleway signposted 'Stenbury Trail'. Climb steeply for 100m before forking → onto Rew Down. After 800m you meet a concrete path at the foot of a cemetery and this leads you back to the road; turn ←. Climb for a further 100m and take a → onto Down Lane. Climb steeply through a couple of switchbacks until you top out on Wroxall Down and enjoy the breathtaking views in all directions.

Ticket to Ryde

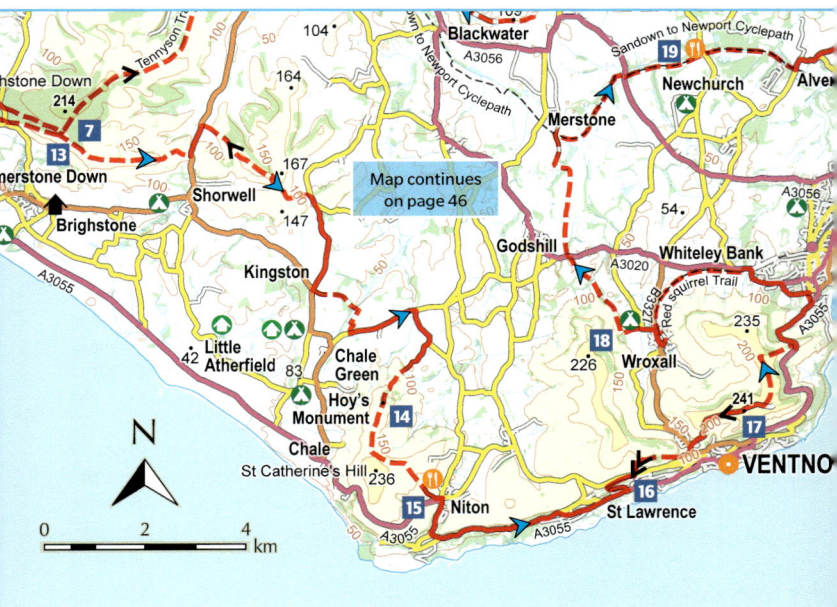

17 ■ When the road runs out and becomes a car-wide gravel track, continue east. After 100m turn ← through a gate and join a bridleway heading over Luccombe Down. After 1km take a sharp → onto a bridleway that soon becomes a singletrack green chute and drops you to the A3055. Turn ← and continue towards Shanklin.

> To **skip the stone steps** in the next section, continue along the A3055 and turn ← onto Rectory Road to rejoin the route.

Just outside **Shanklin**, carry your bike up a set of stone steps and follow the path for 80m until you join Rectory Road; turn ←. At the junction with Westhill Road, turn ←. Continue to Victoria Avenue; turn ←. Follow the road as it bears → and crosses an old railway bridge with a concrete path below. Bear ← with the road and descend. As the road begins to climb once more, turn ← onto a concrete drive signed as a bridleway. After 50m, turn → onto the **Red Squirrel Trail** (formerly the Sunshine Trail). Continue on this for 2.5km.

When the trail reaches **Wroxall**, follow signs to the left for the Red Squirrel Trail. Turn → onto suburban Yarborough Road, and at the junction with Castle Road turn →. Continue to the junction and take the → onto Station Road. When you meet the larger St John's Road, turn → and continue past the church. As the road dips, look for signs on your right for the cycleway and Appuldurcombe House and Gardens; turn ← onto Appuldurcombe Road. Climb gently out of town and up the hill until you reach the grounds of the ruined mansion. It's free to visit the remnants of Appuldurcombe House, which makes an interesting 15min detour.

18 ■ Opposite the white wooden gates that lead to Appuldurcombe House, turn → onto a gravel track that heads uphill. After 800m, bear ← and join the Stenbury Trail. Follow this through the ornamental Freemantle Gateway and descend on a good track through woods and over a stream. Climb Godshill Park Road to the junction with Shanklin Road near **Godshill**, then turn ← and immediately → to rejoin the Red Squirrel and Stenbury Trails.

Continue north past Moor Farm Cottages. Bear ← with the good gravel track past Great Budbridge Manor and continue to an old railway bridge. Here, take a footpath that joins you to the cycle trail; turn ← onto the trail from

Ticket to Ryde

Big skies above the Stenbury Trail

the footpath. Continue on the cycle trail for 1.5km to Horringford. Continue through a white wooden gate, turn → and follow the lane to the A3056. Use the pedestrian crossing to reach the Yar River Trail, and follow this to the Pedallers Café on your left. The cycle-friendly Pedallers Café is a must for a cream tea.

19 ■ After the café, continue down the Yar River Trail to the road at **Alverstone**; turn ←. Climb through the village and bear →. When the road forks, take the ← signed 'Adgestone Quiet Road'. After 2km of climbing on Upper Road, turn → at the blue cycleway sign onto Lower Adgestone Road. After a short climb, descend into **Yarbridge**, cross the busy road and take the Marshcombe Shute over the railway line.

Continue on this fast road to an awkward corner where the detour to Culver Down begins: as the road begins to climb once more, take the → signposted 'Culver Haven Inn'. If time or the weather is against you and you wish to exclude the detour to Culver Down, bypass the right turn at the awkward corner. After a steep climb, the road opens up and the views back onto Sandown Bay are stunning. Head to the end of the road at Culver Down.

20 Retrace your route back to the road; turn →. After 1km when the road bears left, you join a byway. Climb gently through woods to regain the road and bear ← past Glover's Farm. Descend Peacock Hill and turn →. After 150m, turn ← onto Commonwood Lane. When you meet Sandown Road, turn →. After a short descent of 50m, turn ← onto a bridleway, signposted for the Bembridge Windmill. Climb past the windmill, meet the road and bear ← into

Great cream teas at the Pedallers Café

Bembridge. Follow High Street to a small green with a bench, turn ← and follow the road past the church. Continue to the B3395, turn ← and follow this road as it traverses Bembridge Harbour.

21 ■ Continue to Bembridge Marina on your right, head through the car park and cross the wooden bridge that spans the Yar River. Take the gravel drive through the wooden gate, turn → onto Latimer Road and turn ← at the end of the stone way when you reach the harbour. Now turn ← inland and climb up Mill Road to the green. Turn → and continue to rejoin the busy road. Turn → then follow the road as it bears ←, becoming Eddington Road. At the next bend you leave the fast road and take the asphalt bridleway, R84, towards Nettlestone.

Climb, ignoring the entrance to the Nodes Point Holiday Park, and bear ← following signs for the coastal path. Prior to the two large stone gateposts, fork ← onto a rough gravel track. In 150m, at the next junction, turn → and then immediately sharp ← and follow this track to the B3330 on the edge of **Nettlestone**; turn →. Bear ← at the green and continue to descend, bearing ←. On a tight corner on Nettlestone Hill, by a bench, turn → onto a narrow singletrack onto Fairy Hill and follow this to the Alan Hersey Nature Reserve. Turn → and continue to Duver Road and the seafront: you are on the final stretch now. Turn ← and follow the road along the front. Bear ← on Puckpool Hill before taking the cycle path on the → past the Puckpool Mortar Battery. When you meet the sea wall once more, turn ← and continue to **Ryde Pier**.

71% off road

3

Route 3 – Surrey Hills

A Tower, a Temple and a Punch Bowl

Start/Finish	Godalming, Railway Station
Time	2–3 days
Total distance	132km (82 miles)
Off-road distance	93.5km
Percentage off-road	71%
Total ascent/descent	2050m
Grade	Moderate ▲
Terrain	Singletrack 49%, track 22%, road 29%
Bike choice	Gravel/MTB

Surrey is a bikepacking/gravel rider's dream, offering 1238km (769 miles) of bridleways and unrestricted byways. This route introduces you to the most dramatic, well-maintained selection of these in an exceptional two- to three-day ride, giving you the best of the North Downs Way, Serpent Trail, Greensand Way and Downs Link while introducing you to some wild and out-of-the-way corners. The landmarks of Leith Hill Tower, Peaslake, Pitch Hill, Temple of the Winds and the Devil's Punch Bowl are connected by singletrack and good car-wide byways.

Route options

Alternative start/finish: The Portsmouth Direct Line from London Waterloo touches or passes near the route at (north to south) Godalming (Stage 1), Witley Station (Wormley, Stage 12), Haslemere (Stage 14 or 16) and Liphook (Stage 17), so any of these could be used as starting or ending locations. Dorking (Stage 5) is also a great place to join the route, via the Mole Valley Line from Waterloo, or you could join at Coldharbour (Stage 6) if you alight at Holmwood and journey west.

Shortcuts and extensions: Leave the route at the end of Stage 13 or end of Stage 15 to return from Haslemere (reducing the route by 47km or 37km respectively) or

Route 3 – Surrey Hills

Summary table

Waypoint	Section	Distance (km)	Ascent (m)	Descent (m)
1	Godalming Station – Downs Link	9.1	150	160
2	Downs Link – Newlands Corner	9	230	110
3	Newlands Corner – Hogden Lane	9.1	90	60
4	Hogden Lane – Ranmore Common	7.4	160	160
5	Ranmore Common – The Plough pub (Coldharbour)	8.2	170	150
6	The Plough pub (Coldharbour) – Leith Hill Tower	1.4	60	20
7	Leith Hill Tower – Peaslake	8.3	90	230
8	Peaslake – Pitch Hill	2.2	100	0
9	Pitch Hill – Shamley Green	7	70	230
10	Shamley Green – Hascombe	8.3	130	80
11	Hascombe – Hambledon	4.5	80	110
12	Hambledon – Chiddingfold	3.4	20	60
13	Chiddingfold – Tennyson's Lane	7.1	140	40
14	Tennyson's Lane – Temple of the Winds	5.1	160	30
15	Temple of the Winds – A286 (Bell Road)	4.9	10	130
16	A286 (Bell Road) – Liphook Station (nr)	7.5	100	120
17	Liphook Station (nr) – Bramshott	7.2	60	70
18	Bramshott – Thursley	12.3	180	180
19	Thursley – Godalming Station	10	50	110

at Liphook (removing the final 30km). You can exit the route after Stage 10 by riding north to Godalming from Hascombe, or from Dorking after riding Stages 1–4.

Big Gravel Days: Godalming is roughly the central point of two legs: east to Hascombe via Dorking, and west to Hascombe via Liphook. The eastern leg (70km plus 5km back to Godalming) contains many of the route's big attractions such as the North Downs Way, Polesden Lacey, Coldharbour and Leith Hill Tower, while the western leg (62km plus 5km to the start) is more peaceful and less

A Tower, a Temple and a Punch Bowl

Surface	Grade	Description
mixed	🟩	Stretch your legs on the way to the Downs Link
mixed	🔴	Some steep singletrack climbing
off-road	🟩	Follow the North Downs Way singletrack through the woods
mixed	🔺	Rough car-wide track followed by forested singletrack climb
off-road	🔺	Tough singletrack descent before crossing the valley and climbing to Coldharbour
off-road	🔺	A hard climb on a byway past a pocket-sized cricket pitch to a medieval tower overlooking southern England
mixed	🔺	Singletrack descent followed by climb into Peaslake
off-road	🔺	Wooded singletrack climb
mixed	🟩	Hugging the shoulder of the hill, heading west
off-road	🔺	Minor roads and isolated bridleways
mixed	🟩	Through the Hurtwood, taking green chutes and the Greensand Way
mixed	🟩	Unkempt bridleway delivers you to Chiddingfold for a snack stop
paved	n/a	Road riding along the valley towards Haslemere
off-road	🔺	Breathtaking scenery crossing Black Down to the Temple of the Winds
off-road	🔺	Descending through heathland along a magical valley
off-road	🔺	After a tough singletrack climb, it's a fun descent to Liphook
mixed	🟩	Tricky wayfinding
mixed	🟩	Urban route to Devil's Punch Bowl
mixed	🟩	Change of terrain over Thursley Nature Reserve before an easy finish at Godalming Station

well-trodden but no less dramatic, traversing Temple of the Winds and the Devil's Punch Bowl as well as sections of blissfully wild and raw heathland. Both legs have excellent options for wild camping on common land.

Another option would be to start at Dorking and ride to Liphook following the more southerly routeline of the north-east to south-west axis (2km to the start plus 68km), or reverse that. I wouldn't recommend the more northerly routeline, Liphook to Godalming, for a big day.

Route 3 – Surrey Hills

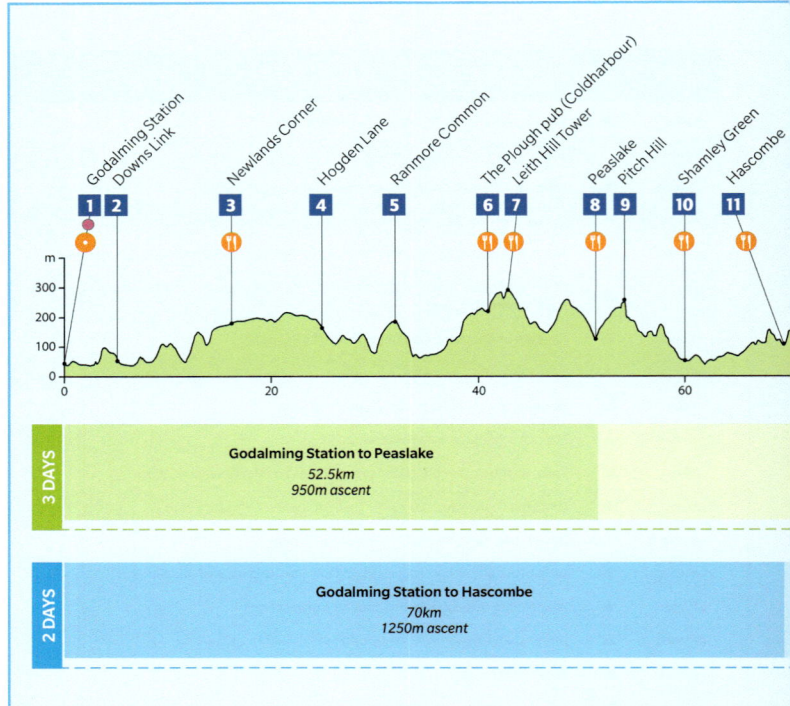

Directions

1 ■ Leave Godalming Station precinct and turn →. Continue ↑ and turn ← onto Flambard Way. After 500m, turn → onto Brighton Road. After 1km, past the village hall, fork ← onto Heath Lane. At the Munstead Heath Road, turn ←, then after 500m drop onto a bridleway on your ←. Follow this good track to Catteshall Lane; turn →. It's a shallow climb for 300m before you fork → onto Fox Way. Cross Foxburrow Hill Road and continue through a golf course to Horsham Road. Turn → and then immediately ← onto Station Road in **Bramley**.

After 100m you cross a disused level crossing and immediately turn ←, signed NCN 22 (National Cycle Network). Follow this for 800m to the Wey

A Tower, a Temple and a Punch Bowl

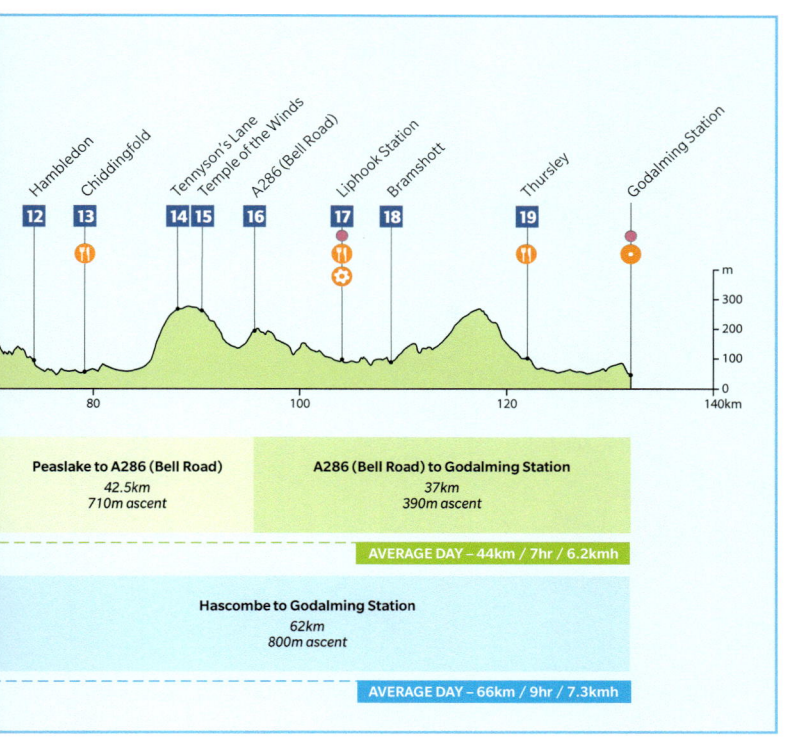

and Arun Canal and then head ➔ over the old bridge. Bear ⬅ and continue to Tannery Lane; turn ➔. At the junction with Chinthurst Lane, continue ⬆ and join the Downs Link. The Downs Link follows the course of two disused railways and links the North and South Downs.

2 ● Continue, bearing ➔ and with **Chinthurst Hill** to your right, to the busy road. Cross this and continue on a bridleway past Great Tangley Manor Farm. Climb steeply through the woods and onto **Blackheath**. Cross Sample Oak Lane, pass a small gravel passing place and take the broader of the two tracks to your right before almost immediately forking ➔ into a shallow climb to the war memorial. Bear ⬅ and descend to a good car-wide track heading north. Cross the red-brick railway bridge and continue across the Dorking Road

Route 3 – Surrey Hills

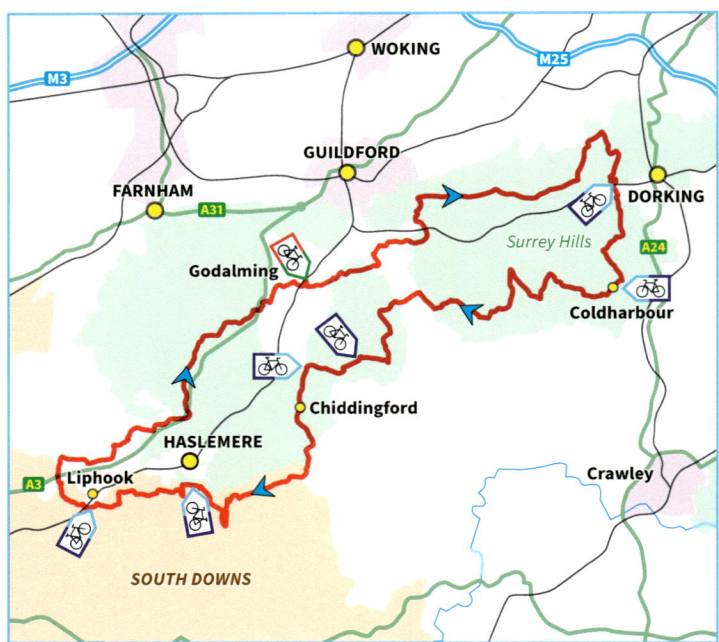

onto a track that descends to the Tillingbourne River. Take the Downs Link on the ➔ as it begins to climb. When the roads runs out, bear ➔ and enter the wood onto **St Martha's Hill**. St Martha's Church can be visited on a short detour as you climb towards Newlands Corner. To bypass the church, continue on the Downs Link.

For St Martha's Church, fork ← and hike-a-bike yourself for 50m before joining a bridleway on your ←. After visiting the church, return to where the path intersects and turn ← onto the bridleway, which takes you back to the Downs Link. Continue to the road and climb steeply until it bears sharply left; here, you should jump off your bike and push to the bridleway beyond the trees before riding into **Newlands Corner**. Newlands Corner Visitor Centre is popular with cyclists and provides a limited range of snacks.

> Criss-crossed by mountain bike trails, the **North Downs** are a paradise for riders. Cicerone's ***Mountain Biking on the North Downs*** covers 21

A Tower, a Temple and a Punch Bowl

mountain biking routes throughout the area, including the Downs Link. The North Downs Way Riders' Route (www.cyclinguk.org/north-downs-way) links bridleways, byways and quiet roads to create a continuous rideable trail from Farnham in the west to Dover in the east.

3 ■ Continue east through the woods on the **North Downs Way** (NDW) for 2km. Cross Staple Lane and join Combe Lane for 50m before taking a sharp →. After 300m turn ← and continue on the NDW for 2.5km. When the NDW forks right, you continue ↑ on a good bridleway that becomes a byway and continues through the wood. Continue east on this to the road at Ranmore Lodge. After 300m, turn ← onto the **Hogden Lane** byway.

Hogden Lane is a fantastic byway that takes you past Polesden Lacey House before the route heads south once more. If time is tight, you can skip this section by continuing east along the road and rejoining the route at the start of Stage 5.

4 ▲ Descend on Hogden Lane for 2km, then ascend bearing → and then ← before reaching a gate on your right. Take this bridleway and continue towards the lodge ahead of you. Join Polesden Road and climb for 300m before turning → onto a bridleway (Connicut Lane). Continue south through the woods. After 1.3km the route bottoms out and you turn ← through a gate. For Tanners Hatch YHA (300m off the route), ignore the left turn and continue

Lush views along the Surrey Hills

on Connicut Lane. Descend gently through pasture to Bagden Farm. Beyond the farm, turn → onto a bridleway and now climb steeply into Dorking Wood. Continue to the road at Ranmore Common.

5 ▲ At the road, turn → and continue past the impressive St Barnabas Church to Ranmore Road; turn ←. After 300m, turn → onto a bridleway and descend very steeply through the wood to open ground. Bear → and cross the railway at a level crossing. Follow the car-wide track into the copse ahead of you, then 300m beyond the wood turn → towards Milton Court Farm. After 100m turn ← onto Lince Lane. Cross the bridge and then cross the A25 onto Milton Street.

Continue south on this bridleway through the Bury Hill Fisheries and beyond as it climbs towards Chadhurst Farm. Bear → at the ponds and climb steeply into the wood. When you meet Logmore Lane, turn → and descend. After 100m, ignoring the footpath to your right, turn sharply ← and continue on a good car-wide cinder bridleway that shortly becomes a concrete driveway. At Squires Farm, turn ← and then → 25m later. Now hike-a-bike through the wood on a thin singletrack for 200m to Wolvens Lane byway. Continue south on this good sandy byway for 2km before descending to the Plough pub at **Coldharbour**. The Plough pub is in a magical location and a popular lunch stop for road and mountain bike riders.

A Tower, a Temple and a Punch Bowl

6 ▲ Opposite the pub, climb on a rough byway past the Coldharbour Cricket Ground and on through the Mosses Woods to Leith Hill Tower on **Leith Hill**. Leith Hill Tower marks the highest point in south-east England. The views are breathtaking.

7 ▲ With the views over southern England in front of you, descend to the right of the tower on the Greensand Way (GSW). Cross the road and continue, bearing → then ← towards High Ashes Farm. Now follow a sweeping descent that maintains altitude through Pasture Wood before dropping to the road; turn ←. Continue through Bulmer Farm, turn → and continue into **Holmbury St Mary**.

With the church above you to the left, hug the left of the green, ride past the Royal Oak pub on your left and climb gently along a row of detached houses towards a village hall in a woodland bowl. Continue through a gate

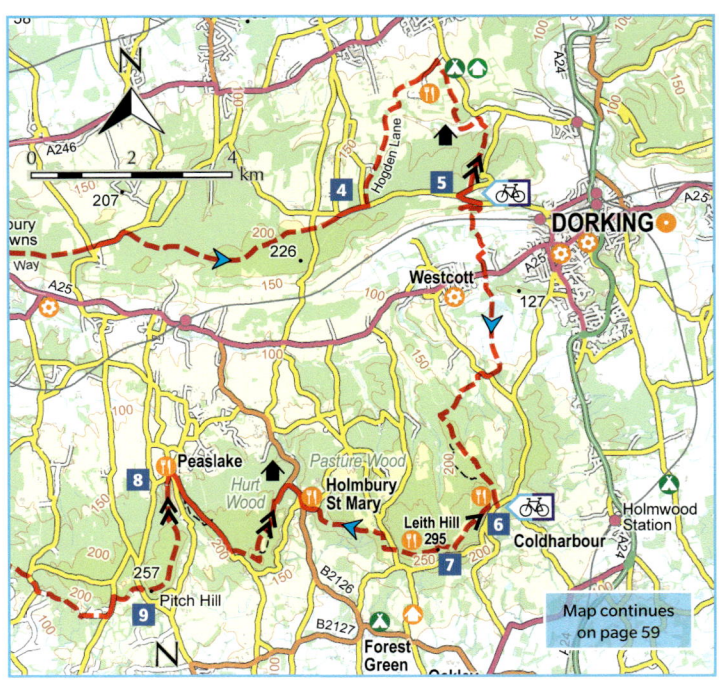

57

Route 3 – Surrey Hills

The Plough at Coldharbour is a gem

that marks the entrance to the Hurtwood (or Hurt Wood), following a good sandy bridle path into the mixed woodland; 800m beyond the start of the track, fork ← and follow the forestry track to Holmbury Hill viewpoint on the site of an old fort. Descend on a forestry track on the right to the car park. Drop onto Radnor Road, turn → and continue for 1.5km into **Peaslake**. The pretty village of Peaslake has a village shop and a pub.

8 ▲ Keeping the pub on your right, bear ← towards the Memorial Hall and follow an asphalt drive that continues beside it, signposted as a bridleway. Continue on this car-wide track up into the western section of the Hurtwood. Take the ← when the bridleway forks. Follow this as it bears → to **Pitch Hill**.

9 ■ To the right of the trig point, take a bridleway that descends steeply to the road; turn →. Climb past the sadly defunct Windmill pub before following an asphalt bridleway for 500m and rejoining the road; turn ←. After 200m turn →

A Tower, a Temple and a Punch Bowl

onto an asphalt drive, signed 'Winterfold House, bridleway'. Follow this as it bears ← before forking →. Now continue on a rough singletrack through the wood then along Dick Lane. When you meet the road, turn →. Climb steeply on Alderbrook Road, bearing ← and then forking ← onto a bridleway that cuts into the wood. After 700m fork ← and drop into Willinghurst Farm. Continue until the B2128 (Guildford Road), turn → and head towards **Shamley Green**. Shamley Green has a pub and a village store.

10 ▲ Unless heading into the village to refuel, turn ← onto the GSW opposite the church. Continue on this over the Wey and Arun Canal, across the Downs Link to the busy Rooks Hill Road; turn →. After 50m turn ← onto Brookwell Lane. After 200m, bear ← and rejoin the GSW. This bears ← and runs along the side of Gatestreet Farm. Meet the road and continue to Selhurst Common; turn →. After 400m, head past a gate on the left on a good cinder track. Continue south on this for 1.5km towards Nore. Now fork sharply → and climb into the Creek Copse on a steep, rough bridleway. When you reach open land and top out, fork ← and descend into **Hascombe**.

> If you're riding this route on a two-day schedule, **Hascombe** is the recommended finish for Day 1; it's also 4km from Godalming, if you need to cut the ride short. Perhaps refuel at the White Horse pub and then plan to wild-camp. See Appendix A for camping and glamping options.

Route 3 – Surrey Hills

11 ■ Opposite the White Horse pub, take the bridleway and follow it round to the → to Hoe Farm. Turn sharply ← up a bridleway into Hurtwood Copse. Bear → and continue on the sandy track for 1km. Drop to the road and turn ←, ignoring the bridleway in front of you. After 25m turn → onto the GSW once more. Continue for 1km and follow the GSW when it forks ←. Meet the road, pass a church and bear ← onto Hambledon Road. Turn ← and head through **Hambledon**.

12 ■ The road bears right and you drop ← onto a bridleway running alongside a terrace of houses. When this drops to the road, turn → and then immediately take the bridleway signposted on the left. Continue over a footbridge to Hambledon Hurst and Petworth Road beyond. Turn ← and continue on the A283 to **Chiddingfold**.

> As you approach **Chiddingfold**, the Roberts Post Office on the left is a good place for snacks, as is Elliott's Coffee Shop on the south of the green. There is also a pub, and a butcher's selling rolls.

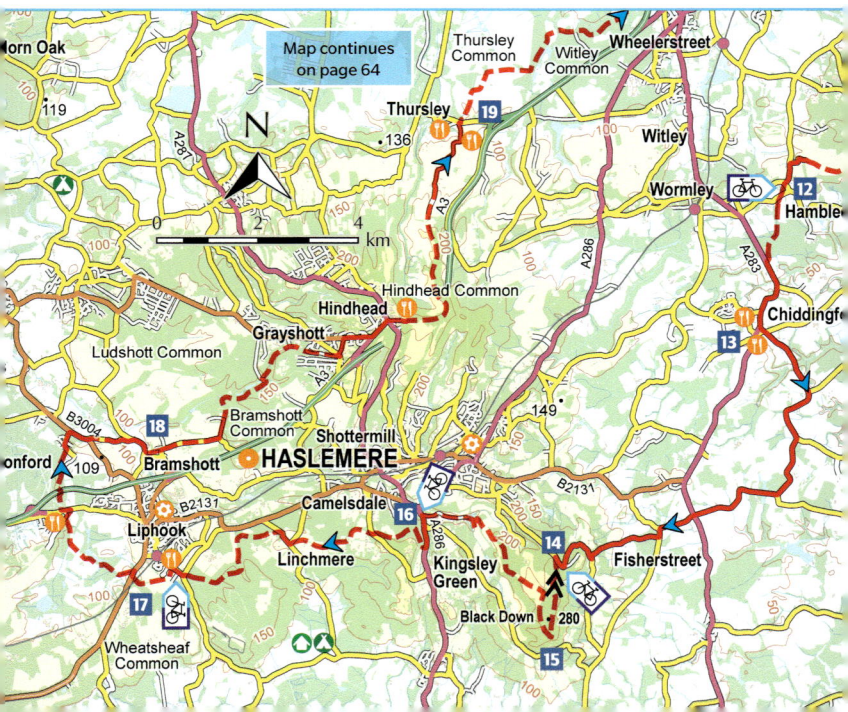

A Tower, a Temple and a Punch Bowl

Leith Hill Tower, the highest point in south-east England

13 Leave the A283 in Chiddingfold and skirt round the left of the green onto Pickhurst Road. Continue south on the road for 2km, turn → onto Plaistow Road, signposted 'Shillinglee Park Road', and enjoy a gentle climb through the woods. On reaching a green with three willow trees, turn → onto Shillinglee Road. Follow this road for 1.5km as it passes the ponds, then cross the A283.

At Gospel Green, turn ← onto Jobson's Lane, then 70m into the wood take a tight → onto Jay's Lane. A steep climb onto the shoulder of Black Down takes you to a junction, where you turn → onto Tennyson's Lane. Climb, bearing first ← then →. Just prior to a large car park in the woods, take the sharp ←.

14 ▲ Turn ← onto the Serpent Trail and continue into the heath. Take the left fork when it's offered, and maintain a course along the edge of the escarpment to the viewpoint: Temple of the Winds.

Route 3 – Surrey Hills

Descending on the Greensand Way

15 ▲ After enjoying breathtaking views over to the South Downs, turn around and ride slowly around to your right, enjoying spectacular vistas towards your next long-term goal: Beacon Hill. Continue north on the Serpent Trail as it hugs **Black Down** and bears ← before you fork ← and take a shallow descent on the Sussex Border Path (SBP). Continue to bear → and head north to Chase Wood. Bear ← then turn → and follow the vague bridleway along the edge of the wood and down towards the river; bear ← now and exit onto an asphalt drive. Continue past Stedlands Farm to the A286 (Bell Road).

16 ▲ Turn ← onto the busy Bell Road, head south for 700m before taking an asphalt bridleway on your → into Marley Wood. Bear → and climb on this rough track before turning ← onto Marley Common. Follow this good car-wide track west for 1km before bearing ←, descending and forking →. Back on the SBP now, you follow this west for 1km before descending slowly back to the road at **Linchmere**. Turn →. After 200m, fork → and then immediately turn ← onto the SBP. Continue west for 1km along the edge of Linchmere Common. When the SBP becomes a footpath, fork → onto the bridleway. Continue south for 1km before forking → and rejoining the SBP. Follow this to Highfield Lane and continue ↑ onto New Lipchis Way.

A Tower, a Temple and a Punch Bowl

> **Liphook Station** is easily accessed from the start of Stage 17: after the 200m climb, ignore the byway on the left and continue along New Lipchis Way for 300m. The station is on the same line as Godalming and Waterloo.

17 ■ After a 200m climb on New Lipchis Way, turn ← onto a rough byway marked with a wooden post. Climb slowly and then bear → and descend to the tunnel under the railway line. When you meet Portsmouth Road, turn →. Continue towards the Links Tavern before taking a signed singletrack heading back into the woods: you are now on the Shipwrights Way (SWW). After 150m fork →. Follow this for 1km past Foley Manor. Where the SWW intersects with two bridleways, fork →. Continue past the Deers Hut pub onto a small singletrack cutting across the grass. When this reaches the road, the bridleway is opposite you. Enter the drive and turn immediately ←. Continue and bear → through the wood. Take the bridge over the A3.

Continue north, bearing ← past some buildings and over a footbridge. When you reach the road at **Conford**, turn ← and then bear → and follow the road out of the village. At the junction, turn →, then after a further 200m fork ← signed 'Bramshott village only'. Continue on Burgh Hill Road before turning → onto Tunbridge Lane. After 300m turn ← onto a byway that's a shortcut to Rectory Lane in **Bramshott**.

18 ■ Continue for 1km until you reach the edge of **Bramshott Common**. Turn ← at the junction signed 'Rectory Lane'. When the road runs out, continue into the Bramshott Common car park and take the bridleway. This descends to a river; don't cross it, but instead bear → on a bridleway. Continue through Waggoner's Wells and Croaker's Patch to a car park where a number of bridleways intersect. Now cross the stream and immediately turn → onto a byway. Follow this for 200m as it bears → and becomes a good car-wide track. Continue ↑ at the intersection with a footpath into **Grayshott**. Follow the asphalt drive to the road and turn ←.

After 100m turn → onto Boundary Road. At the junction turn → onto Headley Road and continue to a roundabout; take the first exit, signed 'Hindhead, Haslemere, Devil's Punch Bowl'. At the next roundabout take the second exit, signed 'Devil's Punch Bowl', and begin a shallow climb up London Road. Continue into the National Trust car park for **Hindhead Common** and the Devil's Punch Bowl. Join a cycle path running adjacent to the road. Follow this as it bears ← around the edge of the Devil's Punch Bowl, with fantastic views of Beacon Hill to your left and Gibbet Hill to your right. Maintain the ridge and head north for 1km before descending on the eastern buttress of

Route 3 – Surrey Hills

the hill on the GSW to Little Cowdray Farm. When you join the road, follow it north to **Thursley**.

19 ■ Fork → at the green and continue onto a rough asphalt driveway opposite, signposted as a bridleway. Climb on this rough track until it becomes a raised walkway that crosses the heathland of Thursley National Nature Reserve. After 1km, ignore the first bridleway offered to you on the right and take the second at the junction. Turn → onto this and descend slowly for 1km to an intersection with a second bridleway with a building on the right; turn ←. Continue for 800m with a pond on your right. Turn → onto a good car-wide track and head → over the river. Climb gently to the road, turn ← and then, after 50m, turn → onto a bridleway.

Follow Lower Moushill Lane through the woods east for 1km until you reach the road; take the bridge over the A3 and bear ← onto a bridleway. In 200m turn ← back towards the A3 and then follow the bridleway around to your →. Continue to the busy A283 and turn →. After 100m take the road on the ← signed 'Eashing, Abbey Mill, The Stag PH'. Bear → and continue on Eashing Lane for 1km before turning onto Halfway Lane. After 500m take a bridleway on the → signed 'Fox Way'. Follow this road ← to **Godalming Station**.

56% off road **4**

Route 4 – Chiltern Hills
The Chilterns Off-Road Cycleway

Start/Finish	Wendover, Railway Station
Time	2–3 days
Total distance	133km (82.7 miles)
Off-road distance	74.8km
Percentage off-road	56%
Total ascent/descent	2210m
Grade	Difficult ●
Terrain	Singletrack 39%, track 17%, road 44%
Bike choice	Gravel/MTB

The Chilterns National Landscape offers fantastic off-road riding. One moment you'll be sweeping steeply down the edge of a field of shoulder-high wheat, and the next plunged deep into an ancient forest. As you grind your way up a chalk bank in the granny ring, spectacular views into secluded valleys give you vertigo. With a seemingly endless procession of tough climbs followed by technical descents and river valley traverses, it's a hard two days, but a three-day schedule gives you loads of options for pub lunches, cake shops and perhaps a swim in the river. Highlights are many, but Whiteleaf Hill, Coombe Hill and the village of Turville stand out.

Route options
Campsites in the Chilterns are scarce. The three-day schedule includes a relatively short first day to take advantage of one east of Turville (Chiltern Retreat). The two-day schedule makes use of the YHA at Goring: take this option, leave the camping gear at home and travel light over this tough route. Having said that, there is no shortage of first-rate spots for wild camping here.

Alternative start/finish: You are spoilt for choice when it comes to alternative start locations. Princes Risborough or Saunderton could be easier options for you, on the same line as Wendover. Pangbourne and Goring are also good choices.

Route 4 – Chiltern Hills

Summary table

Waypoint	Section	Distance (km)	Ascent (m)	Descent (m)
1	Wendover Station – Little Hampden	6	230	140
2	Little Hampden – Lacey Green	6.7	110	90
3	Lacey Green – Bledlow Ridge	7.3	85	115
4	Bledlow Ridge – Horsleys Green	4	90	120
5	Horsleys Green – Turville	7.7	110	230
6	Turville – Nettlebed	12	280	200
7	Nettlebed – Stoke Row	5	70	65
8	Stoke Row – Whitchurch-on-Thames	10.5	45	170
9	Whitchurch-on-Thames – Goring & Streatley Station	4.8	20	30
10	Goring & Streatley Station – Nuffield	13.3	210	55
11	Nuffield – Cookley Green	8.3	110	130
12	Cookley Green – Christmas Common	6.1	120	80
13	Christmas Common – Northend	9.2	130	135
14	Northend – M40	5.3	110	110
15	M40 – Hempton Wainhill	10.6	160	190
16	Hempton Wainhill – Princes Risborough (outskirts)	7	150	90
17	Princes Risborough (outskirts) – Chequers (gates of)	5	100	140
18	Chequers (gates of) – Wendover Station	4.2	80	120

Shortcuts and extensions: By starting and finishing at Princes Risborough, you slice the top off this route and reduce the length to 110km.

Big Gravel Days: The obvious choices here are Wendover to Goring or vice versa: two of the best Big Gravel Days in this guide, and wild riding you won't forget. A loop from Goring to Nettlebed and back is 38km, while the top section, a Princes Risborough–Wendover loop, is a spectacular 25km.

Directions

1 ▲ Leave the station precinct, turn → and continue to the main road; turn ←. At the mini-roundabout, turn →. South Street becomes London Road and you

The Chilterns Off-Road Cycleway

Surface	Grade	Description
mixed	▲	Easy exit from Wendover and quickly into ancient woodland
mixed	▲	Rolling off-road trails and possible refreshments
mixed	■	Across the valley on good bridleways
mixed	■	Some steep off-road climbing
mixed	▲	Over the big road and then great off-road to a magical hamlet
off-road	▲	Fantastic car-wide gravel tracks
mixed	▲	Steep climb into Stoke Row
off-road	▲	Magical wooded singletrack
off-road	■	Following the Thames into Goring, with dizzying views of the river below
mixed	■	Riding the Icknield Way north
mixed	■	Onto the Chiltern Way before some steep off-road
mixed	▲	Steep off-road through a wild wood
off-road	▲	The best descent in this route and a savage climb to match
off-road	▲	Remote section up to the M40
off-road	▲	Gentle descent to the foot of a good off-road climb
mixed	▲	Easy riding and a steep road climb
mixed	▲	Big descents and fast wooded tracks
mixed	▲	Down the nose of Bacombe Hill to Wendover

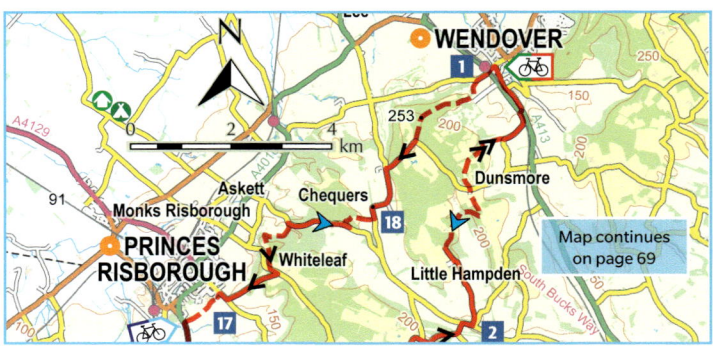

Route 4 – Chiltern Hills

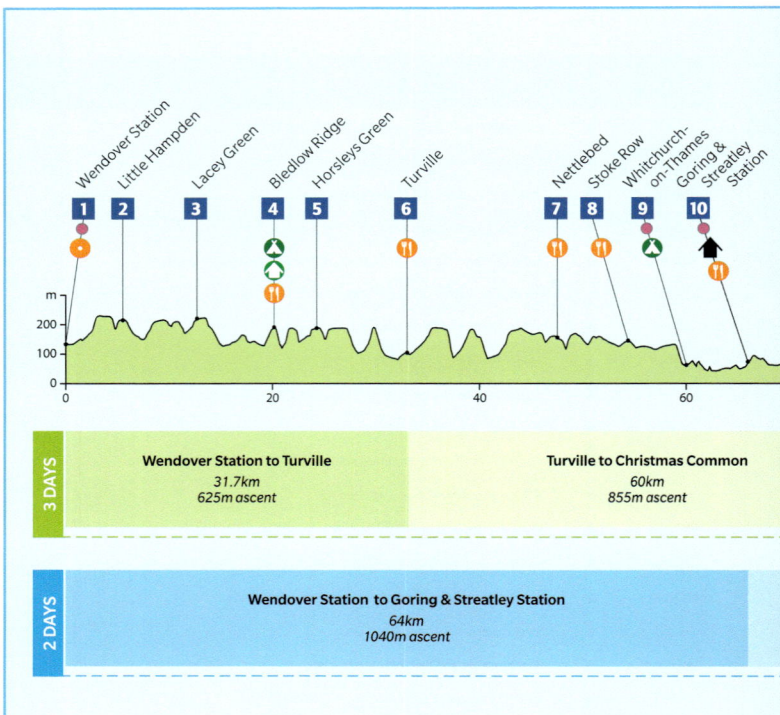

continue to a large roundabout. Take the second exit and climb on Small Dean Lane. You are now on the Chiltern Way (CW). Continue to the right of Small Dean Farm on a good car-wide track. The track skirts the left of the woods as you continue to climb. Turn ← when you meet the bridleway and continue through **Dunsmore** on the CW. After 200m take a steep → and drop into the wood. At the bottom of the slope, where the tracks intersect, turn ← onto the second track on the left and climb up to **Little Hampden**.

2 ▲ Turn ←, continue past the church and descend to the junction. Turn → onto Rignall Road. After 100m, turn ← signed 'Prestwood, Great Hampden'. Climb Glade Road, bearing →. When you reach the crossroads, continue ↑ on NCN 57 (National Cycle Network). Bear ← and follow the road through **Great**

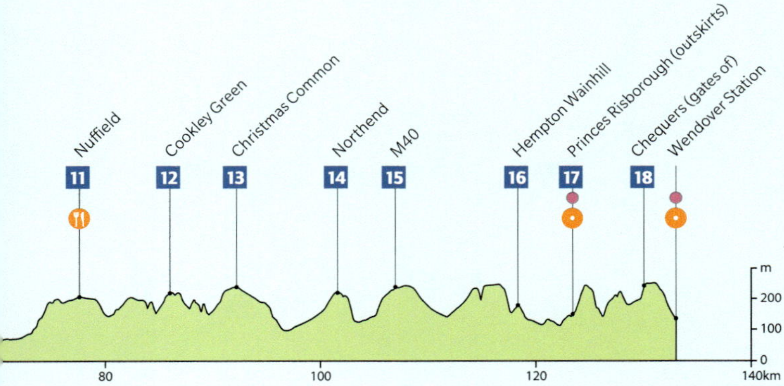

The Chilterns Off-Road Cycleway

Christmas Common to Wendover Station
41.3km
730m ascent

AVERAGE DAY – 44.3km / 6hr / 7.3kmh

Goring & Streatley Station to Wendover Station
69km
1170m ascent

AVERAGE DAY – 66.5km / 8hr / 8.3kmh

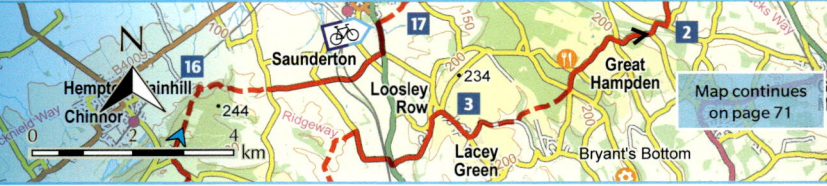

Hampden. Continue 100m past the pub before taking a ← and heading steeply downhill to a junction. After crossing the road, turn → onto the singletrack heading into the woods. Continue for 1km and then descend to Highwood Bottom on a steep rough trail. When you meet the asphalt, turn →

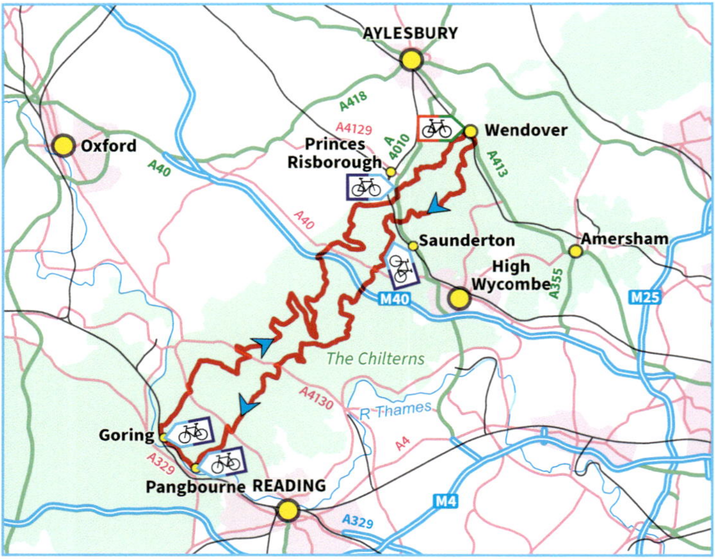

Route 4 – Chiltern Hills

and climb uphill on Kiln Lane. Take time to stop and enjoy the sculptures on Kiln Lane. Bear ← and continue to **Lacey Green**.

3 ■ Turn →, continue to a crossroads and turn ← opposite the pub, onto **Loosley Row**. Enjoy great views and a fantastic descent on Lower Road and Little Lane. At the A4010 turn → and then immediately ←, signed 'Saunderton Lee, Bledlow'. Bear ← with the road and take a bridge over the railway line. Bear → and at the next junction turn ← onto a bridleway that heads across the

Sculpture park near Kiln Lane, Lacey Green

The Chilterns Off-Road Cycleway

field. When a footpath continues onto the Ridgeway, bear ←. Descend and then take the ← that maintains the same altitude and hugs the shoulder of the hill. Continue on this to Haw Lane, turn → and climb steeply to **Bledlow Ridge**.

4 ■ Turn ←. After 25m turn → onto a bridleway and descend to Bottom Road. Turn ← and after 25m turn → onto a wide track bordering a field and follow it to the road beyond; turn ←. After 300m turn → through a small metal gate to access a bridleway on your right. Drop steeply into Bottom Wood and turn → when the bridleway forks. Continue out of the woods, across the field and into **Beacon's Bottom**. Turn ← and continue to the A40. Turn → and after 100m turn ← to **Horsleys Green**.

5 ▲ Descend on Bigmore Lane through the woods and continue over the M40. At the junction, turn → signed 'Stokenchurch' before immediately crossing the road and taking a ← onto Chequers Lane. Descend on this for 500m

Route 4 – Chiltern Hills

before peeling off to your → on a bridleway that heads past Harecramp Cottages. At the foot of the hill turn → onto a bridleway. Weave through the woods on a great singletrack.

At the intersection of three tracks, take the bridleway into the woods. Climb steeply on this and follow the signs as the track runs parallel to a concrete drive. When you reach the road, turn ← and then follow the road round to the →. Before reaching St Nicholas Church follow Ashfield Barn Road as it descends steeply ← to Holloway Lane. Turn ← and continue to **Turville**. Turville is an exceptionally pretty, secluded hamlet with a fantastic pub, the Bull and Butcher.

6 ▲ With the church to your right, follow a little lane on your left as it cuts between two cottages, and follow the CW until it meets Dolesden Lane; turn ←. After 100m turn → onto a bridleway that follows the edge of the wood. Continue on this and climb through Kimble Wood, past Kimble Farm to the road; turn →. Follow the road as it bears ←. After 1km the road turns sharply left, but you fork → to the right of two large metal gates and continue on a good car-wide track. After 100m take the → fork and descend through the woods on a good singletrack to **Stonor**; turn →.

After 50m take the ← signed for the Five Horseshoes pub. Climb through beech woods towards **Maidensgrove**. Fork ← into the woods on a bridleway and continue past Lodge Farm. Slog it up through the woods on a decent

Wild cornflowers near Mongewell Woods

The Chilterns Off-Road Cycleway

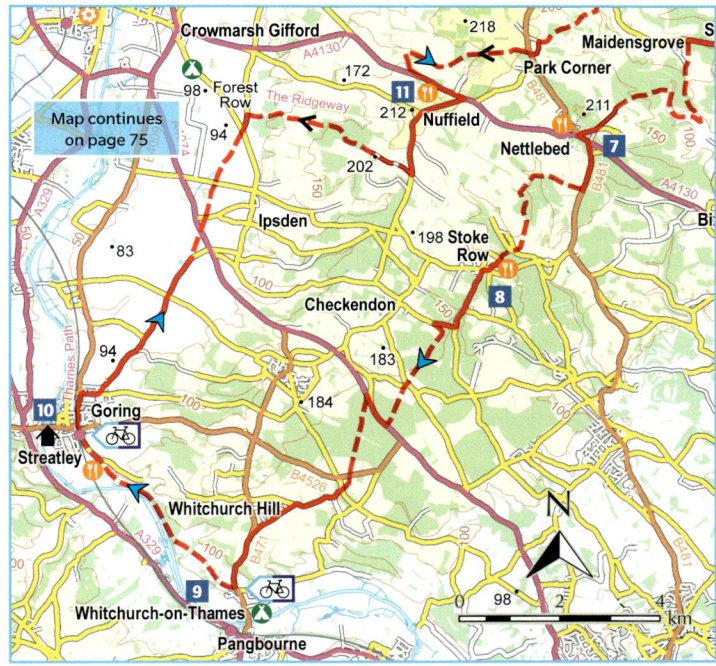

singletrack. The views here are exceptional. Descend on a car-wide flint track to Bix Bottom and take a sharp →. Climb the restricted byway for 500m and then fork sharply ← and climb into the woods once more. When you meet the road, turn → and continue into **Nettlebed**. There are refreshment options (a coffee shop and a pub) in Nettlebed.

7 ▲ At the green in Nettlebed, turn ← onto the A4130. At the roundabout, take the second exit onto the B481. Follow this for 1km before taking a → onto Deadman's Lane. Descend at first, then bear ← and climb along the edge of the woods. Fork ← into Nott Wood and keep following this south. When you meet the road at Newnhamhill Bottom, take a bridleway into Bush Wood and climb to Newlands Lane. Follow this into **Stoke Row** and turn →.

Route 4 – Chiltern Hills

8 ▲ After 100m turn ← onto Busgrove Lane. After 1km turn → onto Emmens Lane. As the road continues to bear right, you take a sharp ← onto a gravel drive signposted 'Larchdown Farm'. Follow this good track as it bears →. Descend through Beech Wood, past Heath End and on to Lower Farm. At Hook End, continue south on a bridleway through mixed plantation. Your path forks → and you continue through the woods adjacent to the busy A4074. After 400m your track meets the fast road and you cross it to take the well-defined path into Ashlee Wood. Continue south on this for 1km through Abbot's Wood. *Wayfinding in Abbot's Wood is tricky without GPX; head south.*

Cross the B4526 and join a bridleway that runs past Black Dog Pots. Cross the next junction and take the sign for 'Hill Bottom, Whitchurch Hill' onto Goring Heath Road. Follow this towards Hill Bottom, continuing to bear ← when the road forks. When you meet the B471 turn ← signed 'Whitchurch, Pangbourne'. Continue towards **Whitchurch-on-Thames** until you reach the Hartslock Bridleway on your right.

> The **Hartslock Bridleway** (Stage 9) is a stunning section, and light relief after the previous climbs. Enjoy the spectacular views over the Thames to your left but don't get too close to the edge!

9 ■ Turn → onto the Hartslock Bridleway. Follow this great concrete drive for 1.5km until you reach Hartslock Wood, where it becomes a path and edges closer to the Thames. Follow this track to **Goring & Streatley Station**.

Thirsty work

The Chilterns Off-Road Cycleway

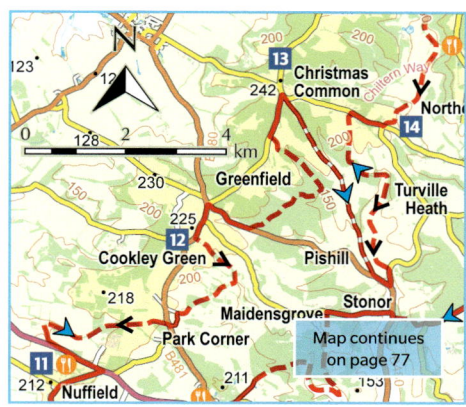

The second half of this route criss-crosses the **Icknield Way**. To bypass it on Stage 10, ignore the turn-off onto the Icknield Way, stay on the road and head towards Braziers, then turn ← and continue to Ipsden. Continue north on NCN 5 to rejoin the route 2km north at Forest Row.

10 ■ Continue past the station on Gatehampton Road as it follows the railway for 1km, then turn → onto Elvendon Road. After 500m fork ← onto Icknield Road. After a shallow climb you top out to spectacular views. Continue north on the road for 1.5km past Icknield Farm on the left before branching onto the well-defined Icknield Way as it heads out over the fields. Continue through the fields for 2.5km to **Forest Row**, then turn → onto a restricted byway. Head past Woodhouse Farm and climb into Mongewell Woods. When you meet the road, continue ↑. At the junction turn ← and head to **Nuffield**.

11 ■ Continue on Timbers Lane to the A4130; turn ←. After 1km turn → onto a concealed restricted byway as it heads into a copse. Climb towards Ambrose Farm and fork → onto the CW. Continue for 2km to the road at **Park Corner**. Turn → and then immediately ← and continue to the junction. Turn → and immediately join a bridleway heading into Priors Wood. Descend to Redpits Manor, head through the farmyard and descend to an intersection; turn ← at the foot of Devil's Hill. Next, bear ← and ascend to **Cookley Green**.

> In Stage 12, if time is tight, follow signs for **Christmas Common** instead of taking the → onto Patemore Lane.

12 ▲ Turn → onto the B481 and continue for 800m before turning → onto Patemore Lane. Descend to Grove Farm and turn ← onto the bridleway at Pishill Bottom via a wide metal gate with vertical bars. Climb into Shambridge Wood, bear ← and continue on the CW. After 1.5km, when five tracks

Route 4 – Chiltern Hills

intersect, take the only bridleway. Continue on this for 1km to the road. Turn → and head towards Christmas Common.

> In Stage 13, you can jump directly to **Northend** if necessary by forking → off Hollandridge Lane and skipping 12km of (fantastic) off-road.

13 ▲ Before reaching **Christmas Common**, turn → signed 'Northend' and continue on Hollandridge Lane. When the asphalt runs out, continue on the byway for 5km to the road; turn ←. After 200m, take a sharp ← signed 'Turville Heath, Northend'. Continue along Balham's Lane for 200m before turning ← onto a restricted byway. After 2km you pass Turville Park Farm, bear ← and continue into the woods. After 1km fork → and rejoin the CW. Continue to **Northend** and turn → onto Holloway Lane.

14 ▲ Continue for 500m into Northend and fork ← at the green. To the right of a lawn in front of a garden wall, take the good car-wide track leading into the wood. At the next intersection bear ← and continue north to Wellground Farm. Follow the bridleway as it heads between the farm buildings and ascends along the nose of the hill and into Langleygreen Plantation along a stunning singletrack, until it climbs steeply to meet the road. Climb over the low barrier, turn → and cross the M40.

15 ▲ Continue for 1km, across the A40. When the road bears left, you fork → onto an asphalt drive. Continue to bear → and descend along Collier's Lane. When you reach Grange Farm Road, turn ←. After 300m the road runs out and you join a bridleway for a climb into Crowell Wood. After Crowellhill Farm, turn → towards Sprig's Alley. After 100m turn ← onto a bridleway that runs between two houses. Follow the track as it flanks Venus Wood. Ignore the tight right and instead climb steeply through Sunley Wood before topping out and meeting a road. Turn ← onto Chinnor Road before forking → onto Hill Top Lane. Continue to a small car park, ignore the bridleway to the left and instead join a bridleway ↑. Descend steeply to an intersection with four other bridleways at **Hempton Wainhill**.

16 ▲ Take the good byway on the right which makes up part of the Icknield Way. Continue ↑ at the next two crossroads, cross the railway twice, first under then over a bridge. Cross Shootacre Lane and continue to the junction with Wycombe Road. Turn ← onto the busy road, descend for 300m and turn → to regain the Icknield Way byway. At the road, turn → and then shortly ← onto

The Chilterns Off-Road Cycleway

Kop Hill on the outskirts of **Princes Risborough**. Princes Risborough is well connected if you need to cut the ride short.

17 ▲ Climb Kop Hill and turn ← at the junction. After 100m turn → into the car park for Whiteleaf and Brush Hill Local Nature Reserves. Follow the bridleway past the Whiteleaf Cross before descending steeply to Whiteleaf Golf Club.

Route 4 – Chiltern Hills

The Ridgeway long-distance route: both a bridleway and a footpath

Turn ➔ and follow the bridleway as it skirts the wood. On reaching Cadsden Road turn ➔ and climb Hobb's Hill. Turn ⬅ onto a byway before shortly taking a bridleway into Pond Wood. Bear ➔ and descend to the road, turn ⬅ and continue to the gates of the Prime Minister's country residence, **Chequers**.

> In Stage 18, if you have time, take a few minutes at **Coombe Hill Monument** to enjoy the view north across the Three Hundreds of Chiltern, the stewardship of which was briefly held by Alexander Boris de Pfeffel Johnson in 2023 on his resignation from the House of Commons.

18 ▲ Continue and follow Missenden Road as it bears ⬅. After 800m fork ➔ taking signs for Dunsmore. Climb Lodge Hill. Coombe Hill Monument can be accessed through the car park on your left. When the road bears right, continue through a car park onto a bridleway. When it forks, bear ➔ and descend the nose of Bacombe Hill. When you meet the road, turn ➔, cross the railway line and turn ⬅ for **Wendover Station**.

38% off road

5

Route 5 – Kent Downs

Come on Pilgrim

Start/Finish	Otford, Railway Station
Time	1–2 days
Total distance	76.2km (47.5 miles)
Off-road distance	28.9km
Percentage off-road	38%
Total ascent/descent	1050m
Grade	Moderate ▲
Terrain	Singletrack 23%, track 15%, road 62%
Bike choice	Gravel/MTB

The Kent Downs National Landscape is one of the closest wild landscapes to London and forms part of the North Downs. Proximity to London dictates that the modern infrastructure of motorways, orbitals and train lines are never far away, and this route circumnavigates one of the capital's largest satellite towns: Sevenoaks.

However, the landscape is dramatic and steeped in history. The Pilgrims' Way, made famous by Geoffrey Chaucer's 14th-century Canterbury Tales, runs along the shoulder of the North Downs and is your first destination, followed by Chartwell, Winston Churchill's family home. Toy's and Ide Hill are here too, as well as Ightham Mote, a fine example of a medieval manor house, and Knole Park. The off-road riding is a mixture of challenging, wooded singletrack and decent gravel.

Route options

This route can definitely be ridden in a day (starting early in midsummer), but if you prefer a more relaxed adventure you can stop around halfway at Little Elses Glamping. Alternatively, there are many wild camping options in The Chart and Goathurst Common. There is a National Trust campsite at Oldbury Hill on the penultimate section.

Route 5 – Kent Downs

Summary table

Waypoint	Section	Distance (km)	Ascent (m)	Descent (m)
1	Otford Station – The Pilgrims' Way	8.1	110	40
2	The Pilgrims' Way – Evelyn Avenue	7.1	60	40
3	Evelyn Avenue – The Chart	3.4	75	30
4	The Chart – Chartwell	4.3	70	80
5	Chartwell – Toy's Hill	3.6	90	70
6	Toy's Hill – Ide Hill	3.5	80	60
7	Ide Hill – Sevenoaks Weald	6.2	65	160
8	Sevenoaks Weald – Ightham Mote	9.1	140	150
9	Ightham Mote – Plaxtol	3.3	10	50
10	Plaxtol – New Pound	6.2	120	60
11	New Pound – Ightham	11.4	80	110
12	Ightham – Oldbury Hill	1.7	95	40
13	Oldbury Hill – Otford Station	8.3	55	160

Alternative start/finish: You could join the route at Stage 4, having caught a train to Oxted, east of Sevenoaks. To begin the route at the halfway stage, continue on the train past Otford to Hildenborough Station and ride 3km north to Stage 8 at Sevenoaks Weald.

Shortcuts and extensions: To leave the route around the halfway point, you could extricate yourself at Hildenborough Station. At Ightham Mote (end of Stage 8), you could head north and rejoin the route at Oldbury (start of Stage 13), removing 24km and nearly 300m of climbing.

Big Gravel Days: This route is a Big Gravel Day!

Directions

> **Otford village** is the perfect place to pick up any snacks you need for the ride.

1 Exit Otford station, turn → and then ← following Station Approach to the A225; turn ←. Follow the road around the pond, join High Street and continue through the village; you are now officially on the Pilgrims' Way. Continue west

Come on Pilgrim

Surface	Grade	Description
paved	n/a	Leaving Otford for the Pilgrims' Way
paved	n/a	Following the Pilgrims' Way along the shoulder of the North Downs
off-road	■	Gravel bridleway takes you over the M25 to The Chart
mixed	■	Fantastic wooded off-road tracks take you to Chartwell
off-road	▲	A steep off-road climb delivers a singletrack descent to Toy's Hill
mixed	▲	A car-wide bridleway through the woods then on to Ide Hill
mixed	▲	Climbing on minor roads followed by a gravel bridleway to a pub
mixed	▲	Cross a nasty intersection to a stunning gravel byway that takes you to Ightham Mote
mixed	■	Mainly car-wide byways
mixed	▲	Into the woods on car-wide gravel tracks to the Moody Mare
mixed	■	Skirt the wood on a car-wide track
mixed	■	A steep climb on a byway to Oldbury Hill
mixed	■	Back to the Pilgrims' Way and on to Otford Station

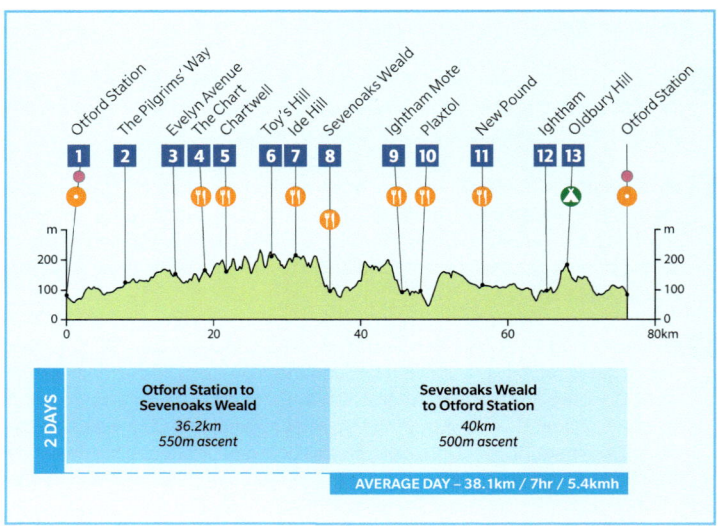

Otford Station to Sevenoaks Weald
36.2km
550m ascent

Sevenoaks Weald to Otford Station
40km
500m ascent

2 DAYS

AVERAGE DAY – 38.1km / 7hr / 5.4kmh

Route 5 – Kent Downs

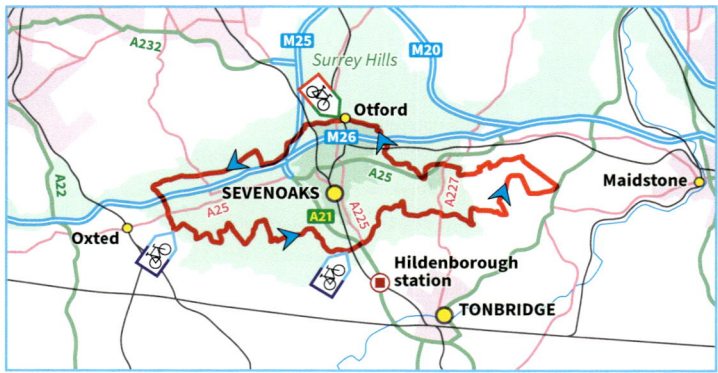

for 2km under a railway bridge and bear ←. Take a →, signed 'M25, Bromley, Sevenoaks, Dunton Green' and take the bridge over the M25. Turn ←, continue over the next roundabout and follow the B2211 as it heads into open countryside. Continue ↑ for 1.5km before turning → onto Ovenden Road, your route for the next 1.5km to Sundridge Hill. Enjoy wonderful views into the valley to your left. Turn tight ← at the foot of Hagbush Wood, rejoining the **Pilgrims' Way**.

2 Now you follow the Pilgrims' Way west for 7.1km as it hugs the foot of the North Downs. Opposite a row of houses signed 'Evelyn Avenue', turn ← onto a gravel track marked with a stone bridleway sign.

3 ■ Drop onto the bridleway and continue over the valley floor, into a copse and on over a bridge spanning the M25. Now on the Vanguard Way, you continue through a farmyard onto Broomlands Lane. Cross the busy A25 and descend on the bridleway, cross a stream and begin to climb into the woods until you reach **The Chart**.

4 ■ On returning to asphalt, turn ← onto Moorhouse Road. After 700m, turn → onto a gated bridleway and climb through the High Chart to the road; turn → onto Goodley Stock Road. After 400m turn ← onto a bridleway, signed 'Hunters Lodge'. Bear ← and climb through Crockhamhill Common, bearing → at Crockham House. Drop onto Hosey Common Road and immediately descend further into the woods. Bear ← over Mariners Hill then weave along

Come on Pilgrim

singletrack to the road and Chartwell; turn ←. If time allows, Chartwell is worth a look, and there's a café and toilets here.

5 ▲ Continue to a tight bend and fork onto a bridleway that climbs very steeply through the woods. The bridleway crosses Hosey Common Lane and begins to descend. At French Street Farm you turn → and pick up the Greensand Way (GSW). The Greensand Way is a long-distance path that tracks a ridge of green sandstone through the Surrey and Chart Hills. A solid climb is rewarded by a fast descent and you pop out halfway up **Toy's Hill** on Puddledock Lane by a phone box. Cross the road to Scords Lane.

6 ▲ Descend on the asphalt bridleway and then climb into the wood, bearing ← into some tough climbing through Scords Wood before turning → onto Emmetts Lane. When you reach Sundridge Road, turn → and climb to the pretty village of **Ide Hill**.

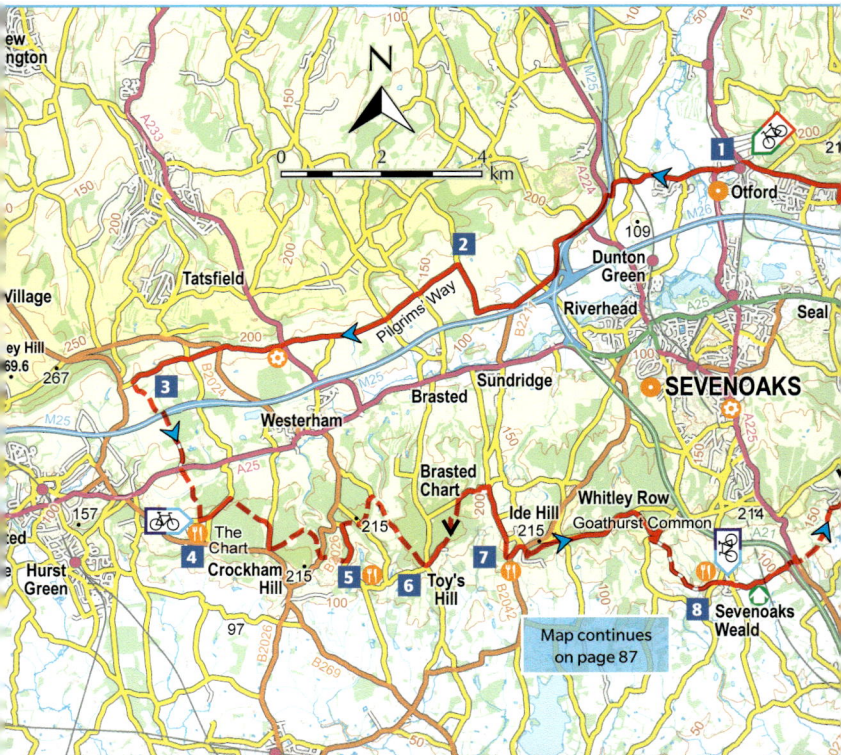

Route 5 – Kent Downs

A wild descent drops you outside Chartwell

7 ▲ Follow the road ← past the Cock Inn and then bear → and continue to the junction at Wheatsheaf Hill; turn ←. Climb gently before forking → onto Gracious Lane and bear ← over Sheephill Wood. Turn → down Rycroft Lane; continue for 1km as the road bears ← and immediately take a very tight → signed 'Weald 2'. Continue to Wickhurst Road and turn ← onto the asphalt bridleway. This is yours to the Windmill pub at **Sevenoaks Weald**.

8 ▲ Follow Windmill Road past the garage onto Morleys Road and over the railway bridge to a huge roundabout. Turn ← onto this fast road and bear →, signed 'Sevenoaks'. Head over the A21 and then fork ←, signed 'Knole 2, Riverhill Himalayan Gardens'. At the next road, turn →, cross the road and join the pavement. Turn ← onto a signed restricted byway by a small stone cottage.

Follow this charming track through George's Shaw woodland and then out over the shoulder of the hill to Kettleshill Farm. Here, turn ← and climb Carter's Hill, just east of Knole Park. Cross the road and continue through the wood on a singletrack. When you meet the road once more, turn → and follow this to the crossroads. Cross onto Bitchet Green Road, cross Bitchet Common to Bitchet Green, turn → and then → again, signed 'dead end'. When the road bears right, you turn ← onto a wooded bridleway. The bridleway meets the GSW and you continue past the oast houses at Mote Farm to Mote Road; turn →. After 25m, take a sharp ← onto a bridleway that runs along the eastern edge of the medieval moated manor house Ightham Mote.

9 ■ Turn →, keeping the moated Tudor manor on your ←. Continue on the gravel track and bear →. After 750m, briefly dismount and follow a footpath 50m to the road. Turn →, and after 25m turn ← onto an asphalt bridleway. This crosses the grounds of Fairlawne Park to School Lane; turn ← and continue to **Plaxtol**.

10 ▲ Turn →, signed 'Old Soar Manor'. Head past the green, with a phone box on your right. Turn → onto Brook Lane and continue to Allens Lane; turn ←. When the road bends left, bear → onto a gravel byway that flanks the stone

The Kent Downs are criss-crossed with singletrack

Route 5 – Kent Downs

Ide Hill Community Shop is popular with cyclists; the views south are breathtaking

wall. When you drop to the road, turn →. After 200m, turn ← onto Brooks Road. At the green metal gate, join the bridleway and head into **Hurst Wood**, taking the middle of three possible car-wide tracks up the hill. You dip and cross an adjacent track before climbing to a junction. Turn → and continue to the road and the Moody Mare pub at **New Pound**.

11 ■ Take Beech Road opposite the pub and continue to the outskirts of **Kings Hill** and a group of red-brick houses; turn ←. After 25m turn ← onto a bridleway (Lords Walk) into a wood. Follow this very straight track to Bramble Hall Cottages and onto the road. Turn ← onto Comp Lane, which joins Beechin Wood Lane. At the three-road junction, turn → and climb Long Mill Lane; bear ←. After 200m, turn ← onto a concealed bridleway beside a red-brick house.

When you regain the road, turn → and after 50m turn ← onto a bridleway: look for a stone bridleway marker and a track on your left that takes you back

Come on Pilgrim

the way you came, adjacent to the road, for 200m before bearing →. Follow this up the nose of the hill to **Basted**. Follow the sign for the restricted byway past the red postbox next to the stone wall. Now join a narrow singletrack, with a stone house on your left. Continue to the road and turn →. After 150m, turn ← onto Mill Lane and progress to the junction. Turn → for **Ightham**.

12 ■ After 100m, turn ← onto the Sevenoaks Road. Cross the **A25** on a footbridge. On the far side, turn ← by the white house onto Oldbury Lane. Climb gently and bear ← after the green. The byway continues but you turn ← into woods on a good track and climb Oldbury Hill. The best campsite on this route is here at Oldbury Hill (see Stage 13).

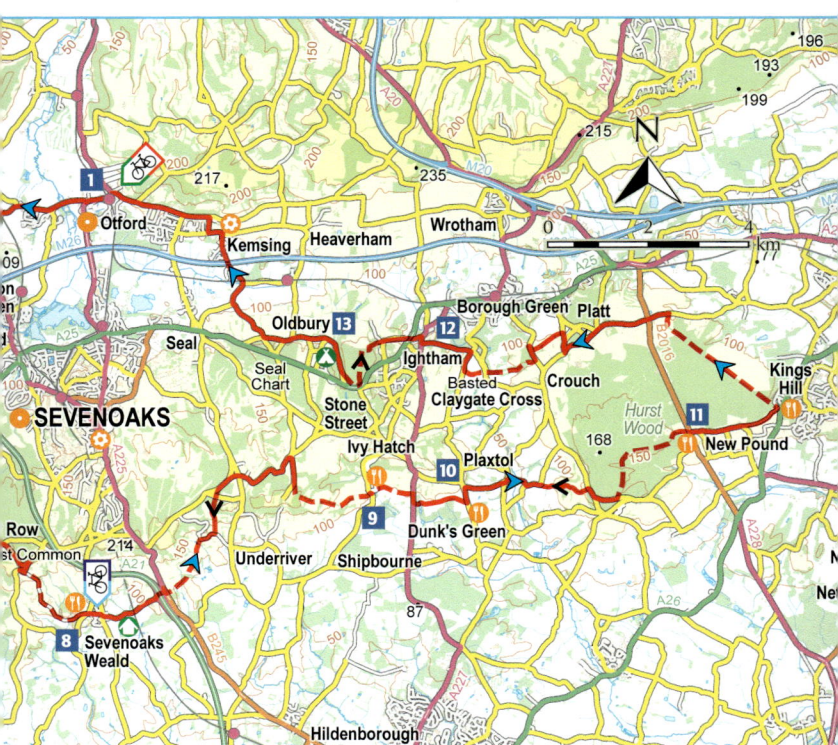

Route 5 – Kent Downs

Ightham Mote

13 ■ From the hilltop, follow the bridleway → as it drops through the woods. On meeting the road, turn →. Passing Oldbury Hill National Trust Campsite on the left, bear ← and continue for 2km. At the crossroads, turn → for Fullers Hill. At the junction with Church Lane, turn →. Descend and cross the railway bridge. Climb and then cross the **M26**. At the junction in **Kemsing**, turn ←. Continue to Childsbridge Lane and turn →. Climb gently and rejoin the Pilgrims' Way once more; turn ←. After 1km, at the junction, turn ← and take the first ← for **Otford Station**.

44% off road

6

Route 6 – East Sussex/Kent
High Weald Drifter

Start/Finish	Eridge, Railway Station
Time	2–3 days
Total distance	159km (99 miles)
Off-road distance	69km
Percentage off-road	44%
Total ascent/descent	2320m
Grade	Moderate ▲
Terrain	Singletrack 21%, track 23%, road 56%
Bike choice	Gravel/MTB

The High Weald is England's fourth-largest National Landscape, yet despite this its off-road routes remain relatively unexplored. Cycling is mostly restricted in Ashdown Forest, and the area lacks the dramatic mountain biking terrain of the Surrey Hills. However, the heathland, woodlands and sandstone outcrops are home to medieval monuments and ancient bridleways. This route connects the best off-road sections from Ardingly in the west to Bedgebury Forest in the east, combining green trails, hardpack forestry roads and tree-lined country lanes, far from busy roads and urban areas.

Route options

This route is demanding and certainly best done over a minimum of two days, with three days being preferable. Reaching Crowborough after a big day, head to Crowborough Camping and Caravanning Club site (if not wild-camping). If you are doing the route over three days, make Bluebell Camp your first night's stop and Cairds Camping your second.

Alternative start/finish: If you catch a train to East Grinstead and ride south, you could join the route at Forest Row (Stage 3) or Stone Farm Rocks climbing area (Stage 4). You could also start the route from Groombridge Station (Stage 1).

Route 6 – East Sussex/Kent

Summary table

Waypoint	Section	Distance (km)	Ascent (m)	Descent (m)
1	Eridge Station – Hartfield	8.8	50	60
2	Hartfield – Forest Way	8.3	160	140
3	Forest Way – Stone Farm Rocks climbing area	10.7	170	120
4	Stone Farm Rocks climbing area – Priest House (West Hoathly)	6.4	130	60
5	Priest House (West Hoathly) – Ardingly	4.4	40	90
6	Ardingly – Cinder Hill Lane	3.7	30	70
7	Cinder Hill Lane – Horsted Keynes	4.4	60	40
8	Horsted Keynes – Warren Farm House	1.7	20	10
9	Warren Farm House – Chelwood Beacon	6.6	140	90
10	Chelwood Beacon – Crowborough Road	3.5	70	80
11	Crowborough Road – A26	9.3	200	120
12	A26 – Crowborough Station (nr)	4.5	20	120
13	Crowborough Station (nr) – Burwood Farm	3.4	80	50
14	Burwood Farm – Argos Hill Windmill	3.7	90	80
15	Argos Hill Windmill – Mayfield	2.4	20	100
16	Mayfield – Mutton Hall	5.8	140	70
17	Mutton Hall – Rock Farm	3.4	10	70
18	Rock Farm – Red House Farm	6.6	140	170
19	Red House Farm – Stonegate Station	6.5	40	90
20	Stonegate Station – Berner's Hill (Bedgebury MTB Trails)	7.1	150	80
21	Berner's Hill (Bedgebury MTB trails) – Berner's Hill	14.3	140	140
22	Berner's Hill – Wadhurst Station	21.2	230	230
23	Wadhurst Station – Nap Wood	6.6	150	80
24	Nap Wood – Eridge Station	5.7	40	160

Shortcuts and extensions: Bail out at Crowborough Station (end of Stage 12) if Stages 1–12 have wiped you out, or from Stonegate Station (end of Stage 19) or Wadhurst (end of Stage 22) if you want to finish the route early (but note that both Stonegate and Wadhurst stations are on a different line from Eridge). Skip Stage

High Weald Drifter

Surface	Grade	Description
mixed	🟩	You quickly join a cycleway on a disused railway
off-road	🔺	Head to Pooh Sticks Bridge before climbing through the woods
paved	🟩	Pass the ancient ruins of Brambletye House and climb over the heath
mixed	🔺	Past the sandstone climbing rocks, through the vineyard and into the forestry – stunning
off-road	🔴	Wild singletrack is followed by a stop at the post office
paved	n/a	Paved linking section
mixed	🟩	Optional section includes fast descent
paved	n/a	Short linking section
off-road	🔺	Two optional off-road descents
mixed	🔺	Wooded descent and a steep climb
mixed	🟩	Long section includes fast cinder descent into the woods
paved	n/a	Linking section ends near station
paved	n/a	Linking section
mixed	🟩	Byway descent and climb to the windmill
mixed	🔺	Great descent past Pages Farm
mixed	🔺	Join the off-road NCN 21 (Sussex Diamond Way)
paved	n/a	Linking section
off-road	🔺	Fast bridleway and singletrack descents
mixed	🔺	Wild wooded descents and a climb to Stonegate Station
paved	n/a	Linking section
off-road	🔴	Optional wildcard: free MTB trails
mixed	🟩	Lakeside singletrack (mud permitting)
paved	n/a	Heading west to Nap Wood
paved	n/a	Final push back to Eridge Station

21 if you have no love of mountain bike trails, and avoid the lakeside trail around Bewl Water outside of summer months as it gets very muddy! There are a number of ways to miss out a few of the off-road sections by journeying on road: these modifications are described in the route directions.

Route 6 - East Sussex/Kent

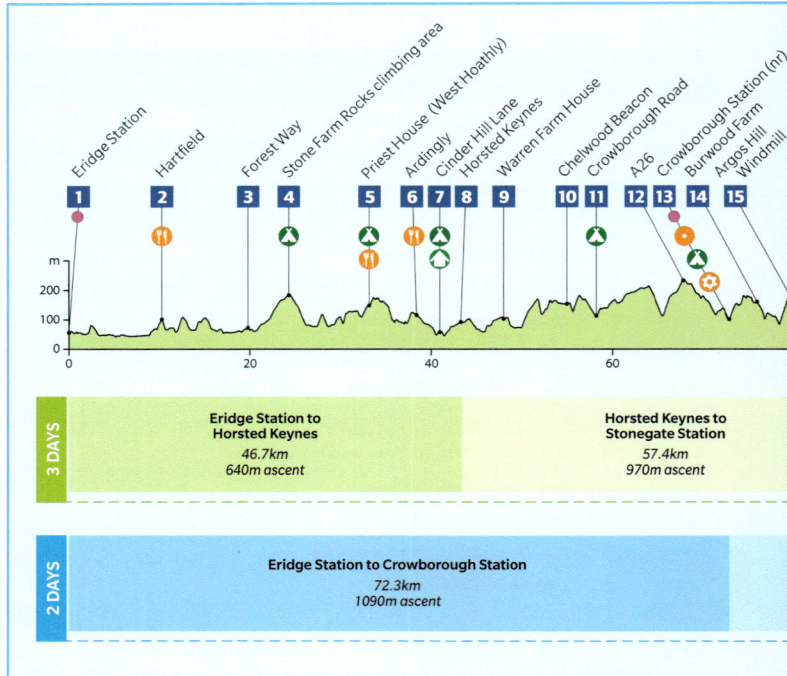

Big Gravel Days: An incredible day's riding would be to start at Groombridge and end your day at Crowborough. This 70km section includes the most variety and the wildest sections. If you fancy taking on the red mountain bike trails in Bedgebury Forest and the track around Bewl Water, start at Stonegate Station and finish at Wadhurst Station (40km).

Directions

1 ■ Once out of the station, turn → over the bridge before turning → onto Forge Road, signed NCN 21 (National Cycle Network). Head along the Spa Valley for 2km until you reach the junction with Corseley Road. Turn → and take signs for Groombridge. Cross the railway bridge and bear ←. Shortly after

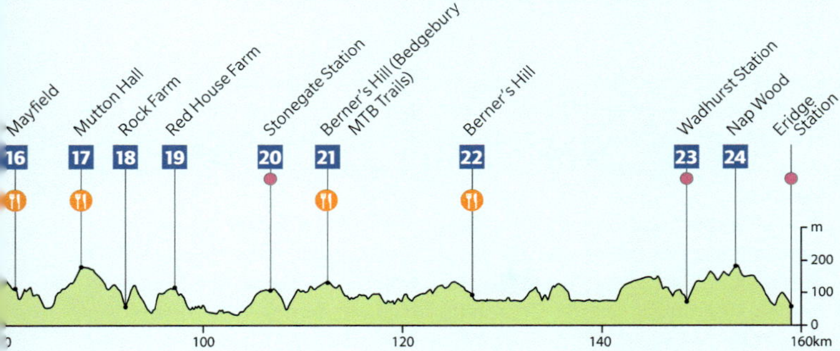

Mayfield
Mutton Hall
Rock Farm
Red House Farm
Stonegate Station
Berner's Hill (Bedgebury MTB Trails)
Berner's Hill
Wadhurst Station
Nap Wood
Eridge Station
16
17
18
19
20
21
22
23
24
m
200
100
0
100
120
140
160km

Stonegate Station to Eridge Station
54.9km
710m ascent

AVERAGE DAY – 53km / 7hr / 7.6kmh

Crowborough Station to Eridge Station
86.7km
1230m ascent

AVERAGE DAY – 79.5km / 9hr / 8.8kmh

SEVENOAKS
A26
ROYAL TUNBRIDGE WELLS
EAST GRINSTEAD
Groombridge
A21
Eridge Green
Crawley
Bewl Water
Forest Row
Crowborough
Wadhurst
Mayfield
Ashdown Forest
A22
High Weald
HEATHFIELD

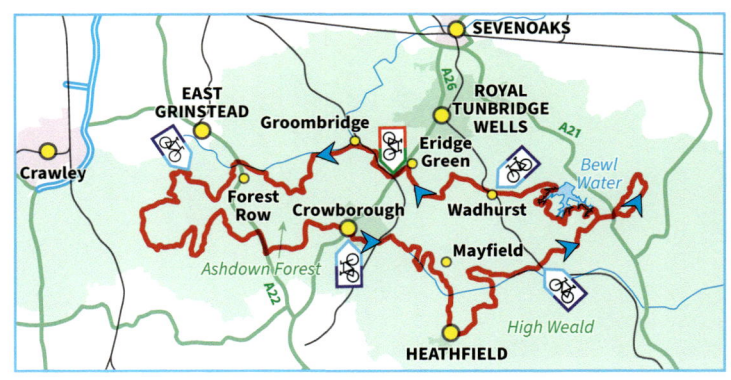

crossing a small stone bridge, look for signs on your right for NCN 21 and now turn ← to join the **Forest Way**. Continue on this disused railway track for 5km to **Hartfield**.

2 ▲ Leave the cycleway on an asphalt path to meet Edenbridge Road; turn ←. Climb through Hartfield. After a short steep descent, turn → onto an asphalt bridleway. After 800m fork ← and descend to Pooh Sticks Bridge. AA Milne grew up close to here and this is the bridge where Piglet and Pooh used to hang out.

Follow the bridleway as it climbs through the wood, fork → before the car park and descend to the road. Continue to the bottom of the hill and fork → over the bridge. Climb to the B2110. Turn ← and continue on Shepherds Hill past the Holy Trinity Church. On a sharp left corner, turn → and drop onto an asphalt bridleway, signed 'Ashdown House Prep School'. The road crosses a bridge over the Forest Way, and after 50m you take a small path to the → that takes you back to the **Forest Way**.

Snack time on the Forest Way

High Weald Drifter

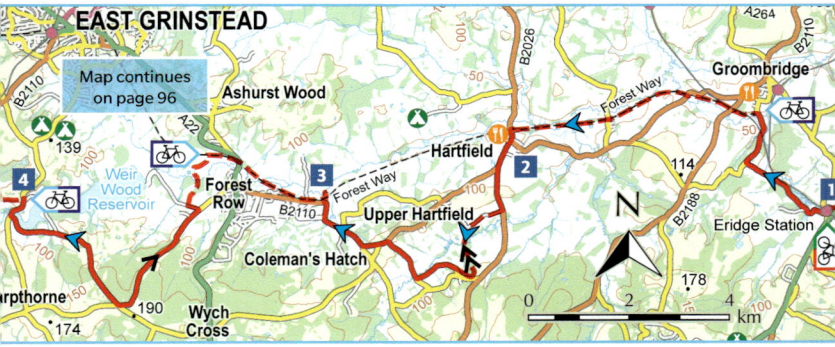

3 ■ Follow the Forest Way and cross the A22. After 300m turn ← onto a bridleway, pass the impressive ruins of Brambletye House, turn ← and climb through the woods to Kidbrooke Farm; turn ←. At Priory Road, turn → and continue for 2km over wooded common land. At the junction, turn → on Legsheath Lane, signed 'St Hill Green'. At the T-junction turn →, cross the bridge at the head of **Weir Wood Reservoir** and climb steeply for 250m. Turn ← onto a bridleway that passes the impressive Stone Farm Rocks climbing area.

4 ▲ Descend on the bridleway, through Mill Place and the Kingscote Vineyard. Ice creams (and wine!) are available at the Kingscote Vineyard shop. Pass below the Bluebell Railway Line bridge, bear → and climb on a good asphalt road before taking a sharp ←, signed 'Bush Farm'. This is the start of a permissive bridleway, known as the Yellow Brick Road, that criss-crosses the Gravetye Estate. The William Robinson Gravetye Estate is a 600-acre woodland given over to public access.

After 200m turn → and descend before a steep climb. Bear → and follow this great track through the wood before bearing ← and descending to the road. Turn → and continue past the head of the rail line to the Top Road; turn → and climb through **Sharpthorne**. Turn ← at the Fox pub and continue to **West Hoathly**. Bear ← past the church and Priest House.

5 ● When the road bears left, you continue ↑ onto a bridleway, where a large carved sandstone sign soon marks the entrance to Philpots Quarry. Continue on this good track, through Philpots Manor School. The next section is a candidate for the most stunning and exciting singletrack in this guidebook. Turn → onto a green chute to the right of the stables courtyard and drop into

Route 6 – East Sussex/Kent

Stone Farm Rocks is popular with climbers

the woods. Bear ← and continue on the High Weald Landscape Trail past waterfalls and over two footbridges. This good track hugs the edge of the valley for 2km before meeting the B2028. Turn ← and head into **Ardingly**. The Ardingly Post Office staff are very friendly and it's a great place to grab a snack.

6 Bear ← and descend before turning ← onto Burstowhill Lane. Take the next → signposted 'Bluebell Railway'. Follow this past **Horsted Keynes Station** (preserved) before meeting Cinder Hill Lane.

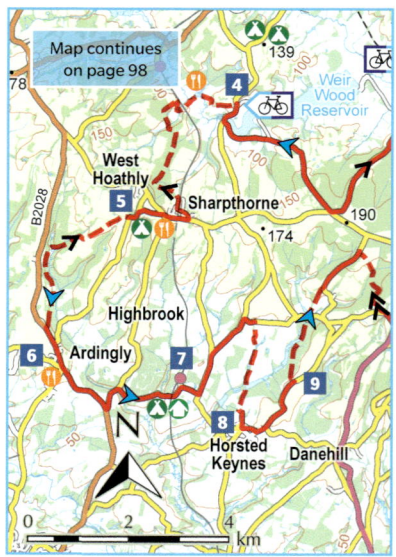

High Weald Drifter

> To **skip Stage 7** if you are short of time, fork → on Cinder Hill Lane and follow signs for Horsted Keynes.

7 ■ Turn ← on Cinder Hill Lane. After 800m fork → onto Chilling Street. Take the next → onto Broadhurst Manor Road. After 100m, turn → onto a bridleway. Follow this past a series of impressive lakes on a good cinder track for 2km. Take the car-wide path signed 'No Vehicle Access' to the left of a brick wall to reach the green in **Horsted Keynes**.

8 Head through the village and bear ← onto Birchgrove Road. After 100m, pass a junction on your right signed 'Danehill, Chelwood Common'. Stay on Birchgrove Road for 1km to Warren Farm House, then continue for 100m.

> To **bypass Stage 9** and its two off-road sections, continue on Birchgrove Road past Warren Farm House (on your left) to Chelwood Gate.

9 ▲ Turn ← onto a hidden bridleway and descend on a cinder singletrack. This opens out and descends through a plantation flanked by a series of ponds on your left. Shortly you meet the road.

Taking a breather in Giffard's Wood in the Gravetye Estate

Route 6 – East Sussex/Kent

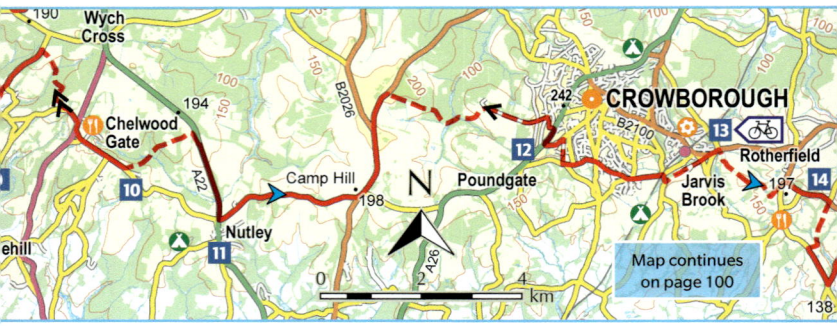

> To omit the next off-road section and take a **shortcut to Chelwood Gate**, turn → onto the road and head east on School Lane and Birchgrove Road.

Turn ← onto the road and cross a ford. Immediately turn → onto a good track. Climb through a wood to the road. Continue ↑ for 800m before turning → onto a bridleway; this opens up into fields, with spectacular views to the south. A steep descent on a stepped singletrack takes you over a wooden bridge. Climb through the plantation on a good track. When this tops out, bear → and meet the road opposite the Red Lion pub at **Chelwood Gate**. Turn → and continue towards Chelwood Beacon.

> To **bypass Stage 10**, continue on the road to Outback Farm and meet the A22 on the edge of Nutley.

10 ▲ Turn ← onto a bridleway into the woods. Descend on a wide path to a ford. Climb on the cinder track, past Chelwood Vachery, fork → over common land and continue to the A22. Join the road and turn →. First descend and then climb towards **Nutley** before taking a sharp ← signposted to Crowborough.

> In Stage 11, to **go directly to Crowborough**, avoiding the cinder track byway to Old Mill Farm, turn → onto New Road at the junction with the B2026.

11 ■ Continue across Ashdown Forest, with fantastic views to the left and right across the heathland. Turn ← onto the B2026 and continue for 1.2km before

High Weald Drifter

forking ➔, signed 'Groombridge'. After 800m turn ➔ onto a bridleway past a cute mock-Tudor cottage and descend on an exceptional cinder track for 1km; bear ➔ and then ⬅ past Old Mill Farm. Cross a bridge, bear ⬅ and climb to Warren Chimney. Turn ➔ onto the asphalt, continue through Crowborough Warren, then turn ➔ and then ➔ again on meeting the A26.

12 After 300m turn ⬅ onto South View Road. After 300m, turn ➔ onto a byway. Drop down to Hurtis Road and turn ⬅. Continue on this road and cross the railway bridge. Turn ➔ onto Hadlow Down Road and then ⬅ onto Tubwell Lane. Maintain your direction east when the byway bears right. When reaching the road, you are close to **Crowborough Station**. Crowborough Station can be reached 500m off the route.

13 Continue over the junction on Tubwell Lane. After 200m turn ➔ onto a concealed bridleway. Climb past Dewlands Manor Golf Club and then take a ⬅ through a gate onto the golf course; follow the bridleway signs and bear ➔. After 100m, instead of following the bridleway (which is very overgrown), dismount here and push your bike 60m on a well-maintained path to the road. Turn ⬅ onto Cottage Hill Lane. After 100m turn ➔ onto the B2101. After 1.5km you reach Burwood Farm on your left.

> If time is tight or the weather is bad, you can **skip Stage 14** and continue on the B2101 to the Argos Hill Windmill.

Choose your line carefully when riding on ice

Route 6 – East Sussex/Kent

14 ■ Turn → onto a byway that drops into the woods opposite Burwood Farm. Continue to the road, turn ←. After 1km take a sharp ← onto Argos Hill Road. Follow this back up the hill to **Argos Hill** and the Argos Hill Windmill.

15 ▲ Continue with the Argos Hill Windmill on your left. Turn → onto a gravel bridleway and descend through Pages Farm before climbing to the road; turn ←. When you reach the busy `A267` on the outskirts of **Mayfield**, look for the blue NCN 21 sign on the far side of the road. Follow this up a good path to Stone Cross; turn →. After 100m bear ← onto Knowle Hill following NCN 21.

16 ▲ Knowle Hill becomes Newick Lane and you continue south to Old Mill Farm. Here, you join the off-road NCN 21 and climb into the woods on a car-wide track. This joins the Sussex Diamond Way and you climb gently to Mutton Hall and the `A265`.

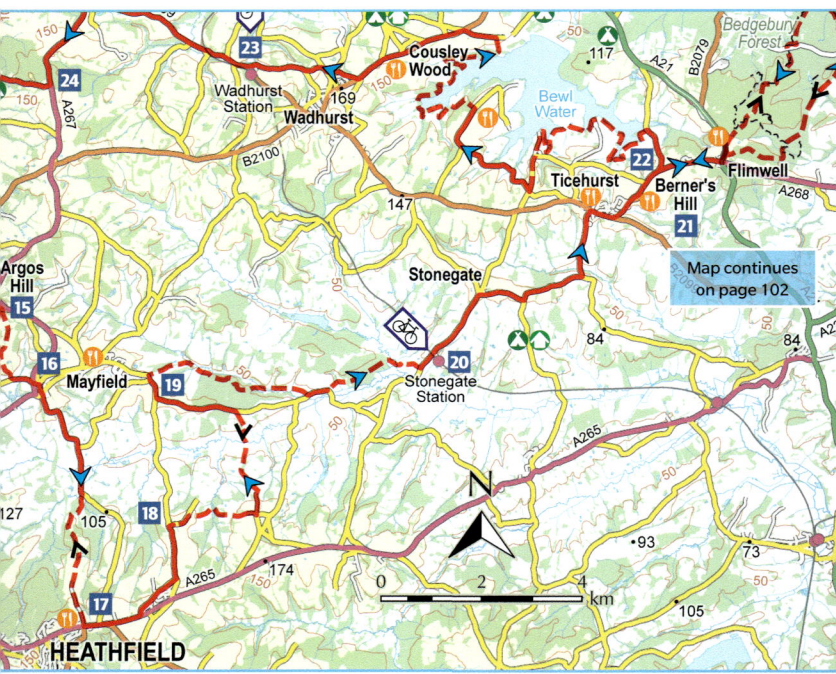

High Weald Drifter

The onset of golden hour

17 Turn ← and continue for 1km before turning onto Street End Lane. At the junction, turn ← onto Scotsford Road. After a further 1km you reach Rock Farm.

> Planning ahead, if you want to **bypass the off-road section in Stage 19**, turn → on joining the road after Froghole Farm in Stage 18.

18 ▲ Take the → onto Pottens Mill Lane and after 500m turn →, signed 'Braylsham Castle'. The asphalt bridleway drops to Pottens Mill Farm. Bear → and climb through a field to the road at Corner Farm; turn ←. When the asphalt runs out, bear ← on the gravel track. This becomes a singletrack and you follow the course of a stream into the valley. Manoeuvre yourself through Froghole Farm and turn ← onto a concrete drive that climbs steeply north. At the road, turn ←. At the junction, turn → and continue, with Red House Farm on your left.

19 ▲ When the road bears sharply left, you turn → onto a bridleway, Merryweather Lane. Bear ← and descend. Before crossing the stream, fork → and enjoy a sweeping rollercoaster of a track through Hawksden Park Wood. Continue east on this to the road; turn ←. When the road bears right, downhill, you turn ← towards Bivelham Farm. The bridleway heads through the farmyard, past the oast houses and into Newbridge Wood. When this spits you out on the road, turn ←. **Stonegate Station** is on the right.

20 Climb Peartree Hill into **Stonegate**. Turn →, signed 'Ticehurst'. Continue through Cottenden and keep following Ticehurst signs until you reach the

Route 6 – East Sussex/Kent

village of **Ticehurst**. Turn → after the phone box. After 300m fork ← signed 'Flimwell, Hawkhurst'. Continue for 1km to **Berner's Hill**.

> When you reach Berner's Hill, you have a choice of routes. If you fancy riding the free mountain bike trails in **Bedgebury Forest** (Stage 21), continue on the B2087 to Flimwell. This is a wildcard: if you like mountain bike trails, you will be in heaven; otherwise, perhaps omit this section.

> If time is tight or the weather isn't in your favour, turn ← onto Rosemary Lane and ride the trail around **Bewl Water** (Stage 22). If the ground is waterlogged or it's been raining recently, avoid the Bewl Water trail as it can be very muddy; instead, follow the minor roads west towards Wadhurst.

21 ● Continue to **Flimwell**. Turn ← onto London Road. After 100m, turn → onto an asphalt bridleway by a small white columnated house. Bear ← and head into the woods to pick up the trails. After 500m on this bridleway, look out for the red mountain bike trail as it intersects the track. Turn → and head round counterclockwise. On leaving the trail centre, retrace your ride to the junction in **Flimwell**, turn → and return to **Berner's Hill**.

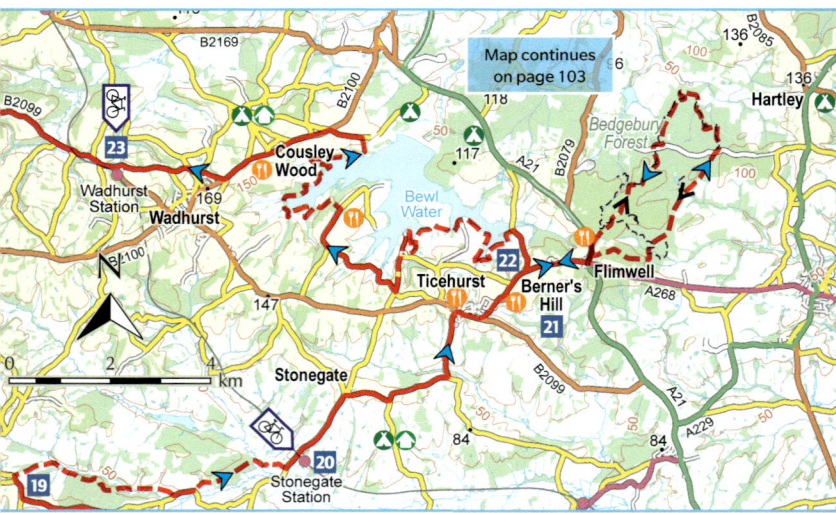

High Weald Drifter

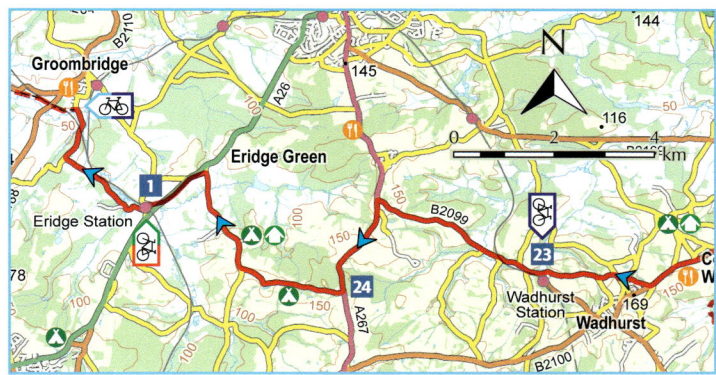

22 ■ Turn → onto Rosemary Lane. Continue towards Bewl Water, and 25m before the bridge turn ← onto a trail. Hug the shore of **Bewl Water** for the next 2km before returning to asphalt. After climbing gently for 1km, turn ←, signed 'Bewl Water Route'. After 2km, bear → and then turn ←, signed 'Bewl Water Route'. When you meet the bridleway, turn ←. Follow the track for 3km around the shore until it terminates at Hook Farm and returns you to the road; turn ← onto Bewlbridge Road.

Continue for 400m to the B2100; turn ←. After 3km, after Pell Green, turn → onto Balaclava Lane, signed 'Woods Green'. At the T-junction, turn →. After 100m, turn ←, signed 'Wadhurst Station'. Continue to the B2099.

> If the train beckons, turn ← here for **Wadhurst Station**. However, if you have a return ticket from Eridge, you will have to continue on the route as these two stations are not on the same line.

23 Turn → and follow the B2099 for 3.5km to Sleeches Cross. Turn ←, signed 'Mark Cross'. After 2km, opposite a sign into the National Trust's Nap Wood, turn → onto Danegate.

24 Head west along Danegate. After the green, turn → onto Sham Farm Road and continue on this for 2km. Before you reach the A26, fork ←, signed 'Eridge Station'. *Enjoy the sweeping views over the valley to your left as you head to the station.* The auxiliary road that runs parallel to the A26 returns to the road, but you turn ← onto a cycle path to the left of the track which drops to a gravel track. Turn → and continue to **Eridge Station**.

7 — 42% off road

Route 7 – Kent/Sussex Coast
Battle Cruiser

Start/Finish	Battle, Railway Station
Time	1–2 days
Total distance	69.4km (43.3 miles)
Off-road distance	29.2km
Percentage off-road	42%
Total ascent/descent	730m
Grade	Easy ■
Terrain	Singletrack 7%, track 35%, road 58%
Bike choice	Gravel/MTB

So much variety and history packed into such a short route! The town of Battle is situated on the high ground above the site of the Anglo-Saxons' most famous defeat to the Normans at the Battle of Hastings. Taking advantage of the 1066 Country Walk (sections of which are a cycle trail) where possible, this route contrasts ancient woodland with coastal scenery and boasts three castles and an abbey. It can be done in one big day or can be punctuated with a stay at Normans Bay campsite.

Route options

This ride is the shortest and easiest in the guide and can be ridden in a day if you make an early start from Battle. However, the majority of the climbing is in the final third, so don't get caught out. A good schedule would be to take it easy over two days, stopping off at Normans Bay campsite in Pevensey Bay, the halfway point of Stage 4.

Alternative start/finish: Continue all the way to the coast on the train to start the route at Hastings.

Shortcuts and extensions: If you start at Hastings and finish at Battle, you can reduce the route to 50km. If you exit the route at Bexhill, you can take the train to Hastings and head north, or head west to Eastbourne.

Big Gravel Days: This route is a Big Gravel Day!

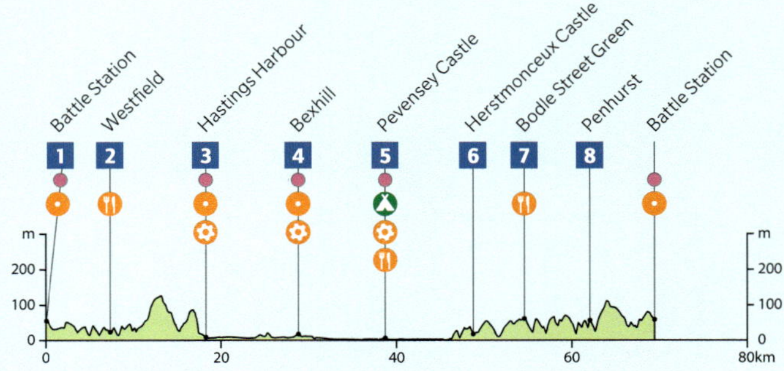

Battle Cruiser

	Battle Station to Pevensey Castle	Pevensey Castle to Battle Station
2 DAYS	*38.8km* *325m ascent*	*30.6km* *405m ascent*

AVERAGE DAY – 34.7km / 5hr / 6.9kmh

Waypoints:
1. Battle Station
2. Westfield
3. Hastings Harbour
4. Bexhill
5. Pevensey Castle
6. Herstmonceux Castle
7. Bodle Street Green
8. Penhurst
   Battle Station

Route 7 – Kent/Sussex Coast

Summary table

Waypoint	Section	Distance (km)	Ascent (m)	Descent (m)
1	Battle Station – Westfield	7	70	90
2	Westfield – Hastings Harbour	11.7	190	220
3	Hastings Harbour – Bexhill	9	30	30
4	Bexhill – Pevensey Castle	11.1	35	30
5	Pevensey Castle – Herstmonceux Castle	8.2	30	20
6	Herstmonceux Castle – Bodle Street Green	6	110	70
7	Bodle Street Green – Penhurst	8	130	150
8	Penhurst – Battle Station	8.4	135	120

Map continues on page 111

Battle Cruiser

Surface	Grade	Description
mixed	🟩	Into the off-road shortly after the start
mixed	🔺	A short road section is followed by a wooded byway before you drop down to the sea
mixed	🟩	An easy, breezy saunter along the seafront
mixed	🟩	Minor roads take you inland to a historic castle
off-road	🔺	Riding across the Pevensey Levels to Herstmonceux Castle
off-road	🔺	Climb through the woods before descending through forestry
mixed	🔺	Tough section on nice byways and minor roads
mixed	🔺	Fast road to the 1066 Walk and onwards to Battle

Directions

1 🟩 Leave the station and turn →. Continue through the car park and follow the walkway, with the train tracks on your right, to Marley Lane; turn → and head over the level crossing. After 500m, turn → onto the 1066 Country Walk (bridleway, marked with a red badge) as it plunges into the wood. The path is narrow and steep at first but broadens to a car-wide gravel track. Continue through Great Wood to the A21; turn →. After 300m turn ← onto Bluemans Lane. After passing Buckhurst Campsite, continue on this tree-lined country road before turning → onto Wheel Lane and continuing to **Westfield**.

2 🔺 With the New Inn pub on your left, head over the busy A28 onto Moor Lane and follow this as it climbs to a staggered junction. Turn → onto Ivyhouse Lane. Immediately after passing Intuitive Horse Guest House and New Coghurst Farm, turn → onto a concrete drive. Follow this restricted byway over a stream and on to Rodger's Farm, where you turn ←. The byway crosses the road and heads into Maplehurst Wood along Beaney's Lane. At the busy road, turn ←.

Opposite the Shell garage, turn → onto a byway (St Helens Park Road) and descend on a great car-wide track into the wood. Exiting the wood, bear ← on Langham Road until you reach Elphinstone Road; turn → and continue to a mini-roundabout. Take the ← onto Mount Pleasant Road. Climb to the junction with Priory Road; turn →. After the large red-brick academy, turn ← onto Croft Road. Bend → with the road and shortly after this dismount and turn ← onto a footpath. Cross the busy A259 onto Harold Road; turn →.

Dropping onto the 1066 Country Walk (bridleway) just outside Battle

Immediately after All Saints Church, join the cycle route to Hastings Harbour along All Saints Street. At Rock-a-Nore Road, turn → and then ← onto East Beach Street. Opposite the London Trader pub, turn ← into a pedestrian zone and follow the blue cycleway signs →. Where this meets the road, immediately turn ← and follow the cycleway to the beach at **Hastings**.

3 ■ Turn →. Keep the sea on your left and continue, first on a concrete esplanade and then a gravel track, to **Bexhill**. You can follow the promenade for many miles as it runs adjacent to the road.

> In Stage 4, on the approach to **Normans Bay**, the Star Inn is a good option for refreshments. Normans Bay campsite is the perfect place to overnight if you are doing this over two days.

4 ■ Turn onto Channel View East and join the promenade once more. When this runs out, join West Parade Road. After 200m, follow the blue cycleway sign, 'Pevensey 6', along South Cliff to Cooden Drive. At the Cooden Beach Hotel turn →, and before the railway bridge turn ← onto Herbrand Walk. Continue as the road bears → along Sluice Lane, then 300m past the Star Inn turn ←,

Battle Cruiser

taking signs for the station. Continue on Coast Road to **Pevensey Bay**. At the traffic lights, turn ➔ and head inland on the A259. When you reach the junction with High Street, turn ⬅ and follow the road to the walls of **Pevensey Castle**. Castle Cottage Tearoom to the left of Pevensey Castle has a great cake selection.

5 ▲ Follow the road as it bends ➔ and hugs the battlements of Pevensey Castle. On the left-hand bend, turn ➔ onto a gravel track that cuts between two houses, signed '1066 Country Walk'.

> The **1066 Country Walk** follows the route taken by the forces of William, Duke of Normandy, as they headed to meet Harold. Sections of it are bridleway so can be cycled.

Cross the busy Pevensey bypass and pick up the track once more. Follow the course of the Pevensey Haven on its southern bank for 2km to Bridge Farm. On reaching the road, turn ➔, continue over a red-brick bridge to Rickney Road, turn ➔ and cross a second bridge. Directly in front of you, a car-wide track heads over the fields following the Hurst Haven. After 2km

Beach huts beneath the esplanade en route to Bexhill

Crossing the Pevensey Levels near Herstmonceux Castle

you leave the eastern bank of the Haven on an indistinct track that becomes a concrete drive after 500m. Turn ← and climb gently towards All Saints Church. Before you reach the church, fork → and continue on the 1066 Walk through a field and then up a singletrack climb. **Herstmonceux Castle** is an imposing sight to your left.

6 ▲ Continue uphill on a tough singletrack, passing the Observatory Science Centre on your left. When you meet the road, turn ←. After 200m turn ← onto a gravel track and enjoy a fast descent through mature plantation before climbing to Little Comphurst Farm and turning → onto Comphurst Lane. When you reach the green at **Windmill Hill**, turn → onto the A271. After passing a Premier shop on your left, turn ← onto Joe's Lane and follow this to **Bodle Street Green**. The White Horse Inn at Bodle Street Green is a possible lunch stop if riding the route over two days.

7 ▲ Bear ← past the White Horse Inn. After the pub, continue for 1.5km until the road turns abruptly left, then turn → onto a restricted byway. After 100m fork → and descend. Fork ← when the drive continues to Water Mill Farm, cross the stream and climb to the road. Turn ←, and after 50m turn → onto a gravel drive. Descend on this byway and follow it as it turns sharply ←. Continue to descend and cross the bridge. Climb on the good car-wide track, turn ← and meet up with the asphalt once more. At the junction opposite Glyde's Farm, turn →. Descend and then climb to **Ponts Green**; turn → onto Church Road. After 500m turn ←, signed 'Penhurst'. Continue to **Penhurst**.

Battle Cruiser

8 ▲ Descend and then climb steeply; at the junction, turn ➔, signed 'Battle'. Follow Penhurst Lane for 2km, cross the A271 and turn ➔ onto Crowders Lane. When you meet the B2204, bear ➔. After 1km turn ← onto a bridleway, signed 'Farthings Farm'. After 500m this meets up with the 1066 Walk once more and you follow this good cycle track to **Battle** and the site of the Battle of Hastings: a nondescript marshy field. Now climb through the left flank of the field and meet a better track that leads to Battle Abbey. On meeting the road once more, turn ➔, continue to the mini-roundabout and take the second exit, signed 'Hastings, Battle Station'. After a second mini-roundabout, turn ← for **Battle Station**.

8 — 51% off road

Route 8 – Kent

The Cantii Way

Start/Finish	Wye, Railway Station
Time	2–5 days
Total distance	249km (154.7 miles)
Off-road distance	127.9km
Percentage off-road	51%
Total ascent/descent	1400m
Grade	Easy ■
Terrain	Singletrack 6%, track 45%, road 49%
Bike choice	Gravel/Hybrid

Launched in 2022; by Cycling UK, the Cantii Way is named after the Celtic tribe that lived in this area. It starts life in the woods of the Kent Downs but the majority of the ride hugs the Kent coast until you reach the windswept headland of Dungeness. It's a long but easy ride with breathtaking scenery, simple wayfinding and a good selection of accommodation options.

Route options

Alternative start/finish: If you are coming from London, there are 14 stations on or near the route, served by the stations King's Cross, Victoria, St Pancras and Charing Cross. The fastest journey times are between St Pancras International and Ashford International. If you are based south of London, consider starting at Winchelsea or Rye. If you are doing this route in stages over a period of time, you are spoilt for choice of ingress and egress stations.

Shortcuts and extensions: A really nice shortcut can be made by skipping from Canterbury (end of Stage 2) over to Sandwich (start of Stage 7) on NCN 1 (National Cycle Network). This slices 60km out of the route and breaks up the

The Cantii Way

sometimes monotonous riding on concrete esplanades that characterises much of the ride. Heading north to Canterbury from Dover on the NCN 16 or from Folkestone on the NCN 17 are also worthwhile prospects if you fancy shortening the route considerably.

Big Gravel Days: If you plan to do this route over a few visits, there are some great options: Ashford to Whitstable (on route, Stage 18 and Stages 1–3) is a great day's riding; along the coast from Whitstable to Folkestone (on route, Stages 4–9) is also totally achievable; the next leg would be Folkestone to Rye (Stages 10–12) plus a further 2km off route to Winchelsea; and lastly, Winchelsea to Ashford (on route, Stages 13–18).

Route 8 – Kent

Summary table

Waypoint	Section	Distance (km)	Ascent (m)	Descent (m)
1	Wye Station – Chilham Castle	13.6	170	190
2	Chilham Castle – Canterbury	9.4	40	60
3	Canterbury – Whitstable Harbour	13.9	100	110
4	Whitstable Harbour – Birchington	19.4	70	70
5	Birchington – Broadstairs	18.4	100	95
6	Broadstairs – Sandwich	15.7	80	80
7	Sandwich – Deal	9.8	10	10
8	Deal – Dover	16.8	170	170
9	Dover – Folkestone	17.9	300	240
10	Folkestone – Dymchurch	20.4	50	110
11	Dymchurch – Dungeness	13.5	10	10
12	Dungeness – Rye	11.3	20	10
13	Rye – Winchelsea Beach	8.9	10	20
14	Winchelsea Beach – Rye	8.1	30	30
15	Rye – Appledore	9.7	10	20
16	Appledore – Shadoxhurst	23	150	110
17	Shadoxhurst – Ashford International	8.8	40	35
18	Ashford International – Wye Station	10.4	40	30

Directions

1 ▲ Head north from Wye Station on Bramble Lane. Cross the A28 and climb White Hill. At Jackets Field turn → across the car park and join the track heading into the wood. Fork → after 200m, fork ← in 1km, and → in 200m. In 200m turn ← onto the North Downs Way. Continue on this for 3.5km to **Chilham**. Turn ← off Mountain Street onto School Hill and continue to Chilham Castle.

2 ■ Turn → across the car park and head through the village and along The Street. Turn ← at the Woolpack Hotel and follow Bagham Road as it bears →. At the junction on your left, turn →. Follow the A28 for 800m before turning →

Surface	Grade	Description
mixed	▲	Some tough singletrack on the North Downs Way
mixed	■	NCN 18 into Canterbury
mixed	▲	The Crab and Winkle Way is one of the highlights of this route
mixed	■	Easy riding on the esplanade
mixed	■	Pick your way around the historic seafront of Margate
mixed	■	Tricky wayfinding
mixed	■	Skirt around Pegwell Bay
mixed	■	The White Cliffs are a worthwhile detour
mixed	■	Skirt around the top of Folkestone, past the Abbot's Cliff Sound Mirror
mixed	■	Back to the coast after a brief sojourn inland
mixed	■	Stunning unique habitat
mixed	■	Across the wild marshes
mixed	■	A loop around the nature reserve
mixed	■	Pick up the 1066 Country Walk and return to Rye
paved	n/a	A dull but necessary section
mixed	▲	If there's been rain, take the road from Woodchurch to Shadoxhurst
mixed	■	Head into Ashford on the banks of the Stour
mixed	■	Easy rolling on the last few kilometres back to Wye

onto Pickelden Lane. Follow this over the railway crossing and climb through the woods on NCN 18 before turning ← onto Thruxted Lane. After 500m, bear → onto Bobbin Lodge Hill. Continue across a staggered junction at Shalmsford Street onto Bolts Hill and continue on Parish Road across an impressive red-brick bridge to **Chartham**.

Go ↑ at the phone box, down Church Lane. At the junction with Station Road, turn →, signposted 'Pilgrims Cycle Trail, Canterbury 3'. Before the stone bridge, turn ← into a car park indicated with an NCN 18 sticker. Follow this along the banks of the Great Stour into **Canterbury**.

3 ▲ On the path 50m beyond the A2050 bridge on Hambrook Marshes, turn ←. This takes you through a brick doorway onto Whitehall Road. Turn → then

Route 8 – Kent

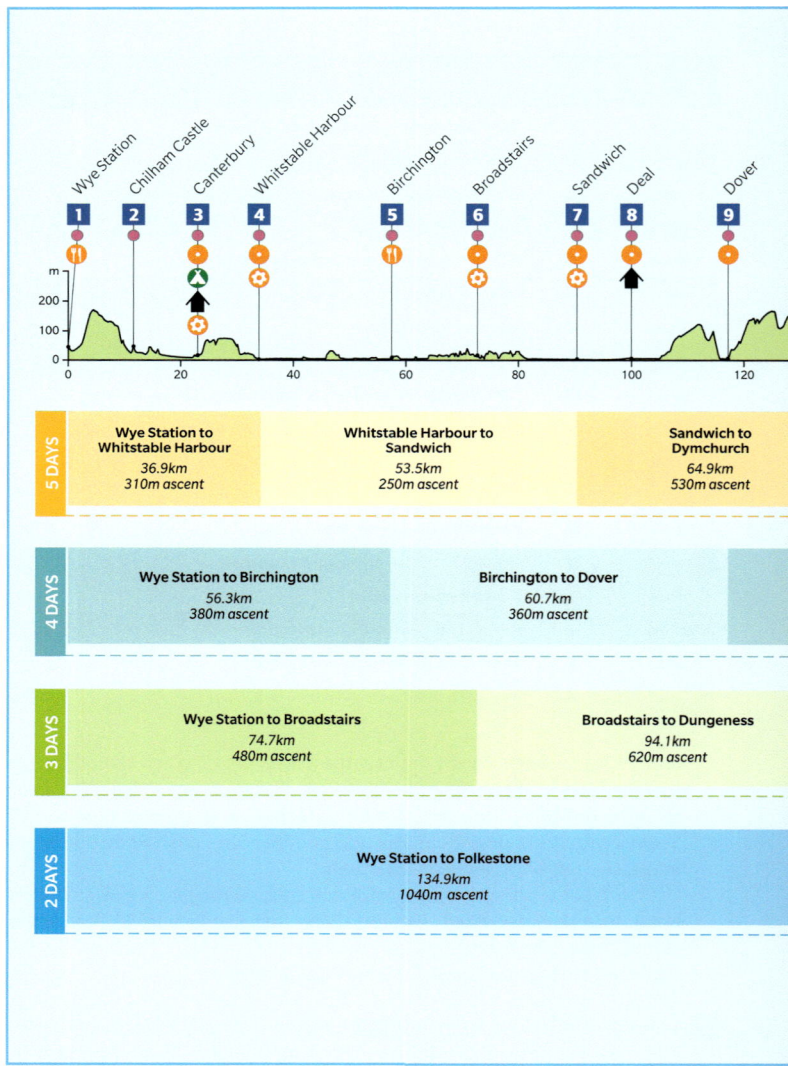

The Cantii Way

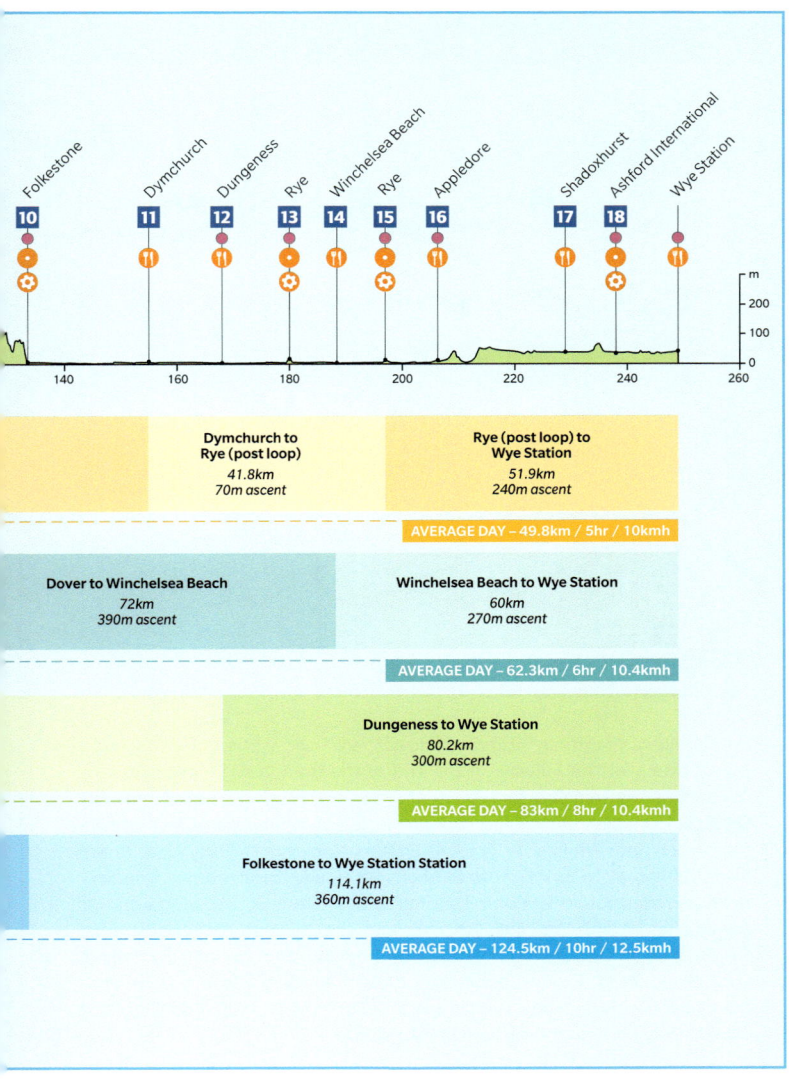

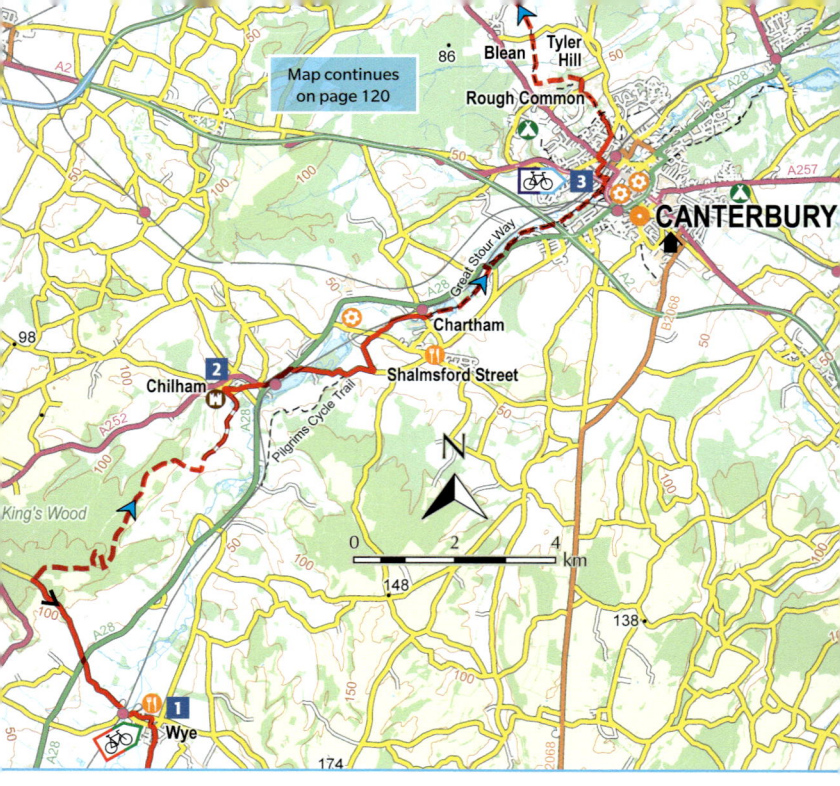

immediately ← onto Whitehall Bridge Road. Follow this before taking a footbridge over the railway. At the end of the road, turn → onto Queens Avenue then → onto Orchard Street. At the end of the street, turn ← onto the A290 (St Dunstan's Street) and continue past the mini-roundabout opposite the church onto Whitstable Road. After 20m, turn → onto Forty Acres Road. After 500m look to fork ← onto St Michael's Road. This becomes Salisbury Road and then you fork → onto Lyndhurst Close. Turn →, following signs for the Crab and Winkle Way. Follow this through the **University of Kent campus**.

Turn → on University Road, then at the mini-roundabout turn ← onto Park Wood Road. Continue for 1km to Oaks Nursery. Here, turn → onto the cycleway, signposted 'Whitstable 5'. Follow the well-marked **Crab and Winkle Way** north to the harbour at **Whitstable**.

The Cantii Way

Heading to Whitstable on the Crab and Winkle Way (photo: Jordan Gibbons)

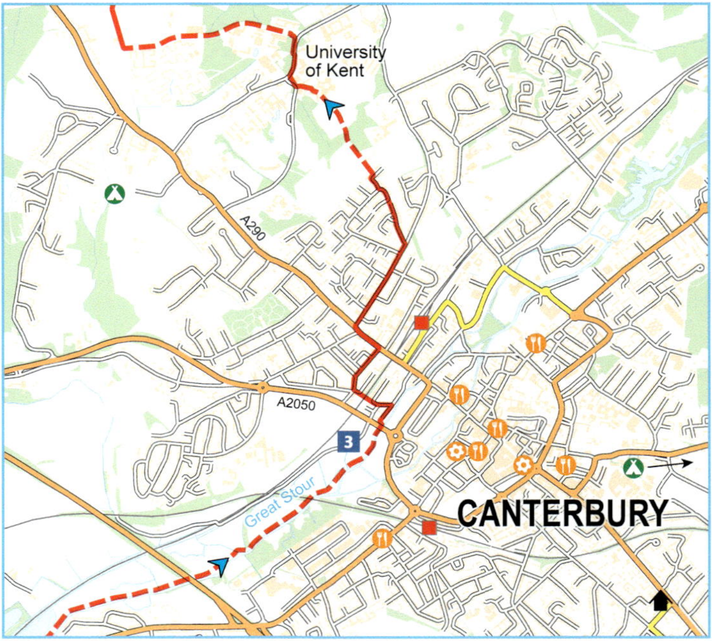

Route 8 – Kent

4 ■ Follow the Saxon Shore Way along the coast, through Hampton and on past **Herne Bay**. Before you reach **Reculver**, the concrete runs out and the path forces you up to the road; turn ←. Head through the town, keeping as close to the coast as the going will allow. Now you are back on the concrete walkway that flanks the Northern Sea Wall; follow this to **Birchington**.

5 ■ Follow this level pathway as it hugs the winding coastline past **Margate**, with the sea as your constant companion to the left. You meet the coast road and follow this for 300m before your route heads back onto the coast path. At Kingsgate, follow the B2052 before dropping back onto the path at Hunton

The Cantii Way

House. Head back to the road once more after 500m and turn ←. Drop to the path and continue to Viking Bay at **Broadstairs**.

6 ■ Bear → and head up Harbour Street. At the junction with Albion Street, turn ← opposite the Dolphin pub. When the road bears right, walk your bike through a cut-through on the left. Bear → along Victoria Parade before taking a cut-through, signposted 'Louisa Bay'. Turn → on the coast path. Continue to **Ramsgate**.

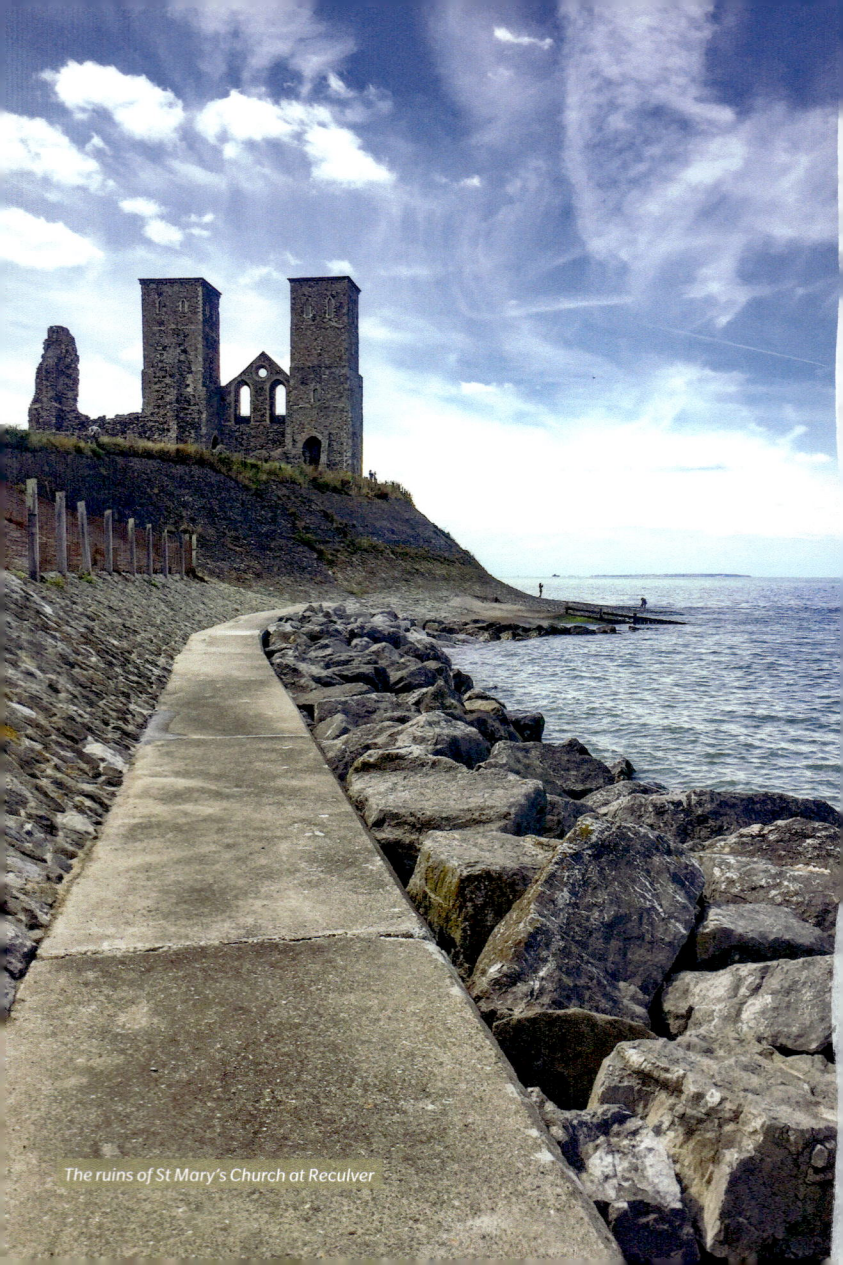
The ruins of St Mary's Church at Reculver

The Cantii Way

Follow the well-signposted Viking Way Cycle Path as it runs around Pegwell Bay beside Sandwich Road. After Sandwich Road becomes Ramsgate Road, maintain your direction for 3km before bearing ← on the asphalt cycleway, following the busy Monks Way auxiliary road. Continue and bear → as your course returns you to Ramsgate Road once more. After the next roundabout, cross the River Stour into **Sandwich**.

7 ■ Turn ← then bear ← and continue on the cycleway as it hugs the Stour before being taken onto Sandown Road. Maintain your course for 6km until you reach the outskirts of **Deal**.

8 ■ Turn ← and take the route onto the seafront. When the road turns right, you continue on the seafront, passing **Deal Castle** on your right. Maintain this for 4km to **Kingsdown** before turning → onto Boundary Road and then ← when this meets Kingsdown Road. Continue along Undercliffe Road and then turn inland onto Oldstairs Road, signposted 'NCN 1'. After 3km, at **St Margaret's at Cliffe**, turn ← through the village before turning → onto Reach Road, signposted 'NCN 1, Dover'. Reach Road becomes Upper Road as you leave the village.

> A kilometre beyond St Margaret's at Cliffe, a gated road on the left provides access to the **White Cliffs of Dover**. You can easily push your bike to this iconic vista.

The White Cliffs of Dover

Map continues on page 126

Follow Upper Road for 3km over open fields of short-cropped grass before the road bears ← and begins to descend. At Fox Hill Down, signposted 'Coastguard Operations Centre' on the left, you join off-road NCN 1. Bear →, rejoin Upper Road and take a bridge across the A2. When you meet the A258, turn ← and descend on Castle Hill Road into **Dover**.

The Cantii Way

9 ■ Cross Maison Dieu Road, taking signs for the town centre. Now bear ← on Kings Street and head towards the sea. Take a foot tunnel under the A20 when you reach the front, and turn →. Continue along the esplanade for 200m into the marina. At the junction with Union Street, turn → and cross a bridge. Continue to the A20 and join a cycle path on the left that follows the big road. Take a crossing over to the right-hand side of the A20 when directed, following NCN 2. At the second roundabout, follow the NCN → up a shallow climb on the Old Folkestone Road.

Continue through suburban estates until you see a cycleway on the left heading up a grass bank. Follow this onto a bridge and across the A20. Continue on this perfect cycleway for 3.5km until you meet the Folkestone Road; turn ← on NCN 2, signposted 'Hastings'. After joining the NCN 2 towards Folkestone, keep an eye out for the Abbot's Cliff Sound Mirror – an incredible place for a wild camp on a warm summer's night.

Morning ritual after a wild camp at the Abbot's Cliff Sound Mirror

Route 8 – Kent

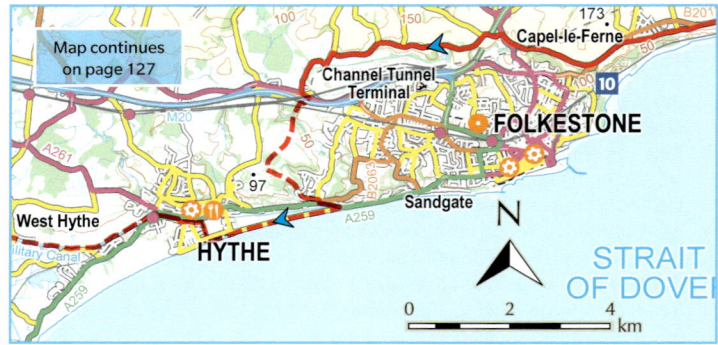

After 200m fork ← onto the Old Dover Road. After 1km rejoin the B2011 and after 500m, with the Valiant Soldier pub on your left, fork → onto a lane, Crete Road East, on the edge of **Folkestone**.

10 ■ After 2km cross the busy A260 and take Crete Road West. Follow this, past the Folkestone White Horse below to your left, for 3km. Fork ← onto Danton Lane. Descend steeply through Peene and Newington on the NCN 17 to the A20. Use the cycleway to continue under the roads and the Channel Tunnel Railway before turning → onto a cycle path that leads you over a bridge across

Good gravel cuts through Dungeness Nature Reserve

The Cantii Way

the M20. Cross a second railway line and bear → on the bridleway to Sene Farm. Take the leftmost of the three options here and descend into Seabrook on Naildown Road. Turn → onto Horn Street, and then ← onto the A259. After 200m turn → onto Princes Parade. After 2km rejoin the esplanade on NCN 2. Follow this beyond **Hythe** as it bears → and then ← and follows the **Royal Military Canal path** for 6km. At Aldergate Bridge follow NCN 2 ←. On meeting Lower Wall Road leave NCN 2 and turn ←. After 100m turn → on a bridleway to the right of a river to **Burmarsh**. With the pub on your right, turn ← onto Thorndike Road. Continue over a level crossing to **Dymchurch**.

11 ■ After 100m turn ← onto Kingsway, followed by a → onto Queensway before a ← onto Hythe Road. After 100m take a → onto a concrete drive before a further → onto the NCN 2. Now follow this uninterrupted for 13km to the Old Lighthouse at **Dungeness**.

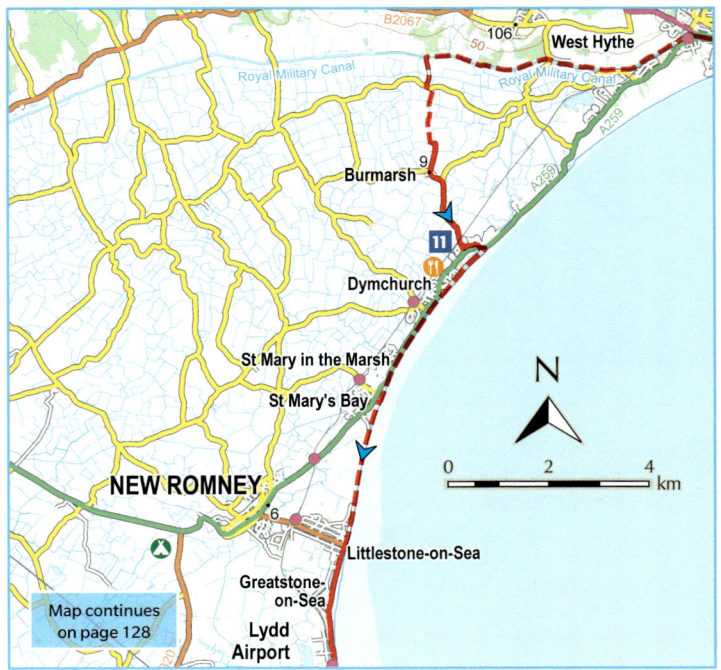

127

Route 8 – Kent

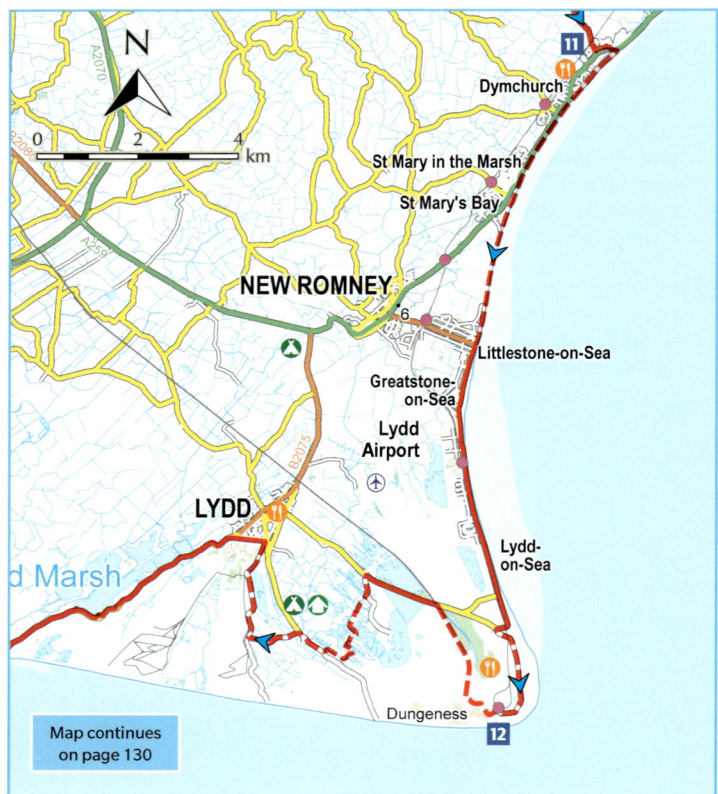

12 ■ Bear →, then take a → on an auxiliary road that crosses Dungeness Nature Reserve for 2km before you meet the Dungeness Road and turn ←. After 1km take a ← before Boulderwall Farm into the RSPB car park. After 2km bear → at Dengemarsh Sewer before a footpath on the left takes you to the road. After 300m turn ← onto a byway, the English Coast Path. After 1km fork → and continue to **Lydd**.

Turn ← onto Tourney Road, bear ← and continue to **Camber**, where you meet the coast once more. Shortly after Camber, the NCN 2 takes a brief sojourn onto a nice track, before delivering you back to the road. After a

The Cantii Way

further 1km the road bears right and you fork ←, following the NCN 2 on a good track to **Rye**. Turn ← and head over the River Rother.

> Stages 13 and 14 detail a loop around **Rye Harbour and Winchelsea**, which are definitely worth a visit. But if time is tight or the weather is against you, skip to the end of Stage 14 and pick up the route again here in Rye.

13 ■ Bear ← at the mini-roundabout. If you are skipping Stages 13 and 14, turn right at the mini-roundabout and jump to the end of Stage 14. At the traffic lights, turn ← onto a path to E Cliff Street. After 100m turn ← onto East Street. Head round the castle, bear → back to E Cliff Street and follow the road to the ←. Cross Wish Ward and head to the river on The Deals; turn →. At the mini-roundabout, turn ← across the bridge. After 300m, turn ← onto Harbour Road. After 3km you reach the coast, turn → and follow NCN 2 once more through Rye Harbour Nature Reserve. After 3km of this you reach **Winchelsea Beach**.

The beach near Rye

Route 8 – Kent

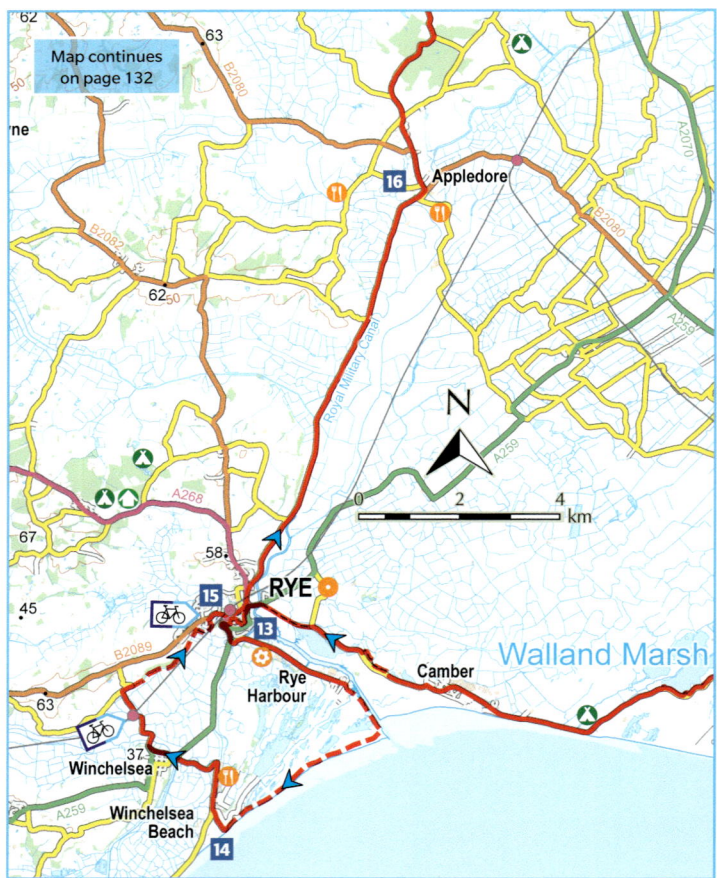

14 ■ Leave NCN 2 and turn → onto Dogs Hill Road. At the junction, fork → onto Sea Road, follow this over a bridge to the A259 and turn ←, signposted 'Hastings', to **Winchelsea**. Bear → and then take a → signposted 'Winchelsea Station, NCN 2'. Follow Station Road over Ferry Bridge as it bears ←. Continue on Winchelsea Lane over a level crossing, and at the T-junction turn →. After 100m the road turns left, but you continue ↑ over a cattle grid onto a gravel

The Cantii Way

drive. Follow the 1066 Country Walk into **Rye**. Turn → onto NCN 2 once more and follow the path to the B2089; turn →. Follow the route over the river, then over a level crossing and immediately turn ← onto an auxiliary road and past the station. Bear → then ← and ← again.

15 ■ Continue over the tracks before shortly forking → onto Military Road, signposted 'Appledore 6'. Continue along the **Royal Military Canal** to **Appledore**.

16 ▲ Turn ← and head through the village, bearing →. Cross Appledore Road and continue on NCN 18 through Great Heron Wood and on to **Woodchurch**, turning → at the inset postbox onto Lower Road. Maintain your direction over the junction onto Place Lane and then Shadoxhurst Road before a → takes you onto Coldblow Lane. If it's been raining, continue north on the Shadoxhurst Road to rejoin the route at Shadoxhurst. At Coldblow, bear → then immediately ←. After 1km take a byway on the ←. After 1km fork ←, then bear → and fork →. Continue on this past Glebe Farm and take Duck Lane before turning ← into **Shadoxhurst**.

On the trail between Ashford and Wye (photo: Jordan Gibbons)

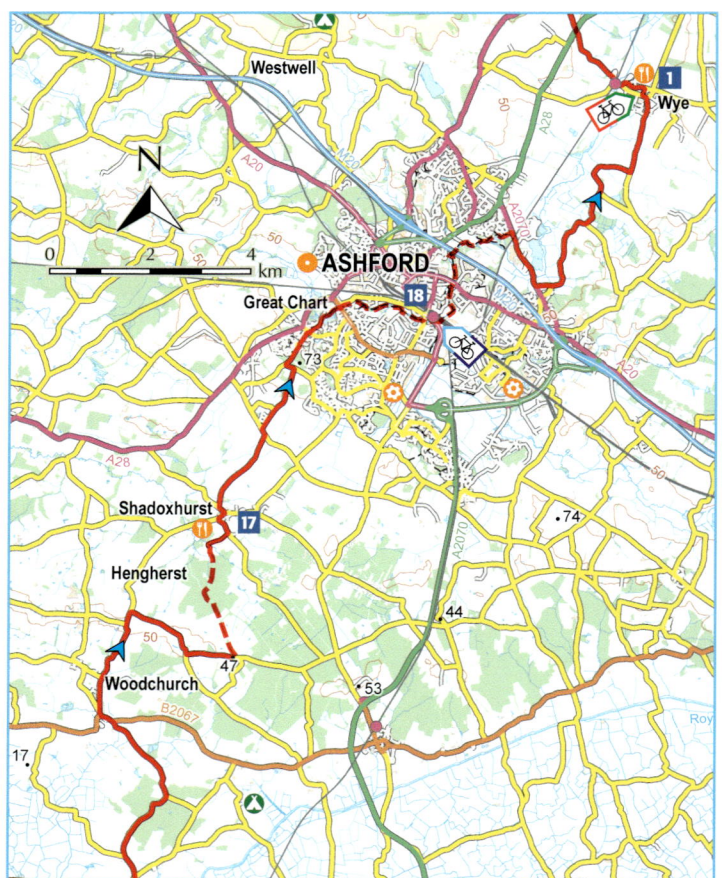

17 ■ At the T-junction turn →, and after 100m fork ←. After 50m fork → onto Criol Lane. After 1.5km turn ← and then immediately → onto Bartlets Lane, signed 'Chilmington, Ashford, NCN 18'. At the T-junction turn ← onto Chart Road, and after 100m turn → onto Singleton Hill. Continue on Singleton Hill to Tithe Barn Lane. Cross the busy Tithe Barn Lane and immediately turn ← onto Bucksford Lane, signed 'Ashford 2' on the NCN. Bear ← around the edge of

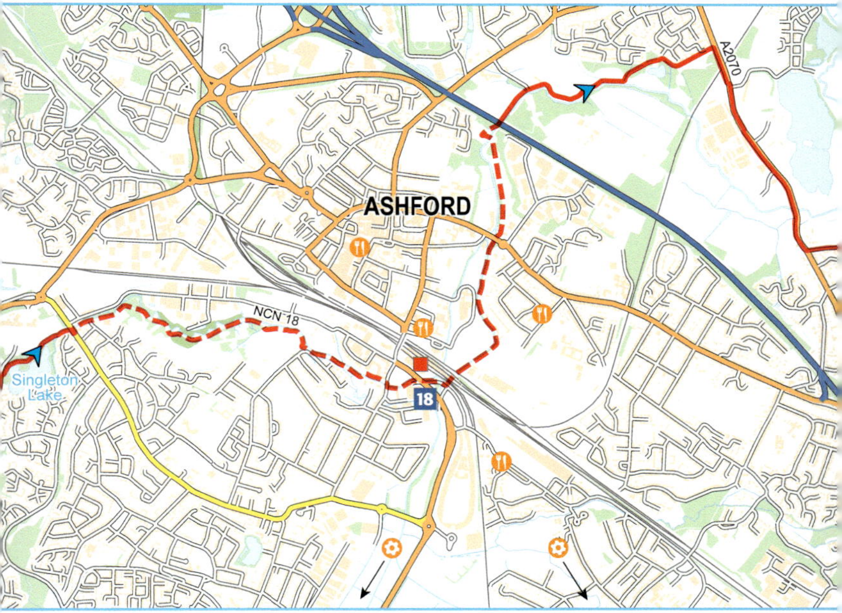

The Cantii Way

Singleton Lake on the NCN route, following the path of the Great Stour all the way to **Ashford International Station**.

18 ■ Follow NCN 18 for 2.5km to the A2070. Turn → onto a cycle path that flanks this busy road and follow it for 1km over Longport Bridge and ← onto Blackwall Road North, signposted 'Canterbury, Wye'. Follow this road for 3.5km before turning ← onto Oxenturn Road. Follow this into **Wye**.

A quick check of the route

9 — 48% off road

Route 9 – London/Essex

The Only Way

Start/Finish	Chingford, Railway Station
Time	2–3 days
Total distance	148km (92 miles)
Off-road distance	71km
Percentage off-road	48%
Total ascent/descent	1020m
Grade	Easy ■
Terrain	Singletrack 16%, track 32%, road 52%
Bike choice	Gravel

The closest route to Central London includes some stunning singletrack and the thrills and spills of the best of Epping Forest. Big skies, endless rural idylls, countless duck ponds and black-timbered barns, and too many pub lunch potentials to mention.

Route options

Alternative start/finish: The advantage to starting this at Chingford is obvious for anyone living in Central London: a few stops on the overground and you are at the start. However, there is a great campsite at Debden Green near Theydon Bois, a few kilometres from Chingford, so if you start at Braintree that would be a great place to spend the night.

Shortcuts and extensions: You can cut the route short by turning back at Ongar (end of Stage 5). Shortly after Cooksmill Green (end of Stage 7), you could head through Writtle to the railway station in Chelmsford. To shorten the ride to 110km, head south at Stagden Cross (near the middle of Stage 10), skipping to Stage 15.

Big Gravel Days: Chingford to Braintree (80km) or Braintree to Chingford (70km). Another big hitter would be Chingford to Toot Hill (Stages 1–4), returning from

The Only Way

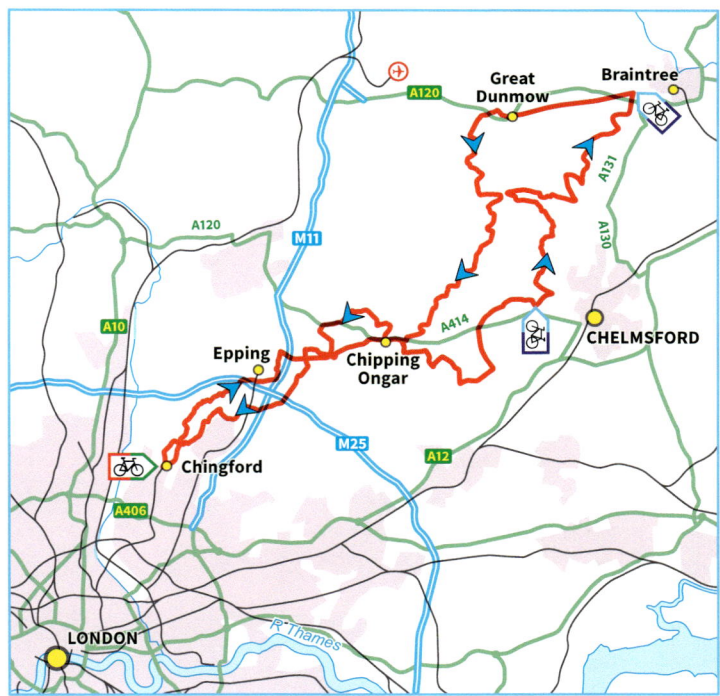

Toot Hill to Chingford via Stages 19 and 20 – a stunning 40km ride not to be missed. For a shorter day in the Braintree area, begin the ride on the Flitch Way and then turn north at Stagden Cross for a nice easy 40km route.

Directions

1 ■ Exit the station and cross the precinct to the road. Turn ➔, and after 100m turn ← onto Bury Road. After a further 100m, turn ➔ into Bury Road car park. Head over to the top edge of the car park before joining a gravel track heading north, adjacent to the road. Take the track on the ➔ into the woods, running alongside Hornbeam Lane. Continue for 1.1km before turning ➔. After 450m,

Route 9 – London/Essex

Summary table

Waypoint	Section	Distance (km)	Ascent (m)	Descent (m)
1	Chingford Station – Green Hut, High Beach	5.3	80	30
2	Green Hut, High Beach – Ivy Chimneys	5.7	35	40
3	Ivy Chimneys – Gernon Bushes Nature Reserve	4.9	60	60
4	Gernon Bushes Nature Reserve – Toot Hill Water Tower	3.9	10	20
5	Toot Hill Water Tower – Ongar	4.8	30	60
6	Ongar – Blackmore	7.9	55	60
7	Blackmore – Cooksmill Green	10.1	70	60
8	Cooksmill Green – Chignall Smealy	10	35	50
9	Chignall Smealy – Pleshey (south)	4.1	40	15
10	Pleshey (south) – Pleshey (north)	5.6	10	20
11	Pleshey (north) – Littley Green	7.9	40	50
12	Littley Green – Booking Hall Café, Rayne	7.3	40	25
13	Booking Hall Café, Rayne – Great Dunmow	8.3	30	50
14	Great Dunmow – High Easter	10.6	80	50
15	High Easter – Good Easter	5.4	35	30
16	Good Easter – Willingale	7.7	50	45
17	Willingale – High Ongar	6.3	20	50
18	High Ongar – Toot Hill Water Tower	12.5	110	60
19	Toot Hill Water Tower – Theydon Bois	9.6	70	120
20	Theydon Bois – Chingford Station	10.1	120	125

fork ← at the intersection of two gravel tracks and climb gently through Hill Wood until you meet the road. Turn ←. After 300m turn → onto Church Lane, with the Church of the Holy Innocents on your right. Turn → onto Manor Road and continue to Pillow Mounds car park at **High Beach**. Mandy's Tea Shack (in the green hut) is a favourite with cyclists and a good place for a cuppa.

2 ■ Fork ← 100m beyond Mandy's Tea Shack onto the Three Forests Way and roll through the woods to Claypit car park. Cross the road and pick up the track once more. Cross the A121 and follow the track as it takes you behind the steak house on the roundabout. The track runs adjacent to Epping New Road;

The Only Way

Surface	Grade	Description
off-road	🟩	Fantastic sweeping tracks through Epping Forest
off-road	🟩	The best of Epping Forest
paved	n/a	Fast road descent to the nature reserve
off-road	🟩	Through the nature reserve, into the countryside and on to the water tower
paved	n/a	Linking section
paved	n/a	Linking section to a favourite cyclists' café
off-road	🟩	Long stretches of low-lying byway
paved	n/a	Minor roads cutting through farmland
off-road	🟩	Tricky wayfinding
mixed	🟩	Minor roads and byways back to Pleshey
mixed	🟩	Leafy neglected byways
mixed	🟩	Delivered to the perfect café
off-road	🟩	Fantastic going on the Flitch Way
mixed	🟩	Picking your way south, avoiding the big roads
mixed	🟩	Join the Essex Way
mixed	🟩	Rural byways to Willingale
mixed	🟩	Cross the old airfield
mixed	🟩	Back to the water tower
mixed	🟩	Great climbing through a lonely wood to a fast singletrack descent
off-road	🔺	Steep climbing and the best sections of Epping Forest back to Chingford Station

follow it for 1km before crossing the road and dropping into the woods once more. After 200m cross a stream and turn ← onto the Green Ride. Maintain this course for 2km until you meet Theydon Road, then turn ←. After 100m turn →, signed 'Ivy Chimneys, Coopersale', towards **Ivy Chimneys**.

3 Follow Ivy Chimneys Road as it becomes Bridge Hill before dropping under the railway bridge and bearing ←. At the T-junction, turn → onto Stewards Green Road. At **Fiddlers Hamlet** turn ← onto Coopersale Street. Follow this road as it bears ← then turn → at the Theydon Oak pub onto Houblons Hill. Climb through **Coopersale**. Immediately after the Garnon Bushes pub,

Route 9 – London/Essex

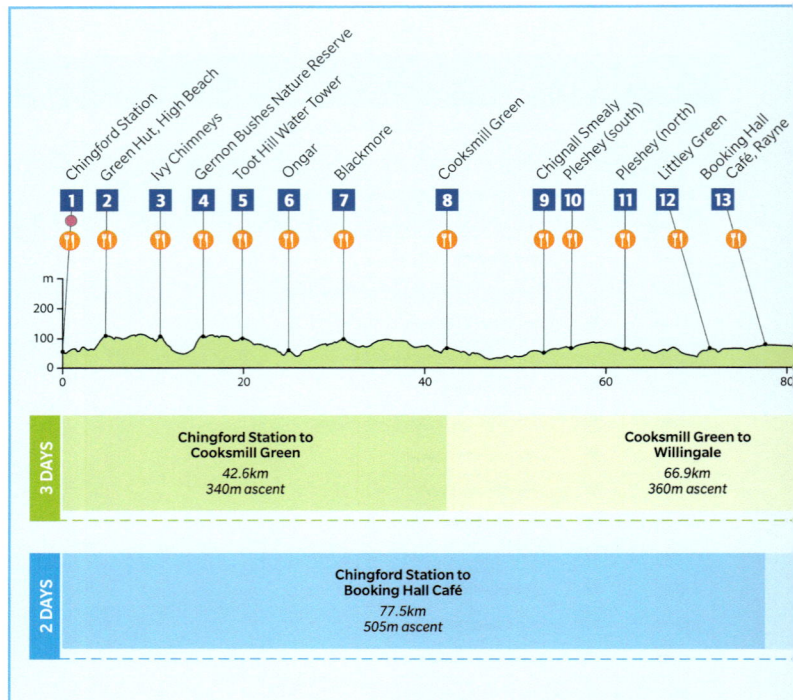

before the railway bridge, turn ➔ onto Garnon Mead. Head up this cul-de-sac and through the gate into Gernon Bushes Nature Reserve.

4 ■ Follow the good track as it weaves through the wood. Cross the M11 on a narrow footbridge. Continue east on the Essex Way, through Birching Coppice and Ongar Park Wood. At a T-junction in the track, head out along the edge of the field and climb towards **Toot Hill**.

5 At Toot Hill Water Tower, turn ➔ along Mill Lane. At the T-junction turn ➔ and after 200m turn ⬅ onto Toot Hill Road, ignoring a turn-off to the right; follow this to the junction. Turn ⬅ onto Drapers Corner, signposted 'Greensted

The Only Way

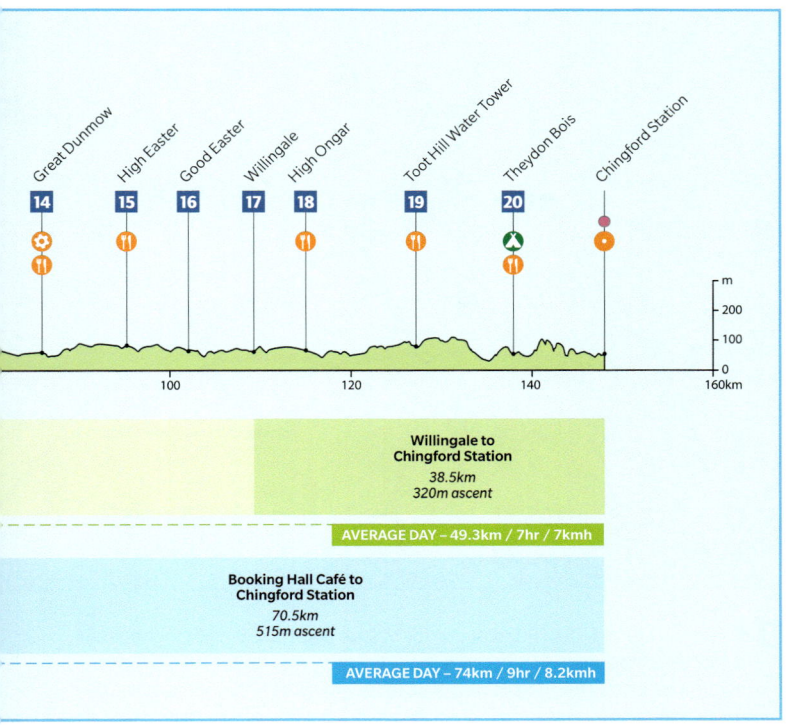

Church, Ongar'. At the next junction take signs for 'Greensted Church, Ongar'. Follow the Greensted Road until it drops you into **Ongar**. Turn →. Fratelli Bites on your left is an ace little cyclists' café with great coffee.

6 Continue up Coopers Hill for 400m before turning ← onto Stondon Road. When the road bears right, fork ← on the corner, signposted 'High Ongar'. After almost 1km turn → onto a bridleway. After skirting a farm on your left, turn → on this car-wide track before dropping to a footbridge; now climb this narrow green lane following St Peter's Way. Turn ← when you meet Nine Ashes Road. After 1km turn → and continue to **Blackmore**. The Blackmore Tea Rooms are a really popular mid-ride stop for coffee and cake.

Route 9 – London/Essex

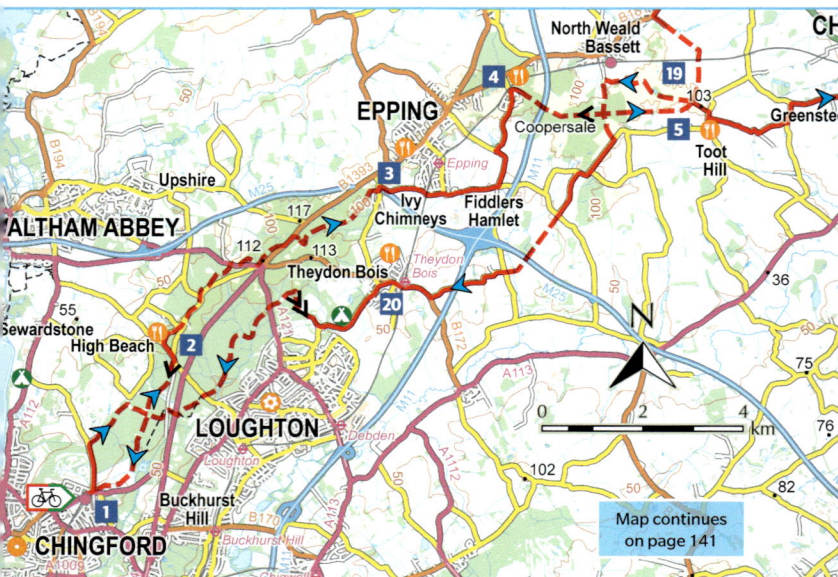

7 ■ Continue along The Green out of the village and turn → onto Ingatestone Road. Take the next ← onto Blackmore Road. After 1km turn ← onto a bridleway into Fryerning Wood and follow Mapletree Lane as it weaves through deciduous trees for 1.5km. At the intersection of two tracks, turn ←. Head through Birch Spring, cross the road and join Old Barns Lane. After 1km you meet the A414; turn → and immediately ← onto Radley Green Road. Shortly after Radley Green, turn → onto a byway (Colley Bridge Lane) that delivers you to the road north of **Cooksmill Green**.

8 Turn ←, then after 100m turn →, signposted 'The Duck'. Continue through Newney Green. Bear → and then ←, then turn ←, signposted 'Roxwell'. Continue on Cow Watering Lane for 1km before turning ← onto an unsignposted road. After the ford, bear ← and continue to the A1060. Turn ← then after 500m take the next → onto an asphalt driveway; continue on this before taking the bridleway across the field. Follow this as it bears →, then ← as it takes a footbridge at Pengymill. Continue ↑, head through a farmyard

The Only Way

Epping Forest is a mecca for mountain bike riders

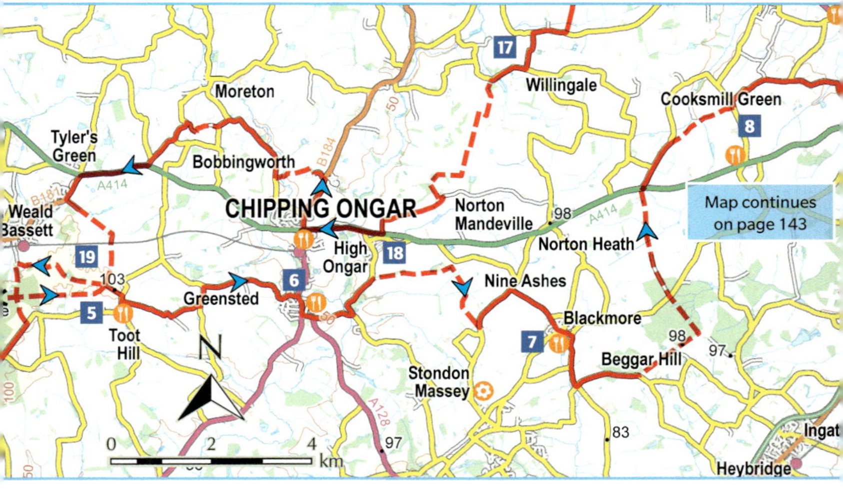

Beyond Gernon Bushes Nature Reserve

and back to the road. Turn ← and continue on the road for 1.2km before turning → for **Chignall Smealy**.

9 ■ Follow the road as it turns sharply →. After 300m, turn ← onto an asphalt road, signed as a dead end towards Beadle's Hall. Continue on this as it bears →, ←, → and then forks ← heading north. Cross Mashbury Road and continue on the bridleway. With Fitzjohn's Wood on your right, bear ← and then → over a footbridge. Bear ← once more and continue to the road south-west of **Pleshey**; turn ←.

> The first half of Stage 10 takes you 2km west to **Stagden Cross**, where you could pick up the return route on Stage 15 and head south.

10 ■ Head west from Pleshey towards **Stagden Cross**, but 100m before the junction turn → onto a byway. This takes you back east to regain the road and bear → to the north of **Pleshey**.

11 ■ At the T-junction turn ←, signed 'The Walthams'. Follow the road to De Lancey Cottages. Turn ← onto Dunmow Lane and continue for 2km to the road at Stumps Cross. Turn → and bear → until you reach the roundabout at

The Only Way

Warner's Farm. Here, take a sharp ← onto a byway and continue north for 1km over a concrete footbridge and past Fair View Farm. At the road, turn ← into **Littley Green**.

12 ■ Turn ←, signposted 'Hartford End'. You are now on the Saffron Trail. After 400m the road bears left, but you turn → onto a bridleway towards a large

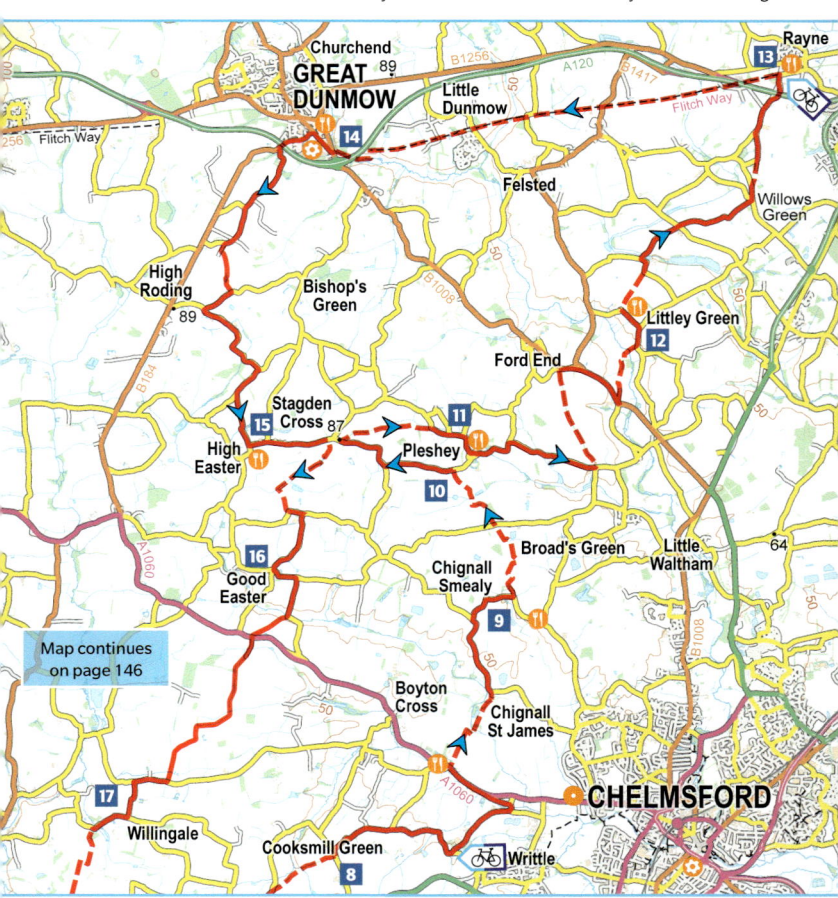

barn. On regaining the road, continue ↑. Bear ← with the road and then fork →, signed 'Felsted', past the remains of Leez Priory. At the crossroads, follow signs for Willows Green. At the T-junction in **Willows Green**, turn ←. After 200m take a byway on the →. Rejoin the road and continue through Bartholomew Green. Follow the road over the A120. When the road bears right on the outskirts of **Rayne**, leave it and head through a white wooden gate to gain access to the **Flitch Way**. The Booking Hall Cafe is a popular spot with cyclists.

13 ■ From the café, turn ← and follow the Flitch Way for 6.5km.

14 ■ As you approach the A120 south of **Great Dunmow**, bear ← with the Flitch Way and head under the road. Cross a footbridge. When you pop out onto the B1008, turn → and shortly take the next ← signed 'High Ongar, The Rodings, NCN 16'. Continue to the junction opposite the Kicking Dickey pub, turn ← and continue for 1km on the B184 over the roundabout and A120, before turning ← onto Clapton Hall Lane. This becomes Philpot End Lane and you continue south onto Watery Lane.

Turn ← onto Dove Lane, then fork ←, signed 'Doves', on a good gravel track before joining a wooded byway that begins to the left of the fence.

The Flitch Way

The Only Way

The Blackmore Tea Rooms are popular with cyclists

Follow this to Barnston House, where it rejoins the road; turn →. Follow the road for 500m and turn ←, signed 'High Easter'. Continue for 2km, over a brook, to Chimballs on Rands Road. At the junction turn →, signed 'High Easter, Leaden Roding'. Bear ← and continue to **High Easter**.

15 ■ Turn ← by the church and continue east out of the village towards **Stagden Cross**. Before you reach the crossroads, turn → onto a bridleway; you are now on the Essex Way. After 1.5km turn ← onto a byway and continue on the Essex Way. On reaching the road, bear ←. At Round Roblets, turn → onto Mill Road. Continue on this through Tye Green into **Good Easter**.

16 ■ Turn ← and continue through the village, past the church. After 400m turn → onto Farmbridge End Road, signposted 'Chalk End, Roxwell, Chelmsford'. At Farm Bridge End, the road bears left but you turn → onto a byway. Follow this to Salts Green. Cross the road and head down to Peppers Green. Continue south, first forking → then bearing ←. On meeting the road turn →. After 400m turn ← into **Willingale**.

Route 9 – London/Essex

17 ■ At the T-junction in Willingale, turn → and follow NCN 1 (National Cycle Network) for 500m until you reach a small marble memorial on the left-hand side of the road, marking the entrance to the historic site of Willingale Airfield. Turn ← onto a good concrete track before bearing → and following this across open land flanked by arable land. When the concrete runs out, follow the bridleway along the join separating two fields. When this meets concrete once more, turn →. After 300m turn ← onto a track marked with two large lumps of masonry. At the gate, fork ← and head into **Norton Mandeville**. At the church, take a sharp → onto a good track. Bear ← at Forest Lodge and continue to the A414 just north of **High Ongar**.

> The first part of Stage 18 is a bit of a dog-leg that takes you to the secluded **St Peter's Church**. If time is tight, you can skip it by turning ← off the B184 onto Moreton Road 200m after the roundabout at the start of Stage 18, signed 'Moreton, The Lavers'.

18 ■ Turn → onto the A414. At the roundabout take the third exit, signed 'Great Dunmow, Fyfield B184'. Continue on the B184 for 1km before turning ← onto Church Lane. Follow this to St Peter's Church. Follow the bridleway as it skirts → then ← behind houses, following the edge of Shelley Common. When you meet Moreton Road, turn →. If you skipped the detour to St Peter's Church, you rejoin the main route here.

The Only Way

After 1km turn ← onto Gainsthorpe Road and follow NCN 1. After 200m fork → and follow this until it turns into a byway. Follow this, bearing ← before turning → and shortly rejoining the Moreton Road. Turn ← and bear → at the next junction. Head through Bovinger to the Epping Road, turn → and head to **Tyler's Green**. At the roundabout take the first ←, signposted 'High Weald, Epping'. After 200m the road bears right, but you turn ← onto a bridleway. Follow this to Ongar Park Hall. Here, turn → and follow the track uphill to the water tower at **Toot Hill**, which you met at the start of Stage 5.

19 ■ Turn → and follow the bridleway on a decent track and then alongside a field. At the gate, turn ← and follow the edge of the field. After Cold Hall Farm turn ← onto an asphalt drive. After 200m turn ← onto a byway; the good car-wide track snakes through the forest. After topping out in the woods you descend to Banks Lane; turn →. Continue south for 1km as the road dips and bears →. After 100m turn ←, signed 'Theydon Mount'.

Descend through Mount End and Sawkins Farm. At the next T-junction, cross the road and join a bridleway; follow this downhill for 1km as it heads under the M25. At Hobbs Cross Farm, keep → on the bridleway and continue to the road. Head up the lane past Theydon Garnon, past the priory and over the M11 on Coopersale Lane. At the B172 turn → and descend into **Theydon Bois**.

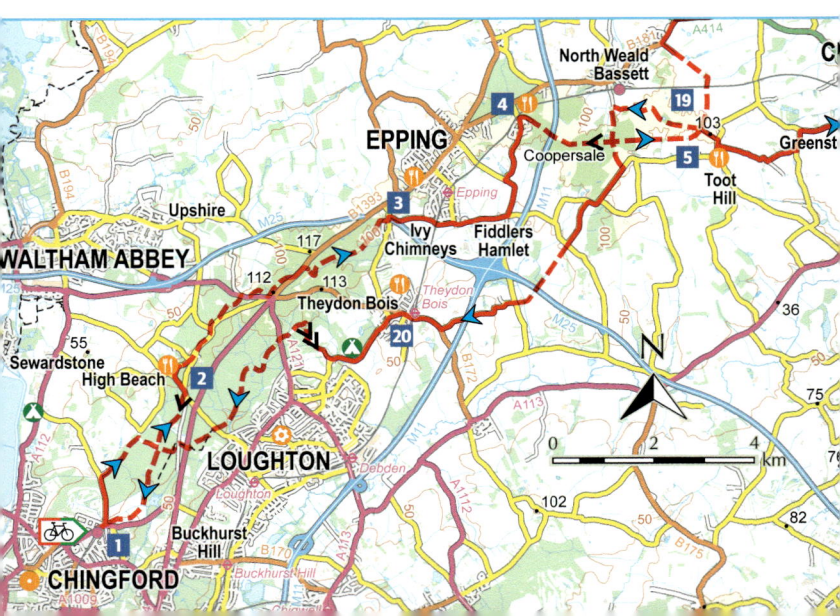

Route 9 – London/Essex

The fantastic Debden House Campsite is the best (only) campsite on the route

20 ▲ Take the second ← that intersects the green. Follow Loughton Lane as it turns into Debden Lane and bears →. Take the → onto Forest Road and past **Debden House Campsite**. Continue for 1km before taking a sharp ← and heading back into Epping Forest.

What follows is a rollercoaster of well-maintained, high-octane, car-wide gravel trails. Head south-west, cross Golding's Hill onto Centenary Walk and then the Green Ride followed by the Three Forests Way. Cross Earl's Path and continue through the woods past Strawberry Hill Pond and over Fairmead Bottom car park. Head over the Epping New Road and then Fairmead Road (track). Now bear → to the intersection in the forest tracks that you reached in Stage 1. Take the ← and follow this down to the open ground and around the back of the Queen Elizabeth Hunting Lodge. From here you meet the road once more. **Chingford Station** is ahead of you on the left.

19% off road

10

Route 10 – Essex/Suffolk
Stour Valley Villages

Start/Finish	Manningtree, Railway Station
Time	2–3 days
Total distance	144km (89.5 miles)
Off-road distance	26.9km
Percentage off-road	19%
Total ascent/descent	1040m
Grade	Easy ■
Terrain	Singletrack 5%, track 14%, road 81%
Bike choice	Gravel

The River Stour still follows the same path as it did when Constable captured the scene at Flatford Mill in 1821 in his painting *The Hay Wain*. Dedham Vale National Landscape offers some of Suffolk's most charming rural scenery and medieval villages. East of Manningtree, the landscape opens up as the river broadens into an estuary and meets the coast. This is one of the easier routes in the guide and a good introduction to bikepacking in south-east England. With a start point just 54min from London Liverpool Street, it's perfect for anyone wanting to squeeze in a two-wheeled adventure at short notice.

Route options

Alternative start/finish: Manningtree sits in the centre of the two legs: the first takes you east to the wide open vistas at the mouth of the estuary in Harwich, and the second west to the ancient market town of Sudbury. You could also start and finish at Harwich (end of Stage 2) and trace the course of the river west before returning; alternatively, start at Sudbury (Stage 9) and head to the mouth of the river before returning inland.

Shortcuts and extensions: Shorten the western section by leaving Stage 7 just before Wormingford, crossing the valley floor and picking up the return route as it

Route 10 – Essex/Suffolk

Summary table

Waypoint	Section	Distance (km)	Ascent (m)	Descent (m)
1	Manningtree Station – Wrabness Station	10.4	90	60
2	Wrabness Station – Shotley Ferry	14.1	70	70
3	Shotley Ferry – Alton Water	13.4	85	80
4	Alton Water – Flatford Mill	19.3	90	120
5	Flatford Mill – Stratford St Mary	7	60	50
6	Stratford St Mary – Nayland	13.9	140	160
7	Nayland – Bures	12	130	110
8	Bures – Sudbury	9.9	95	80
9	Sudbury – Rose Green	14.9	70	45
10	Rose Green – Higham	17	120	150
11	Higham – Manningtree Station	12.1	90	115

heads east to Nayland in Stage 10 (see directions in Stage 7). Shorten the eastern leg (and avoid a busy section at the start) by taking your bike on the train from Manningtree towards Harwich Town Station and alighting at Wrabness Station.

Big Gravel Days: There are four obvious options here: Harwich/Shotley Ferry to Sudbury (Stages 3–8, 75.5km); Sudbury to Harwich (Stages 9–11 then Stages 1 and 2, 68.5km); on the western loop, Manningtree to Sudbury and back (Stages 5–11, 87km); and on the eastern loop, Manningtree to Harwich and back (Stages 1–3 plus most of Stage 4, 50km).

Directions

> Before setting out on your ride, check the timetable for the **Shotley Foot Ferry** (runs April–October), a key link in navigating Stage 3.

1 ■ Turn ← out of Manningtree Station. Turn → at the road, take the first exit at the roundabout and go ↑ along Manningtree High Street. Take the opportunity to pick up some provisions. Continue on the B1352 through **Mistley**. After 4km fork ← onto a byway (rough at first), which drops to the shoreline. Follow the bridleway along the shore for 2km. When the bridleway ends, push your bike for 150m on the coastal footpath until you turn → and

Stour Valley Villages

Surface	Grade	Description
mixed	🟩	Head out of Manningtree and onto a coastal bridleway
mixed	🟩	Take the E2 and NCN 51 to Harwich and the Shotley Ferry
mixed	🟩	Walk with your bike along the foreshore before heading inland and west to Alton Water
mixed	🟩	Take a gentle singletrack around the reservoir before heading to Flatford Mill
paved	n/a	Gentle back roads
paved	n/a	Rolling through iconic villages
mixed	🟩	Stunning bridleway along the Stour basin
mixed	🟩	Follow NCN 13 onto a cycleway on a disused railway track
paved	n/a	Head east on quiet back roads
paved	n/a	Cross the Stour twice
mixed	🟩	Easy rolling back to Manningtree Station

regain the road. Continue on Wall Lane, past All Saints Church and its curious bell tower.

> Look out for the wooden cage-like structure in **All Saints churchyard**. Known as the bell tower, it has housed one of the church bells since the collapse of the original bell tower in the 17th century.

Route 10 – Essex/Suffolk

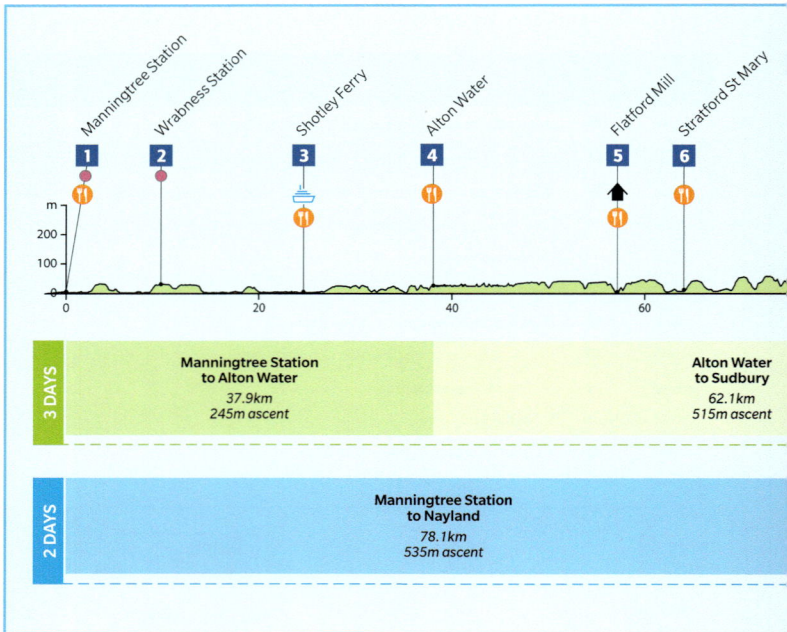

After crossing the railway bridge, turn ←. Follow the road as it bears →, passing **Wrabness Station** on your left. If you are pressed for time, you could catch a train from Wrabness Station to Harwich Town Station.

> Part of Stage 2 follows the **E2 European Long-Distance Route**, which joins northern England with the lowlands of Belgium before heading down to northern Italy. As it approaches Harwich Ferry Terminal, it takes the form of a good car-wide track that runs parallel with the A120.

2 ■ At the junction with the B1352 turn ←, signed 'Wix, Thorpe-le-Soken'. Follow the Wrabness Road for 3km. At the apex of a right-hand bend after Meadowcroft, turn ← onto Ray Lane and the E2. Follow this good car-wide track for 2km until it spits you out at a lorry car park on the edge of **Harwich**.

Follow Dock Road alongside the ferry port car park. Turn → onto Station Road, bear → with the road and continue to a roundabout. Take the

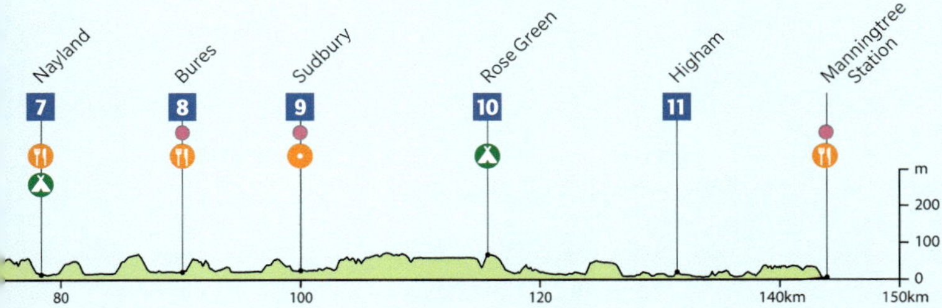

Stour Valley Villages

Nayland	Bures	Sudbury	Rose Green		Higham	Manningtree Station
7	**8**	**9**	**10**	**11**		

Sudbury to Manningtree Station
44km
280m ascent

AVERAGE DAY – 48km / 6hr / 7.9kmh

Nayland to Manningtree Station
65.9km
505m ascent

AVERAGE DAY – 72km / 9hr / 7.9kmh

Map continues on page 155

Route 10 – Essex/Suffolk

The bridleway flanks the coast on the way to Wrabness Station

second exit up Parkeston Road. Your object now is the seafront. At the mini-roundabout turn → onto Main Road. After 200m turn ← at the war memorial. Follow Fronks Road as it bears ← for 300m before you turn → onto Hall Lane. After 400m continue ↑ onto West End Lane and follow this to the beach. When you reach the promenade, turn ←. Join NCN 51 (National Cycle Network) and continue all the way to the Navyard Wharf; look for signs for the Shotley Foot Ferry. Cross the mouth of the estuary, with views of Harwich Harbour.

3 ■ Passing the Shipwreck Bar and Restaurant on your right, continue around the edge of the dock onto King Edward VII Drive and follow the road towards **Shotley Gate**. Opposite the Bristol Arms pub, take a restricted byway following the shoreline. This is yours for 200m, then dismount and follow the footpath for 500m to a caravan park. Now head inland on a restricted byway. When you meet the road at **Shotley**, turn ←. Continue for 800m before forking ←, signed 'Erwarton, Brantham, Manningtree'.

Bear ← and continue past the elaborate domed gateway of Erwarton Hall. The road is yours and you continue through **Erwarton**, **Harkstead** and **Lower Holbrook** to **Holbrook**, where you turn ←. Continue to the church and

Stour Valley Villages

turn ➔. After 1km the road turns sharply ➔ but here you dismount and push your bike down a gravel drive for 150m to intersect with the new cycle path around the shore of **Alton Water**. If you are on a three-day schedule, Alton Water Campsite is a good stop.

4 ■ On joining the cycleway, turn ➔. Continue on this good singletrack around the edge of the reservoir for 3km until you reach Lemons Hill Bridge. Turn ← and head over the bridge. On the other side, take a ←, signed 'cycleway'. Continue on this around the edge of the lake until you meet Church Road; turn ←. Follow this to the junction and turn ➔ onto Stutton Lane. Continue to the busier A137 and turn ←. After 200m turn ➔, signed 'bridleway'. This begins as a concrete drive and you then bear ➔ and follow the bridleway north to Station Road, where you turn ←. Follow the road through **Bentley**.

As you're leaving the town, take a ← onto Bergholt Road. If doing the route in two days, the Briar Campsite on your left is close to the halfway point. At the next junction, bear ➔ and head towards East End. Bear ➔ again, following signs for East Bergholt. At the junction with the B1070 continue ↑. On reaching **East Bergholt**, continue ↑ onto Flatford Road. Continue past the car park to Flatford Mill. Flatford Mill is worth a stop if you are interested in English painters and heritage projects. You can skip it by continuing past the turn-off at the car park.

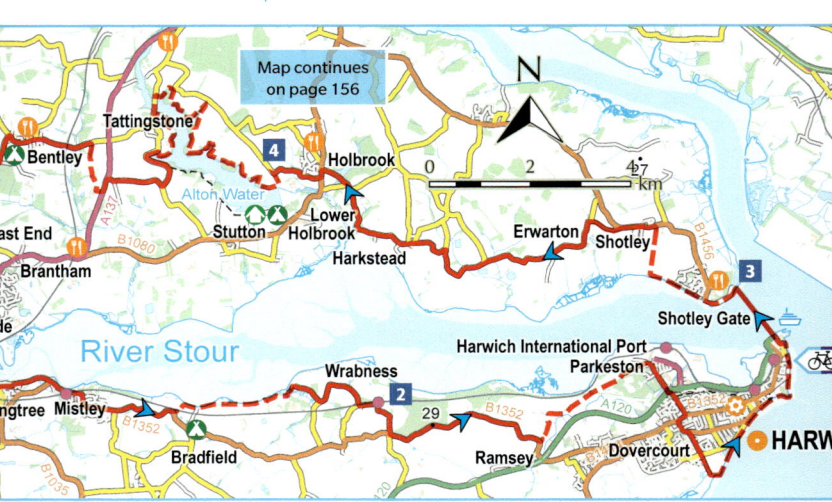

Route 10 – Essex/Suffolk

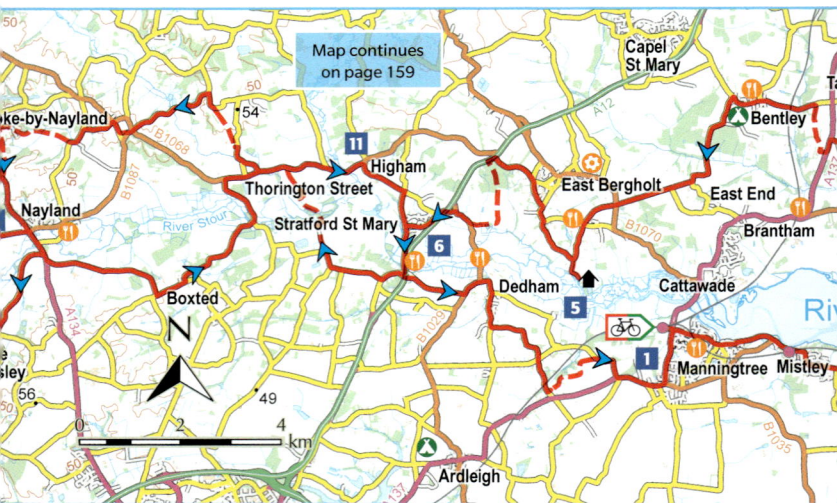

5 Cycle back the way you came. At the car park turn ←, and at the next junction turn ← past the war memorial and church on the edge of **East Bergholt**. Continue ↑ through the town before turning ← onto Hadleigh Road, signed 'Ipswich, Colchester, Dedham'. Bear ← with the road. When you meet the busy A12, take a cycle path running alongside it before quickly taking a ← onto Dead Lane, a fantastic permissive byway that descends into the wood. At the junction with a path, fork → onto Donkey Lane and continue to the road; turn →. After 300m take a ← and head past the parish church of Stratford St Mary. The road dips and you continue under the A12, bear ← and head through **Stratford St Mary**.

6 Continue past the pub and the chapel. Bear ← at the junction, and descend on Lower Street before crossing the Stour. After the bridge, climb on an auxiliary road before forking → onto Stratford Road. After 300m turn → onto Dedham Road towards Langham. Continue ↑ past Whalebone Corner for 1km before forking → opposite an old red-brick wall. After 300m the road turns left but you continue ↑ on an asphalt byway. Follow the route along the right-hand side of the cottages, turning → and then ← after 50m. Ford the Stour and follow the St Edmund Way north on Langham Mill Lane. After 1km reach the B1068 and turn ←.

Stour Valley Villages

Flatford Mill

After 300m, fork → onto Mill Lane and continue to a junction. Turn →, cross the Box River via a small red-brick bridge and bear ← onto Hudson's Lane. After 200m fork ← onto a bridleway and then climb the steep Londs Lane, a good car-wide track. On reaching the road, turn ← and continue for 150m before forking ← onto Scotland Street. Follow this south-west for 1.5km to **Stoke-by-Nayland**.

At the junction, continue ↑ and then bear →. Continue past the church and then turn → onto School Street. After 200m turn ← onto Butt

Fording the Stour near Langham Mill (photo: Luke Morris)

Route 10 – Essex/Suffolk

Descending through woodland on Dead Lane

Road. At the next junction, turn ←, signed 'South Suffolk Route A2'. Descend and cross the river. After a gentle climb, fork → onto a car-wide bridleway, Beachams Lane. The track dips and you cross a stream. Pass Beachams Farm on your left and climb up past Thomsons Farm on your right. Continue ↑ on Cock Street to a junction; turn ← to take the signed bridleway. Continue past Nayland Hall and descend to a stream. The last 200m is hard going, so be prepared to push. On reaching the A134, turn ← and descend on Harper's Hill to the west of **Nayland**, across the valley floor.

> **Nayland** is an archetypal Dedham Vale village, picturesque and dripping with history. If you are doing a two-day schedule, Rushbanks Farm Campsite could be a good choice, 2km west of Nayland.

7 ■ After crossing the Stour, turn → onto Water Lane, signed 'Little Horkesley'. Continue ↑ for 2km to **Little Horkesley**. Turn → at the war memorial, signed 'Wormingford, Bures'. After 150m on School Road, turn ← onto School Lane, an asphalt byway. Descend on this for 500m, bearing ←. Continue on the bridleway to Bowdens Lane.

> To **shorten the western leg of the route**, turn → off Bowdens Lane onto Mill Hill and over Wormingford Bridge, pass Smallbridge Hall on your left and continue to a crossroads. Turn →, signed 'Nayland, Stoke, South Suffolk Route A2', and continue on Stage 10.

Stour Valley Villages

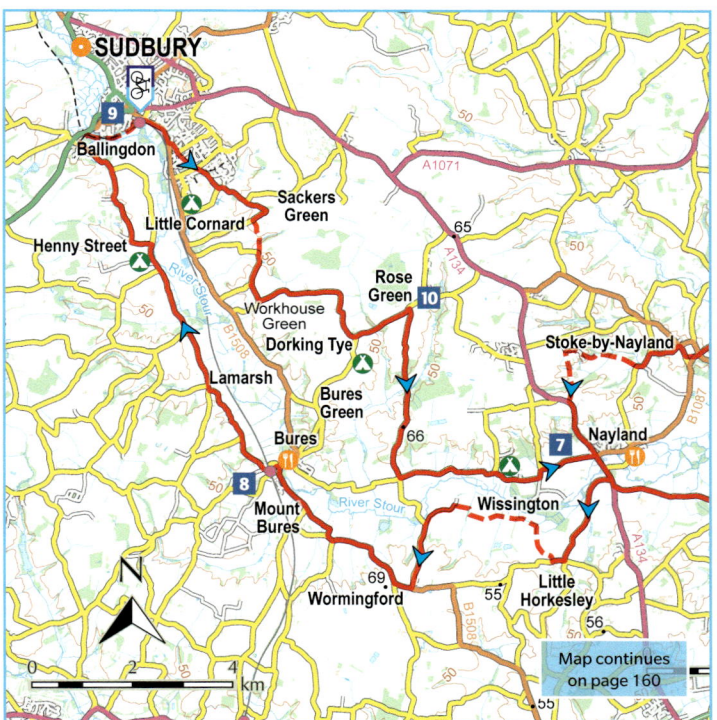

Climb past the church and continue to **Wormingford**. At the road, turn ➜ by the phone box, signed 'Bures, Sudbury'. Continue on the B1508, bearing ➜. Bear ← and climb up Sandy Hill. Follow the road as it bears first ← and then ➜, signed 'Peartree Hill'. Continue to **Bures**.

8 ■ Turn ← and follow the road under the railway line as it bears ➜. Continue north on NCN 13 (National Cycle Network) for 4km to **Henny Street**. Henny Riverside Camping is ideally situated if you are on a three-day schedule. Take the ←, signed 'Middleton only'. Continue on NCN 13 to **Ballingdon**. Before you reach the A131, turn ➜ through a gate that takes NCN 13 into a park. After 200m this continues onto a disused railway; turn ➜ and follow this into **Sudbury**, where the track deposits you in a Waitrose car park.

Route 10 – Essex/Suffolk

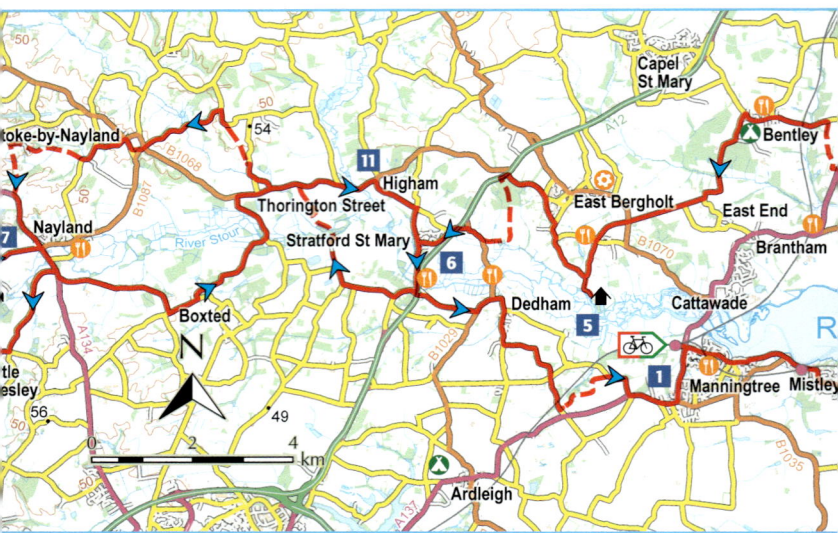

9 Bear → and continue with the station on your right. Turn ← and continue on a cut-through to the road; turn →. Continue for 500m before turning ← onto Stannard Way, signed 'South Suffolk Route A2'. After 150m turn → onto Church Road and then bear ← onto Broom Street. Continue to a staggered junction, and continue ↑ to the end of Wells Hall Road. Bear ← and begin a shallow climb on Prospect Hill. When the road forks, bear →. Continue round a sharp right-hand corner to **Little Cornard**.

   Take a ← and join the South Suffolk Route A2 as it heads south. After 500m rejoin the road and continue ↑ to **Workhouse Green**. Follow Upper Road as it bears ← and continue for 4km, passing **Dorking Tye**.

10 Just before reaching **Rose Green**, take a →, signed 'Arger Fen, Wormingford'. Maintain your course on this minor road for 3km. At the crossroads turn ←, signed 'Nayland, Stoke, South Suffolk Route A2'. Maintain your direction west for 2km on Bures Road to a junction, signed 'Nayland, Stoke-by-Nayland'; turn →. Continue past Rushbanks Farm Campsite and then bear ← and follow the road signed 'Nayland, Colchester'. Next, bear → with the road, signed 'Nayland, Stoke', and join Wiston Road. Continue to the A134; turn →.

Stour Valley Villages

After 500m turn ←, signed 'Boxted, Littlegarth School'. Head along Garth Road before joining Burnt Dick Hill. Continue for 2km to a junction and turn ← onto Church Road, signed 'Boxted, Church Street'. After 500m turn ←, signed 'Higham'. Pass the church and bear →. Descend ↑, pass a weir and bear ←. Continue to a junction, turn → and continue through **Thorington Street** and on to **Higham**.

11 ■ At the green in Higham, turn →, signed 'Stratford St Mary, Colchester'. Continue towards **Stratford St Mary** before turning → to Stratford Bridge. Head over the Stour for the final time and bear ← as you cross the A12. Continue for 500m to a junction, turn ← signed 'Ipswich, Dedham Village', and head through **Dedham**. Dedham is a pretty village with good tea shop options. Bear → and head out of town on Brook Street.

Continue for 600m before turning ← onto East Lane. Follow the road round to the → and climb to a staggered junction; continue ↑ onto Bargate Lane. Follow this as it crosses a railway bridge and climbs gently. Turn ← onto a singletrack bridleway; this shortly becomes a good track as you bear → and continue for 600m on the bridleway to Dedham Road. Turn → and then bear → and continue to the busy Harwich Road; turn ←. Follow this for 1km before turning ← opposite the Jet garage. Descend gently on Cox's Hill before turning ← into **Manningtree Station** precinct.

Looking south across Debden Vale in the afternoon light

11 36% off road

Route 11 – Suffolk Coast

Three Ferries and a Power Station

Start	Felixstowe, Railway Station
Finish	Beccles, Railway Station
Time	2–3 days
Total distance	109km (67.8 miles)
Off-road distance	38.8km
Percentage off-road	36%
Total ascent/descent	470/480m
Grade	Moderate ▲
Terrain	Singletrack 13%, track 23%, road 64%
Bike choice	Gravel

Suffolk isn't known for off-road cycling, but the Suffolk and Essex Coast and Heaths National Landscape offers excellent bridleways, byways and green lanes. The area is criss-crossed by National Cycle Network (NCN) routes, with miles of unspoilt coastline, campsites, nature reserves and quiet pubs. You can enjoy a relaxed ride through heath and woodland in peaceful solitude. Perfect for a lazy summer weekend, don't forget your swimming gear and plan for a pub lunch or two.

The ferry schedules make this route fully accessible from Easter to late summer (see Route options and Stage 9 for alternatives if ferries are closed).

Route options

Alternative start/finish: Begin at Woodbridge and join the route at the end of Stage 2, cutting 13.5km, or start at Wickham Station and head east for 4km to join the route at Tunstall (Stage 5), reducing it by a further 20km. These options are ideal if the first and second ferries (respectively) are not running. For a shorter route, finish at Friston (Stage 6) and head north-west to the train at Saxmundham.

Shortcuts and extensions: See 'Alternative start/finish'.

Three Ferries and a Power Station

Big Gravel Days: This could be a Big Gravel Day. The most exciting sections are between the start and Southwold, but there are no escape options between Southwold and Beccles.

163

Route 11 – Suffolk Coast

Summary table

Waypoint	Section	Distance (km)	Ascent (m)	Descent (m)
1	Felixstowe Station – Felixstowe Ferry	5.2	40	60
2	Felixstowe Ferry – Red Lodge	11.7	50	30
3	Red Lodge – Butley Ferry	7.3	10	30
4	Butley Ferry – Orford	4.8	10	10
5	Orford – Snape	15.4	60	60
6	Snape – Aldeburgh	12.5	70	60
7	Aldeburgh – Sizewell	6.7	20	20
8	Sizewell – Dunwich	11.8	80	50
9	Dunwich – Walberswick Ferry	9.7	40	75
10	Walberswick Ferry – Barnaby Green	9.1	50	20
11	Barnaby Green – Sotterley	5.9	20	15
12	Sotterley – Beccles Station	8.9	50	60

Directions

1 Leave the station, continue ↑ on Railway Approach and turn → onto the High Road. At the roundabout, take the first exit onto Beatrice Avenue. Continue to the roundabout and take the fourth exit, Colneis Road. After 800m take a bridleway on your left. Cross Links Avenue and join a concrete path. Follow this as it bears → and becomes Hyem's Lane. Continue to Ferry Road, turn → and maintain your direction east as the road delivers you to the village of **Felixstowe Ferry**. Take the ferry across the River Deben. The Ferryboat Inn is a lovely pub and a good option for food. The ferry only runs in summer months.

2 ■ Follow the road as it bears ← from the quay. Continue north through **Bawdsey** to **Alderton**. In the village centre, fork → past the Alderton Stores and continue for 2km. When the road bears sharply left, you continue ↑ on a good car-wide track, signed 'Rustic View'. After 1km this becomes a restricted byway and you continue for 100m before forking → onto a bridleway over access land and into Parsnip Plantation. After 200m you intersect with a byway and join the Sandlings Walk. Continue north-east on this to the road, turn → and after 50m turn ← opposite Red Lodge cottage.

Three Ferries and a Power Station

Surface	Grade	Description
paved	n/a	Head north and east to catch the Felixstowe Ferry
mixed	🟩	NCN 1 joins up to Sandlings Walk
mixed	🟩	East through mixed plantation to England's smallest ferry
paved	n/a	Country lanes to the Island of Secrets
mixed	🟩	NCN 1 meets Sandlings Walk on bridleway through coniferous plantation
mixed	🟩	Wild bridleways avoid fast road into Aldeburgh
mixed	🟩	Paved to Thorpeness then open heathland to Sizewell
mixed	🟩	Rejoin Sandlings Walk
mixed	🟩	Quiet road through Dunwich Forest
paved	n/a	2km of coastal riding before taking NCN 1 north
paved	n/a	The start of the warm-down
paved	n/a	Easy back roads to Beccles Station

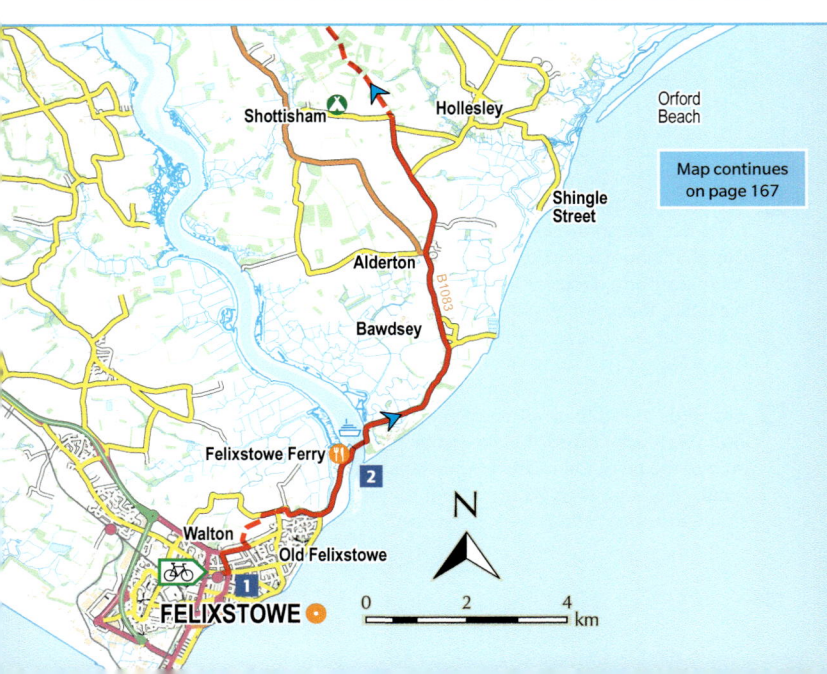

Route 11 – Suffolk Coast

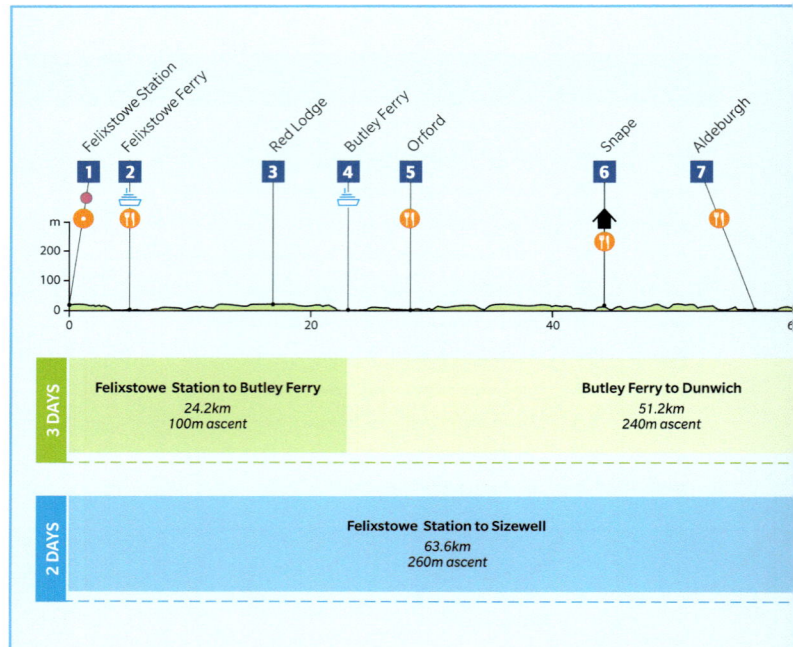

3 ■ Follow the track through Rendlesham Forest. When the Sandlings Walk turns left, you continue on the bridleway to reach the road. Continue ↑ to **Capel St Andrew** and past Home Farm. When the road bears right, you continue ↑ on a good car-wide track to the **Butley Ferry**. Take the ferry across the Butley River. Although the track to the ferry is marked as a footpath only, it is a National Cycle Network (NCN) route and is popular with cyclists. The Butley Ferry runs a seasonal timetable.

4 Bear ← on the footpath and continue past Ferry Cottage and onto the road. In 2km you reach **Orford**. To take in the vista across Orford Ness, turn → and drop to the quay, then retrace your steps to **Orford** and turn → onto Daphne Road. The quay is also a good spot for refreshments. To skip this detour, continue straight ahead on Daphne Road.

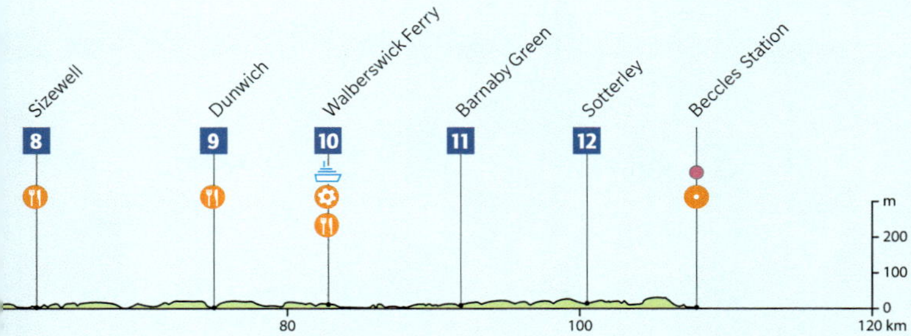

Three Ferries and a Power Station

Sizewell	Dunwich	Walberswick Ferry	Barnaby Green	Sotterley	Beccles Station
8	**9**	**10**	**11**	**12**	

Dunwich to Beccles Station
32.6km
140m ascent

AVERAGE DAY – 36km / 5hr / 7.2kmh

Sizewell to Beccles Station
44.4km
220m ascent

AVERAGE DAY – 54km / 8hr / 6.8kmh

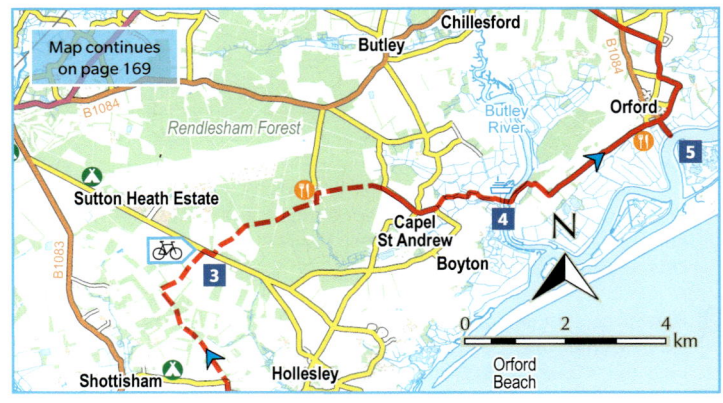

The Felixstowe ferry crossing is popular with cyclists

> **Orford Ness**, the Island of Secrets, was home to top-secret military tests during World War II. If you are on a relaxed schedule, a visit is highly recommended.

5 ■ Follow Daphne Road as it becomes Raydon Lane; continue to the junction and turn ← onto Bullock Shed Lane. After 500m turn → and continue north for 1km on Ferry Road before turning ← onto Hospital Road. Cross Snape Road and join the `B1084`, signed 'Tunstall, Wickham Market, Woodbridge'. Continue on this to **Chillesford** before taking a → onto Pedlars Lane. After 400m turn → and rejoin Sandlings Walk; follow this car-wide bridleway into **Tunstall Forest**.

After 2km you cross a road onto an unmarked singletrack. After 50m turn → onto a restricted byway. After 2km on a very straight track turn ← when you reach the road at the edge of the forest. Continue on this to Snape Maltings, cross the bridge and head into **Snape**.

6 ■ In Snape, turn →, signed 'Golden Key Inn', and continue along Priory Road for 1km. When the road bears left, continue ↑ on a good car-wide track to the road; turn ← onto the `B1121` and continue into **Friston**. In the village centre, at

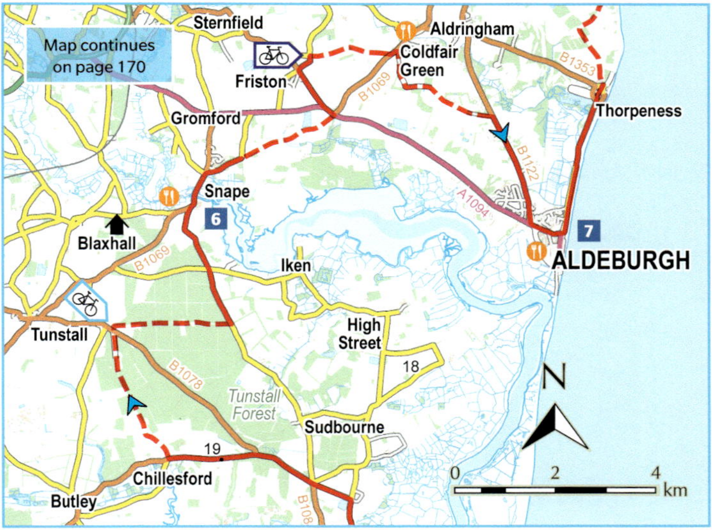

Three Ferries and a Power Station

a crossroads, turn → onto Grove Road. Follow the road as it bears ← and then turn → onto Church Lane. Continue to the road, turn ← and then, after 50m, turn → onto Sloe Lane, signed 'Sandlings Walk'. This is a byway for the first

Choose a good line to prevent sliding about on the sand

Route 11 – Suffolk Coast

kilometre but when you reach the houses it becomes a footpath; dismount and walk the next 700m to the road. When you meet the road, turn → and continue to the seafront **Aldeburgh**.

7 ■ Turn ← by the Tudor Moot Hall. Continue north on the asphalt path for 1km before forking ← to a quiet road when the path runs out. When you reach **Thorpeness**, bear ← by the pond before turning → onto a wide gravel drive (The Sanctuary). Head past the impressive Westgate tower along a decent byway to the road, cross the road, bear ← and follow the byway onto Thorpeness Common. Bear ← and continue until you meet a second byway; turn →. You are on the Sandlings Walk once more. Continue ↑ to join the road towards **Sizewell**. Turn → for the café and beach and a view of Sizewell B. To omit this detour, turn left and then immediately right onto Sandy Lane.

> It's worth a small detour to have a look at **Sizewell B**, the UK's only nuclear power plant with a pressurised water reactor, and to stop for a snack at the Sizewell Tea café.
>
> **Applefields Caravan and Camping Site** (just off route on the way to Leiston Abbey on Stage 8) is a great halfway stop.

Three Ferries and a Power Station

The beach at Sizewell

8 ■ Retrace your steps to **Sizewell** and turn → onto Sandy Lane. After 200m turn ←, then after a further 1km you reach the road and turn →. Shortly, bear ← with the road and continue to Abbey Road. Turn → and then immediately ← onto Abbey Lane. After 150m, dismount, turn → and walk the final 200m to the ruins of Leiston Abbey. Once beyond the abbey, turn → and follow an asphalt drive to the road. Turn ←. When the road bears ← after 150m, take a sharp →, signed 'Eastbridge'. Continue to **Eastbridge**. The Eel's Foot Inn at Eastbridge is a good call for refreshments.

Continue over the bridge, with the Minsmere Level to your right. A gentle climb takes you into Minsmere Nature Reserve, where you bear → on the asphalt bridleway. Continue across Westleton Walks and over Dunwich Heath until you reach Minsmere Road; turn ←. At the junction, turn → and descend into **Dunwich**.

> The famous night ride, the **Dunwich Dynamo**, finishes at the beach here. This 180km ride from London to Dunwich takes place every year in July.
>
> If you are on a three-day schedule and are prepared to walk a further 2km with your bike, you could cross the **Suffolk Coast National Nature Reserve** on a wooden walkway by foot to Walberswick and pick

Route 11 – Suffolk Coast

up the route again there. To do this, turn → onto a cinder track to Dingle Hall Tea Rooms as you leave Dunwich on Stage 9 (after the war memorial and bridge). The track starts as a bridleway but becomes a footpath after 1km.

9 ■ Turn ← and continue past the Ship pub. At the war memorial, bear →. Continue over the bridge, bear ← and follow the NCN 42 through Dunwich Forest to the B1125. Don't join the road, but instead turn → onto the byway signed 'Sandlings Walk'. Continue to Westwood Lodge, where you pick up the road once more. Continue east to **Walberswick** to meet the ferry.

> If you don't fancy the ferry, or it's closed for the off-season, you can **cross the River Blyth** on an old military bridge 800m further upstream. There is a bridleway there that will bring you back to the route.

Three Ferries and a Power Station

10 Once on the north shore of the mouth of the Blyth, turn ➔ and follow the coast road as it hugs the coast and heads into **Southwold**. Climb into the town, turn ➔ by the Red Lion pub and head to the walkway on the foreshore. Continue to the pier before turning ← and heading inland. Follow Pier Avenue to Mights Road and turn ➔. The road bears left but you take a ➔, signed 'Wrentham, Lowestoft'. Continue on Covert Road. When the road bears left,

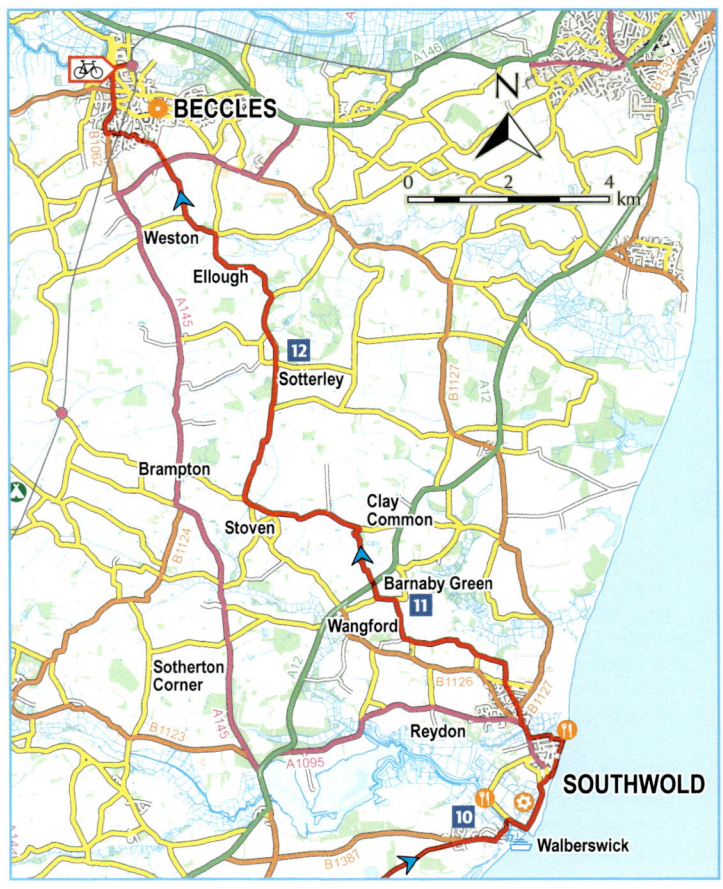

The third and final ferry, at Walberswick

you turn →, signed 'Lowestoft'. Follow Rissemere Lane to Reydon Smear. At the next junction turn →, signed 'Beccles', and continue to **Barnaby Green**.

11 Cross the `A12` and join Kiln Road. Continue north on this before bearing → onto Wash Lane, reaching **Clay Common** after a further 200m. Turn ← and continue to **Stoven**. Turn → opposite the church. Continue 2.2km north to **Sotterley**.

12 Continue ↑ at the crossroads, with the monument on your right, onto Pound Road. After 2km take the ← onto Church Road, signed 'Ellough, Beccles' and NCN 31. Continue to **Ellough** and turn ←. Continue north towards Beccles on Cucumber Lane. When you reach the `A145`, cross to join a cycleway and immediately turn → to join Oak Lane, a passable green lane. Turn ← onto St Andrew's Road, continue ↑ as this becomes St Benet's Drive, and head through the suburbs of **Beccles**.

Turn ← onto Nicholson Drive and after 50m turn → onto Townlands Drive. At the junction, turn → and immediately ← onto Kemps Lane, signed 'High School, Town Centre, NCN 31'. Follow Kemps Lane across the railway and then take a cycle path that delivers you to the `B1062`; turn →. Continue ↑, north, until you reach Beccles town centre. Turn → onto Market Street, signed 'Lowestoft, Norwich, Diss'. After 50m this becomes Station Road. Continue to **Beccles Station**.

30% off road

12

Route 12 – Norfolk

North Norfolk Ways

Start	Diss, Railway Station
Finish	Sheringham, Railway Station
Time	2–3 days
Total distance	179km (111.2 miles)
Off-road distance	52.8km
Percentage off-road	30%
Total ascent/descent	1190m/1200m
Grade	Easy ■
Terrain	Singletrack 3%, track 27%, road 70%
Bike choice	Gravel

On paper this is one of the longest routes in the guide, but progress is quick on quiet roads and flat, direct trails. The route brings together many of the highlights of Norfolk's unique rural landscape: tall coniferous forests, wide open farmland, big skies, ancient castles, a royal residence and a procession of coastal market towns, nature reserves and historical buildings in various states of preservation, all linked by country lanes and drove roads.

Route options

Alternative start/finish: As this route is not a loop, there are no alternative starting points if you are planning to ride the whole route. Having said that, you could definitely reverse the route without issue and start at Sheringham.

Shortcuts and extensions: You could shorten the route by 10km if you start in Thetford and pick up the route in Bridgham.

Big Gravel Days: A really nice day's riding could be had by starting in King's Lynn and picking up the route near Sandringham. Riding from Diss to King's Lynn, a flat 90km, would also be a decent challenge.

Route 12 – Norfolk

Summary table

Waypoint	Section	Distance (km)	Ascent (m)	Descent (m)
1	Diss Station – All Saints Church (remains of)	17.8	60	55
2	All Saints Church (remains of) – Peddars Way	12.8	70	55
3	Peddars Way – Little Cressingham	17.8	70	60
4	Little Cressingham – North Pickenham	7.7	45	60
5	North Pickenham – Castle Acre	11.3	80	80
6	Castle Acre – Gayton	12.1	85	90
7	Gayton – Sandringham	16	90	85
8	Sandringham – Snettisham	6.5	40	60
9	Snettisham – Sedgeford	4.8	50	50
10	Sedgeford – Brancaster	12.1	90	115
11	Brancaster – Burnham Market	9.6	70	70
12	Burnham Market – Holkham Hall	9.6	90	80
13	Holkham Hall – Wells-next-the-Sea	7.2	20	30
14	Wells-next-the-Sea – Binham	10.5	85	65
15	Binham – Blakeney	7.2	65	80
16	Blakeney – Weybourne	11.2	140	120
17	Weybourne – Sheringham Station	4.8	40	45

Directions

1 Head south on Station Road and turn → under the railway bridge. Follow the A1066 for 1.5km. At the mini-roundabout take the first left and after 100m turn ← on Denmark Street, signed 'Angles Way'. Continue for 300m across the bridge before turning →, signposted 'cycleway Thetford 20'. Follow NCN 30 (National Cycle Network) on Ling Road, bearing → and taking signs for 'Redgrave, Hinderclay' for 8km. At Crackthorn Corner turn →. After 1km turn → into **Thelnetham**. Remain on NCN 30 through Hopton and on to a staggered junction at **Knettishall**, close to the remains of All Saints Church.

North Norfolk Ways

Surface	Grade	Description
paved	n/a	Follow NCN 30 to the ruins of an old church
mixed	🟩	Through the Brecks to an ancient Roman road
mixed	🟩	The cycle-friendly sections of the Peddars Way
paved	n/a	Easy section on minor roads
mixed	🟩	Continue north to historic Castle Acre
mixed	🟩	Wild and remote – classic Norfolk
mixed	🟩	Into the grounds of the royal estate
paved	n/a	Following ancient drove roads past the site of a Roman villa
mixed	🟩	A short section to a possible refreshments stop
mixed	🟩	Fast off-road to the coast
mixed	🟩	Back inland and a byway to a market town
mixed	🟩	Holkham Hall – a window into another world
mixed	🟩	Off-road NCN 1 to Holkham Nature Reserve and beyond
mixed	🟩	Remote byways to an impressive ancient priory
paved	n/a	Possible seal-watching opportunity if the conditions are right
mixed	🟩	Minor roads heading east
paved	n/a	A section of fast road to Sheringham Station

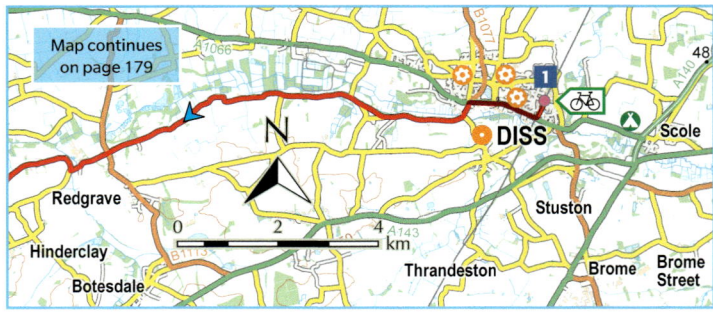

Route 12 – Norfolk

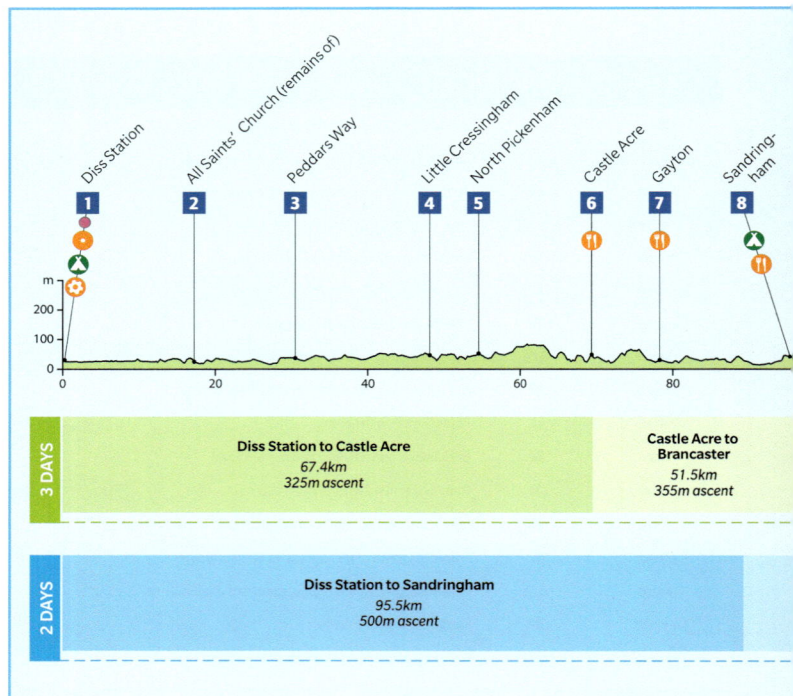

2 ■ Turn → at the staggered junction, signposted 'Gasthorpe, East Harling'. After 4km on an old Roman road, turn ← onto West Harling Road. Follow NCN 30 as it bears ← for 2km before taking a → onto Bridgham Lane, signed 'Peddars Way cycle route/NCN 13'. When you regain the road, turn ←. At the junction, leave NCN 13, turn → and head into **Bridgham**. The route skirts the easterly edge of the Brecks, a unique landscape of heathland and forest.

Turn ← on Timber Hill, and ← at the green, signed 'High Bridgham'. Continue west for 2.5km and turn → onto the **Peddars Way** when it intersects with the road.

3 ■ Continue for 500m, carefully cross the busy A11 and shortly afterwards take care when crossing the railway line. Continue to **Stonebridge**. After 200m fork

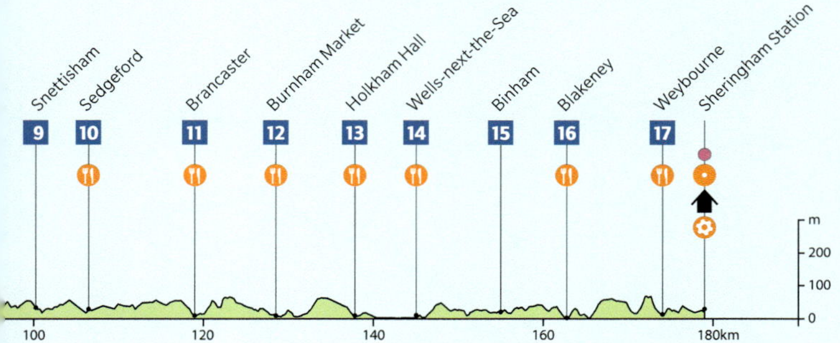

Snettisham
Sedgeford
Brancaster
Burnham Market
Holkham Hall
Wells-next-the-Sea
Binham
Blakeney
Weybourne
Sheringham Station
9
10
11
12
13
14
15
16
17
m
200
100
0
100
120
140
160
180km

Brancaster to Sheringham Station
60.1km
510m ascent

AVERAGE DAY – 59.7km / 8hr / 7.5kmh

Sandringham to Sheringham Station
83.5km
690m ascent

AVERAGE DAY – 89.5km / 9hr / 10km

Map continues on page 181
A1066
Gasthorpe
2
Knettishall
N
Hopton
Blo' Norton
Thelnetham
Redgrave
Hinderclay
Barningham
45
44
57
0
2
4
km
B1113

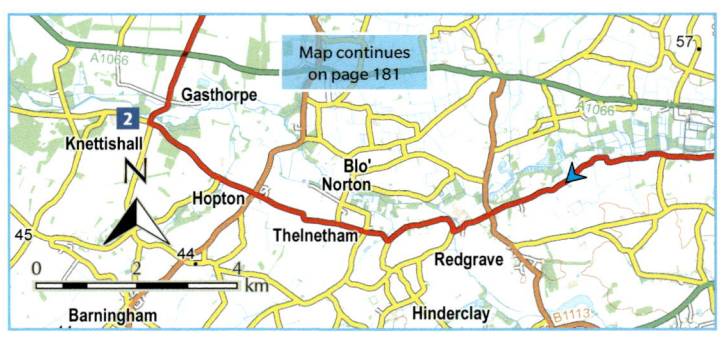

Route 12 – Norfolk

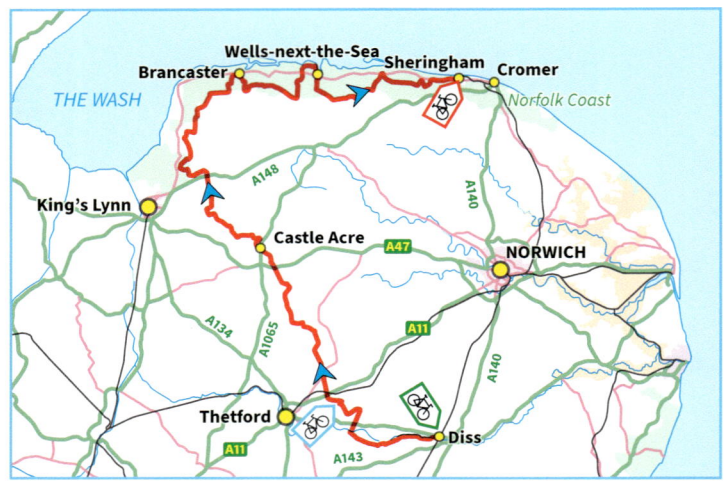

A rider's shadow

North Norfolk Ways

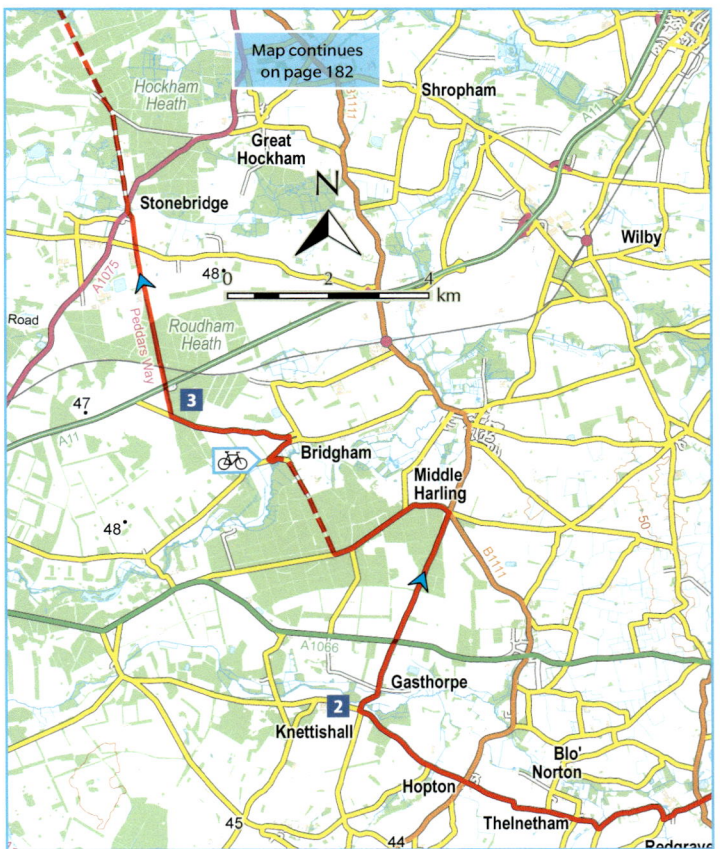

← onto Woodcock Road, signed 'Peddars Way cycle route'. Continue for 2km, turn ← and follow the road as it bears → on the Peddars Way, on a rough track heading north. Follow through the woods and turn → onto a narrow single singletrack, signed 'Peddars Way cycle route'. After 1km fork ← onto Marlpit Road. Continue ↑ and maintain NCN 13, turning ← onto Crow's Lane. Head through **Merton** and bear ←, leaving NCN 13. When the road runs out, continue up a lane on the Peddars Way; fork →. Turn ← and continue to **Little Cressingham**.

Route 12 – Norfolk

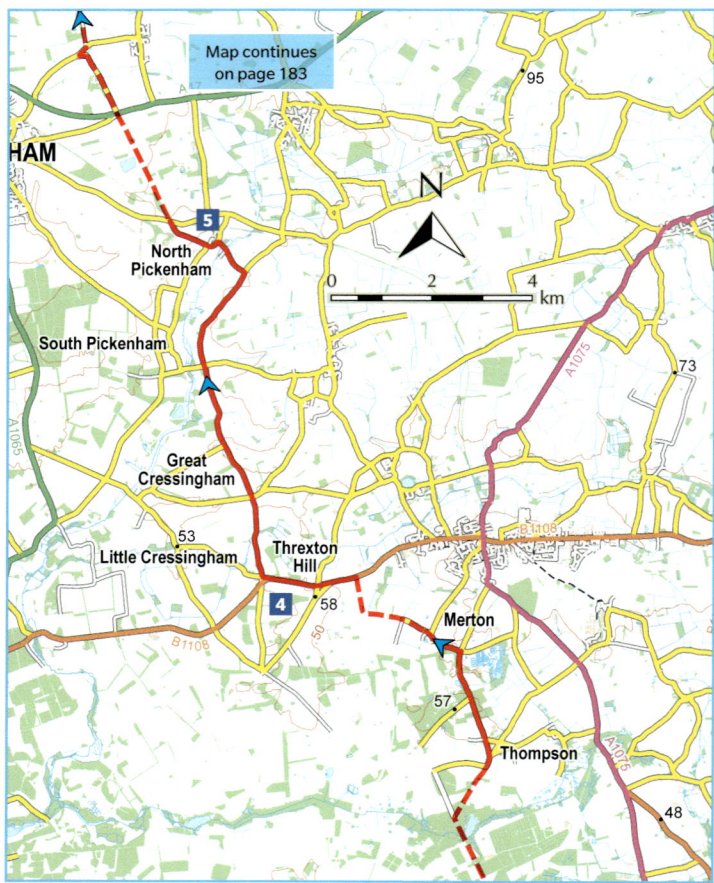

4 At the village centre turn →, signed 'S. Pickenham'. Continue ↑ north for 6km before turning ← onto Houghton Lane and dropping into **North Pickenham**.

> Just off route, down a bridleway to your right shortly before you turn onto Houghton Lane, is **St Mary's Church**, known for its 11th-century interior wall paintings.

North Norfolk Ways

5 With the Blue Lion pub (closed at time of publication in 2025) on your right, turn ←. Follow Procession Lane to the road before crossing it onto the singletrack of the Peddars Way once more. Cross the A47 and onto Procession Lane. At the road, turn → and continue for 150m before turning ← on the Peddars Way. Continue bearing ←, passing Palgrave Hall on your left. At the road, turn ← and follow it to the A1065.

Cross the busy road, take the ← and climb to the junction. Now fork →, signed 'Ford, Deep Water'. Follow this as it bears →, and drop to the ford. Unless you are feeling brave or there has been little rainfall lately, cross via the bridge. After 100m, fork → and climb into **Castle Acre**, heading under the medieval archway. About 1.5km east of here, the George and Dragon pub is a gem, with exceptional food and great local beer.

6 ■ Head through the centre of town, bearing → as you head past the gatehouse for the ancient priory. When you meet the road, turn ←. After 2km turn ← into **West Acre**, head past the Stag Inn and turn →. At the next junction, cross the road and climb on a dirt track. Bear → and continue on a good track over arable land with fantastic views to the north. Descend with the Soigné Wood on your right and drop into **Gayton Thorpe**. Fork → at the church, continue to the road and cross the junction onto Brick Yard Lane. You reach a crossroads after 1km; turn ← and head into **Gayton**.

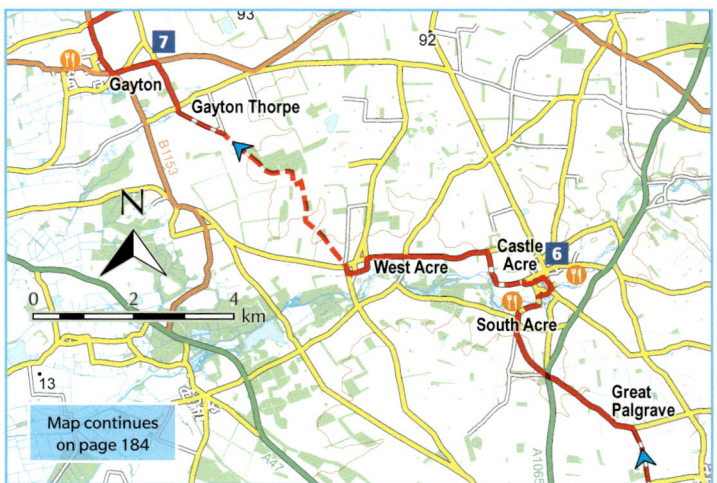

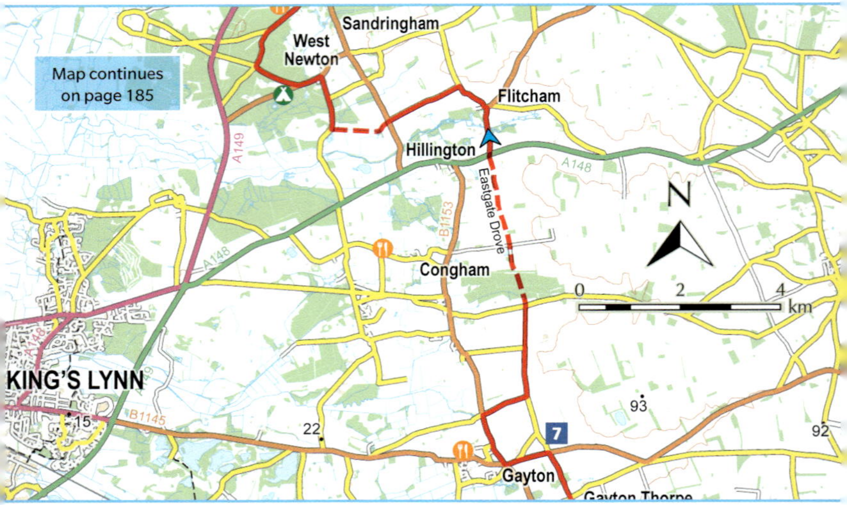

Route 12 – Norfolk

7 ■ With the windmill on your left, turn →, signed 'Grimston'. After 1km fork → at the crossroads, and after a further 1km fork ← on a road. At the next junction you join a good drove road and continue on this ↑ for 3km. Cross the A148 and join the B1153 to **Flitcham**. Turn ← past the community centre and then fork →, signposted 'Sandringham'.

Early spring blossom on the lanes outside Sedgeford

North Norfolk Ways

Pick up a snack at the Fish Shed in Brancaster Staithe

After 500m turn ← onto Common Drove. Pass Flitcham Hall on the left, head over a crossroads and join a dirt track. After 1km on this, rejoin the road and turn →, then head through a wood past Victoria Cottages and turn ←. After 300m fork →, signed 'Camping'. After 1km, turn → and head past the Double Lodges. Bear → onto Scotch Belt and continue to the Sandringham House Visitor Centre at **Sandringham**. If you don't have time to visit the royal household itself, the visitor centre is a great place to grab a coffee and a sandwich.

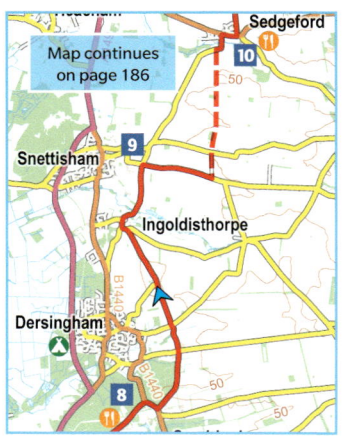

8 Head north past the Norwich Gates and bear → before turning ←, signposted 'Sawmill'. Head over the next two junctions on NCN 1 past Mill Cottages onto Chalk Pit Road. On reaching **Ingoldisthorpe**, take the second right onto Brickley Lane. Bear → on this, cross a bridge and continue on St Thomas's Lane to a junction on the outskirts of **Snettisham**.

9 ■ Turn → onto Bircham Road. After 1km turn ← onto a drove road and head north for 2.5km. At the road, turn → and follow the road into **Sedgeford**.

Route 12 – Norfolk

10 ■ Turn →, signposted 'Fakenham'. After 200m turn ←, following NCN 1 uphill. Top out and begin to descend before turning → onto a drove road after 1km. Follow this for 1.5km and descend. Cross the first road and continue to the next; turn →. Continue on this for 3km east before reaching a small plantation on your right and turning ← onto Chalk Pit Lane. After a short climb, you top out and turn → to follow a car-wide track as it bears ← and drops into **Brancaster**. You can grab a quick snack at the Fish Shed in Brancaster Staithe or at one of the pubs here.

11 ■ On reaching the busy A149, turn →. After 1km, turn → onto Green Common Lane and climb back onto the high ground. Meet the road and turn →, then take the ← after 50m. At the next junction turn → onto a drove road and head away from the coast back to NCN 1. Turn ← and after 800m turn ← onto another car-wide restricted byway and follow it past Sussex Farm to the road. At the next junction turn → and shortly ← and head into **Burnham Market**.

12 ■ With the church on your ←, follow NCN 1 → onto Station Road. Continue over the staggered junction on NCN 1 and follow this as it bears ← through **Burnham Thorpe** and on to **New Holkham**. Follow NCN 1 as it turns ← and

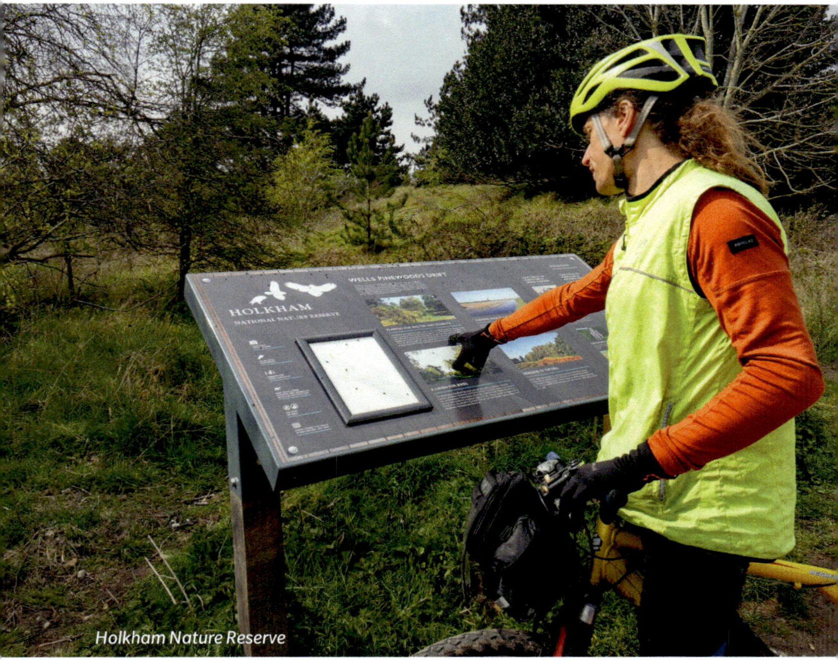

Holkham Nature Reserve

Map continues on page 188

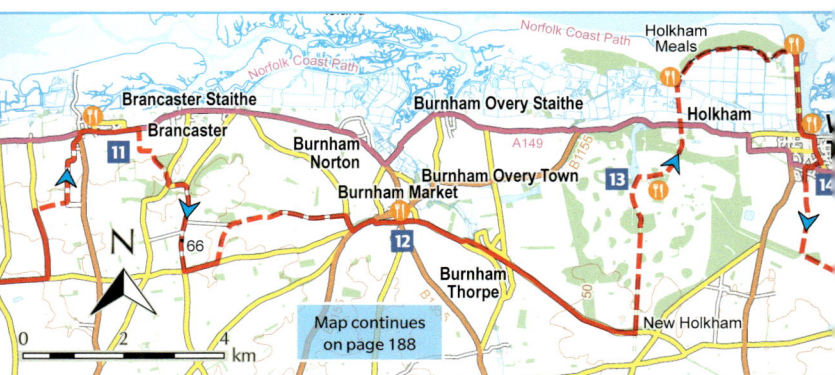

Route 12 – Norfolk

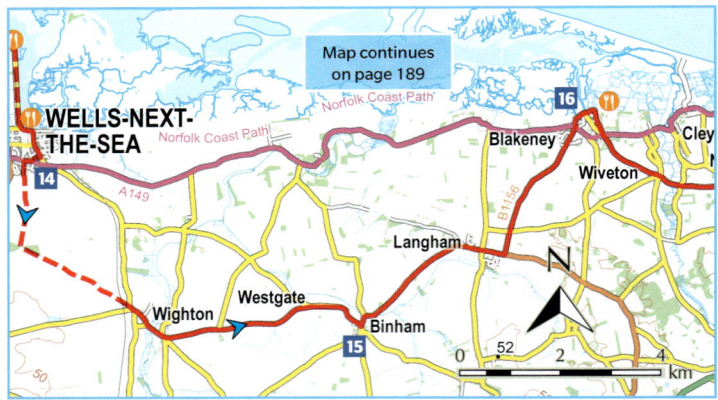

heads through the imposing gates of the Holkham Estate and on to Holkham Hall.

13 ■ You descend slowly to reach the coast road once more at **Holkham**. Cross the road and ride towards Holkham beach. NCN 1 continues east in an arc around the back of **Holkham Meals** before steering you into **Wells-next-the-Sea**. The impressive pines at Holkham Meals were planted in the 19th century by the Second Earl of Leicester to prevent coastal erosion.

14 ■ When the road meets the harbour, follow an NCN sign on the right that takes you along a narrow street. Continue ↑ through these narrow streets, past a school and onto a drove road heading south; climb to Cuckoo Lodge. Take the second ← and descend on a good track. Follow this to the road and into **Wighton**. Leave the town and NCN 1, bear ← and continue to **Westgate**. Continue past the imposing ruins of Binham Priory into **Binham**.

15 ■ Turn ← at the pub, and after 200m bear →, signed 'Langham'. Head through **Langham**, turn ← opposite the pub and continue to **Blakeney**. Cross the coast road and bear ←, following the road along the harbour.

> Europe's largest population of grey seals spends the autumn on **Blakeney Point**. There are a few bridleways that you can use to get closer to the sea if you have the time.

North Norfolk Ways

Windmill near Weybourne

16 ■ Follow the road as it bears →. Cross the coast road and climb gently to **Wiveton**. Head past the church and over the bridge. Continue 2km over Salthouse Heath before forking → onto a restricted byway. When you meet the road, turn ← and head into **Kelling**. Meet the coast road, turn → and then after 200m turn → onto a restricted byway. Climb on this gently for 1km until you meet the road. Turn ← and descend along Holgate Hill into **Weybourne**.

17 Bear ← then turn → to rejoin the coast road for the last time. Continue on this for 5km to **Sheringham**. Sheringham is a great place for some fish and chips – you will have earned them. Turn ← over the railway bridge and descend to the station.

Appendix A
Accommodation

Entries are listed in route order, with off-route locations *shown in italic.*

Location	Name	Type	Tel
Route 1 – From the Forest to the Sea			
The New Forest offers numerous campsites and wild camping options. Forestry England restricts camping in most park areas, but there are opportunities outside these zones. A YHA is also available.			
Brockenhurst	*Hollands Wood Campsite*	🏕	*01590 631641*
	Black Knowl Caravan and Motorhome Club Campsite	🏕	*01590 623600*
	Long Meadow Campsite	🏕	*01590 622489*
	Setthorns Campsite	🏕	01590 681020
Holmsley	*Holmsley Campsite*	🏕	*01590 631641*
	The Old Airfield Campsite	🏕 ⚪	*07476 988855*
Burley	*YHA New Forest*	🏠 🏕	*0345 371 9309*
Linwood	Red Shoot Camping Park	🏕	01425 473789
Breamore	*Dot's Camping*	🏕	*07780 950120*
Hale Park	*Harry's Meadow Campsite*	🏕 ⚪	*07534 006137*
Nomansland	Tanglewood Field Camping	🏕	07563 620678
Fritham	Longbeech Campsite	🏕	01590 631641
	Ocknell Campsite	🏕	01590 631641
Stoney Cross	Ocknell Park Farm	🏕	07825 511096
north of Lyndhurst	Mill House Farm Caravan Site	🏕	023 8028 2798
Ashurst	Ashurst Campsite	🏕	01590 631641
east of Lyndhurst	Matley Wood Campsite	🏕	01590 631641
	Denny Wood Campsite	🏕	01590 631641

Accommodation

Web/Email	Comments/Location
www.campinginthenewforest.com/campsites/hollands-wood	*north of Brockenhurst*
www.caravanclub.co.uk	*north of Brockenhurst*
www.longmeadowcampsite.com	*north of Brockenhurst*
www.campinginthenewforest.com/campsites/setthorns	*south-west of Brockenhurst, close to the route start*
www.campinginthenewforest.com/campsites/holmsley	*south of Burley*
www.harryscampsites.co.uk/the-old-airfield	*south of Burley*
www.yha.org.uk/hostel/yha-new-forest	*the only YHA in the New Forest*
www.redshoot-campingpark.com	
www.facebook.com/p/Dots-Camping-100063522105373	*pop-up campsite, west of Woodgreen*
www.harryscampsites.co.uk/harrys-meadow	*west of Hale*
www.tanglewoodfieldcamping.co.uk	
www.campinginthenewforest.com/campsites/longbeech	
www.campinginthenewforest.com/campsites/ocknell	
www.campinginthenewforest.com/campsites/ashurst	
www.campinginthenewforest.com/campsites/matley-wood	
www.campinginthenewforest.com/campsites/denny-wood	

Appendix A

Location	Name	Type	Tel
west of Beaulieu	Roundhill Campsite	🌳	01590 631641
Lepe	Lepe Meadows Campsite	🌳	0330 100 0842
Lepe	Lepe Beach Campsite	🌳	0330 100 0842
Lymington	Embers Camping	🌳	0345 257 2267
Lymington	Lymington Camping	🌳	07764 603073

Route 2 – Ticket to Ryde

You should have no problem finding a suitable campsite for your Isle of Wight adventure. There are great options for wild camping here too: the Downs (Limerstone, Mottistone, Compton, Tennyson, Wroxall and Bembridge) are all on the route and all are common land. Follow the code in the Introduction.

Location	Name	Type	Tel
Parkhurst	Riverside Paddock Camping Site	🌳	01983 821367
south-west of Newport	Windmill Campersite (Froglands Farm)	🌳 ⚪	07957 572221
south-west of Freshwater	Stoats Farm	🌳 ⚪	01983 759608
Totland	YHA Totland	⬆	01983 752165
north of Freshwater	Heathfield Farm Camping Park	🌳	01983 407822
east of Yarmouth	Camp Wight	🌳 ⚪	07748 844242
Brighstone	YHA Brighstone	⬆	01983 752165
Brighstone	Grange Farm Camping and Cottages	🌳	01983 740296
Shorwell	Troopers View Campsite	🌳	07872 321288
Chale Green	Camp Corve	🌳 ⚪	07815 006450
Chale	Paradise Cottage Campsite	🌳	01983 551375
Little Atherfield	Warren Hill Camp	⚪	07942 893558
Shanklin	Ninham Country Holidays	🌳	01983 864243
north of Wroxall	Appuldurcombe Gardens Holiday Park	🌳	01983 852597
west of Sandown	Southland Caravan and Motorhome Club Campsite	🌳	01983 865385
Brading	Sunrise Hill Camping	🌳	07432 812748
Bembridge	Forelands Pop-Up Campsite	🌳	
south of Ryde	Whitefield Forest Touring Park	🌳	01983 617069

Accommodation

Web/Email	Comments/Location
www.campinginthenewforest.com/campsites/roundhill	*between Beaulieu and Brockenhurst*
www.eazycamp.co.uk	*north of Lepe*
www.eazycamp.co.uk	
www.emberscamping.co.uk/campsites/pylewell-park-the-new-forest	*Pylewell Park, east of Lymington*
www.lymingtoncamping.co.uk	*north of Lymington*
https://riversidepaddock.co.uk	*north of Newport*
www.windmillcampersite.com	*a possible overnight before the steep climb onto the ridge*
www.stoatsfarm.com	*towards the Needles*
www.yha.org.uk/hostel/yha-isle-of-wight-totland	
www.heathfieldcamping.co.uk	
https://campwight.co.uk	
	open late July to end of August; book through YHA Totland
www.grangefarmholidays.com	*on the south-west coast, south-west of Brighstone*
	east of Brighstone
https://www.visitisleofwight.co.uk/accommodation/camp-corve-p2069191	*good option for the second night on a three-day schedule*
www.campingandcaravanningclub.co.uk	
www.warrenhillcamp.com	
www.ninham-holidays.co.uk	
www.appuldurcombegardens.co.uk	*near Appuldurcombe House*
www.caravanclub.co.uk	
https://sunrisehillcamping.co.uk	*west of Bembridge*
www.facebook.com/p/forelands-pop-up-campsite-61560198522342	
www.whitefieldforest.co.uk	*between Bembridge and Ryde*

Appendix A

Location	Name	Type	Tel
Route 3 – A Tower, a Temple and a Punch Bowl			

There are very few campsites on the route itself. However, there are unlimited locations for wild camping on common land at (clockwise from the start) Blackheath, St Martha's Hill, Merrow Downs, Netley Heath, White Downs, Ranmore Common, Squires Great Wood, the Hurtwood, Wotton Common, Hydon Heath, Hambledon Hurst, Frillinghurst Wood, Black Down, Marley Common, Linchmere Common, Stanley Common, Ludshott Common, Conford, Hindhead Common and Thursley National Nature Reserve.

Location	Name	Type	Tel
north of Dorking	Embers Camping – Polesden Lacey	⊗ ⊙	0345 257 2267
north of Dorking	YHA Tanners Hatch – Surrey Hills	⬆	0345 371 9542
south of Dorking	Henfold Lakes	⊗	01306 883346
south of Leith Hill	The Green Escape	⊙	07590 693271
south of Leith Hill	Etherley Farm	⊗	01306 621500
Holmbury St Mary	The Hurtwood Hostel	⬆	01306 730777
north of Hascombe	Firesyde	⊙	
south-east of Hascombe	Springbok Farm Estate Campsite (Care Ashore)	⊗	01403 752555
Haslemere	Night Pastures	⊗ ⊙	01428 610120
Haslemere	Huntingford Camping	⊗	01428 717815
Route 4 – The Chilterns Off-Road Cycleway			

In addition to the viable campsites listed below, there are also pockets of common land along the route that are suitable for wild camping: Park Wood in the Bradenham Beeches south of Loosley Row; Kimble Wood and Highmoor Common Wood, both below Nettlebed; Ipsden Wood near Stoke Row; Nuffield Common and Queen Wood below Christmas Common.

Location	Name	Type	Tel
east of Stokenchurch	Bella Vista Camping	⊗	07976 256641
east of Stokenchurch	Home Farm Camping, Glamping and Caravan Site	⊗ ⊙	01494 484136
east of Turville	Chiltern Retreat	⊗	01494 840243
Pangbourne	Meadow Farm Camping	⊗	07912 068720
Goring	YHA Streatley-on-Thames	⬆	0345 371 9044
south-east of Wallingford	Ridgeway View Campsite	⊗	07552 533381
north of Princes Risborough	Orchard View Farm Camping and Glamping	⊗ ⊙	01844 396301

Accommodation

Web/Email	Comments/Location
www.emberscamping.co.uk/campsites/polesden-lacey-surrey	possible option if doing the route over three days
www.yha.org.uk/hostel/yha-tanners-hatch-surrey-hills	
https://henfoldleisureltd.co.uk	
www.thegreenescape.co.uk	
https://etherleyfarm.co.uk	
www.hurtwoodhostel.com	north-west of Holmbury St Mary
www.firesyde.co.uk	
www.careashore.org	
www.nightpastures.com	*south of Haslemere*
www.huntingfordcamping.co.uk	*north-west of Haslemere*
www.bellavistacamping.co.uk	
www.homefarmradnage.co.uk	
www.chilternretreat.co.uk	
www.meadowfarmcamping.com	*1km from the southern tip of the route; ideal for a two-day schedule*
www.yha.org.uk/hostel/yha-streatley-on-thames	*west of the railway station; apex of the route, recommended for the first night if you are doing the route over two days*
https://ridgewayadventures.co.uk/camping	
www.orchardviewfarmcamping.co.uk	

Appendix A

Location	Name	Type	Tel

Route 5 – Come on Pilgrim

Not so many campsites here but plenty of wild camping options at (counterclockwise from the start) Limpsfield Chart, Crockhamhill Common, Hosey Common, The Chart, Ide Hill and Fawke Common, and a reasonably priced glamping site.

Location	Name	Type	Tel
Sevenoaks Weald	Little Elses	○	07891 626272
Seal Chart	Oldbury Hill Campsite	●	01732 762728

Route 6 – High Weald Drifter

There are plenty of campsites to choose from. Wild camping is also an option: the common land south of Chuck Hatch (Stage 2) and to the north of Priory Road; Camp Hill in the heart of Ashdown Forest is on the route and (if on a two-day schedule) close to the end of the first day; Bedgebury Forest is also common land.

Location	Name	Type	Tel
Hartfield	St Ives Farm Campsite	●	01892 770213
south of East Grinstead	Evergreen Farm Woodland Campsite	●	07377 662852
	Sunnyside Pop-Up Camping	●	07973 600493
West Hoathly	Hook Farm Campsite	●	01342 811113
Horsted Keynes	Bluebell Camp	● ○	07562 710720
Nutley	Tinker's Wood Camping	●	01342 823583
Crowborough	Crowborough Camping and Caravanning Club Site	●	01892 664827
	Idle Hours Owlsbury Park	●	
Stonegate	Cairds Camping	● ○	07765 363546
Hartley	Star Field Glamping and Camping (Charity Farm)	● ○	01580 713189
Bewl Water	Bewl Water Campsite	●	01892 890000
	Cedar Gables Campsite	●	07764 487968
	Hopgarden Glamping and Camping	● ○	07801 491807
south of Eridge Green	Campfire Weekends (Great Danegate Farm)	●	07749 183232
	Deer Park Campsite	● ○	07562 710720

Accommodation

Web/Email	Comments/Location
www.littleelses.co.uk	*just south of Sevenoaks Weald*
www.nationaltrust.org.uk/holidays/kent-surrey-sussex/oldbury-hill-campsite	close to the finish
www.stivesfarm.co.uk	
evergreenfarmland@gmail.com	
www.sunnysidepopupcamping.com	
www.hook-farm-west-hoathly.co.uk	
www.yampcamp.co.uk/bluebell-camp	close to the heritage railway station
tinkerswoodcamping@gmail.com	
www.campingandcaravanningclub.co.uk/campsites	*north of Crowborough*
www.pitchup.com	*south of Crowborough*
www.cairdscampingandcaravansite.co.uk	*east of Stonegate Station, south of the route*
www.starfieldcamping.co.uk	*east of Bedgebury Forest*
www.bewlwater.co.uk	*north edge of Bewl Water*
www.cedargables.org	*north-east of Bewl Water*
www.hopgardenglamping.co.uk	*north-west of Bewl Water*
www.campfireweekends.co.uk	close to the finish
www.yampcamp.co.uk/deer-park	close to the finish

Appendix A

Location	Name	Type	Tel
Route 7 – Battle Cruiser			
Lots of campsites to choose from, although not many options for wild camping (eg Great Wood on Stage 1, or the beach).			
east of Battle	Riverdale Cottage	🏕	01424 756932
	Buckhurst Campsite	🏕	07517 477447
north of Hastings	Hop and Hare Farm Land	🏕	07771 535350
Normans Bay	Normans Bay Camping and Caravanning Club Site	🏕	01323 761190
Pevensey Bay	*Cannon Camping and Caravan Park*	🏕	*07899 651612*
Westham	*Fairfields Farm Caravan and Camping Park*	🏕	*01323 763165*
south of Hailsham	Little Downash	🏕	07763 514566
east of Herstmonceux	*Gardner's Farm Campsite*	🏕	*07758 369572*
west of Battle	*Beech Estate Campsite*	🏕	*01273 980218*
Route 8 – The Cantii Way			
On a 3-day schedule, campsites at Nethercourt followed by Romney Meadows could work; for a 4-day ride, Hawk Place, Coxhill and Herons Park are recommended. There are good opportunities for wild camping before reaching the coast in Clowes Wood north of Canterbury, at Abott's Cliff Sound Mirror, and between Dymchurch and Rye (if you are creative and respectful of residents). There are scant 'legitimate' spots beyond this.			
Westwell, Ashford	Dunn Street Farm Campsite	🏕	
Canterbury	YHA Canterbury	🏠	0345 371 9010
	Canterbury Camping and Caravanning Club Campsite	🏕	*01227 463216*
	The Barn Camping	🏕	*01227 206422*
Herne Bay	Hampton Bay Park	🏕	07925 115741
Birchington	Hawk Place Campsite	🏕	01843 847142
Ramsgate	Nethercourt Touring Park	🏕	07981 029517
Elmstone	*Orchard House Camping and Caravanning Club Campsite*	🏕	*01227 722336*
Knowlton	*Embers Camping – Knowlton Campsite*	🏕	*0345 257 2267*
Kingsdown	Kingsdown Camping	🏕	01304 373713
Shepherdswell	*Coxhill Camping*	🏕	*07869 375034*
Dover	Dover Adventure Backpackers Hostel	🏠	07776 127592

Accommodation

Web/Email	Comments/Location
www.riverdalecottage.com	close to the start
www.buckhurstcamping.com	close to the start
www.popupcampsites.com	
www.campingandcaravanningclub.co.uk	west of Bexhill, on the south coast
www.cannoncamping.co.uk	
www.fairfieldsfarm.com	
www.littledownash.co.uk	
www.pitchup.com	
https://pegsandpitches.co.uk/beech-estate	
www.dunnstreetfarm.co.uk	*west of the route start*
www.yha.org.uk/hostel/yha-canterbury	
www.campingandcaravanningclub.co.uk	*east of Canterbury*
www.thebarncamping.co.uk	*west of Canterbury; requires membership of Camping and Caravanning Club*
www.hampton-bay-park.co.uk	
www.eastkentcamping.co.uk	
www.nethercourt.com	
www.campingandcaravanningclub.co.uk	*north-west of Sandwich*
www.emberscamping.co.uk/campsites/knowlton-kent	*west of Deal*
www.kingsdowncamping.co.uk	
www.coxhillcamping.co.uk	*north-west of Dover*
www.hostelworld.com/hosteldetails.php/Dover-Adventure-Backpackers/Dover/310812	

Appendix A

Location	Name	Type	Tel
Elmsted	The Sunnyfield Campsite	●○	01233 750024
New Romney/Dungeness	Romney Meadows Caravan and Camping Park	●	01797 361499
west of Dungeness	Herons Park Campsite	●○	07585 316316
west of Dungeness	Orca Campsite	●	07751 087800
Rye	Hare & Hounds	●○	01797 230483
Rye	Iden Wood Camp	●	
Kenardington	Battle Hill Farm camping	●	01233 733635

Route 9 – The Only Way

There aren't so many campsites on this route. If you plan to use a licensed campsite within range of the halfway point, consider Sparrows Campsite. Alternatively, start the ride at Braintree and book a pitch at the atmospheric Debden House close to Theydon Bois. For wild camping, there is an area of common land near Coopersale, just east of Epping.

Location	Name	Type	Tel
Sewardstone	Lee Valley Campsite	●	0300 003 0623
Cheshunt	YHA London Lee Valley Hostel	▲	0345 371 9057
north-east of Braintree	Sparrows Campsite	●○	07450 582838
Theydon Bois	Debden House Centre	●	020 8508 3008

Route 10 – Stour Valley Villages

There are a few campsites close to this route, the nearest to the midpoint being the Briar or Rushbanks. Henny Riverside and Alton Water are also nice sites. There is no common land on the route so wild camping choices are few and far between.

Location	Name	Type	Tel
Bradfield	Strangers Holiday Park	●	01255 870304
Stutton	Alton Water Campsite	●○	01473 328268
Bentley	The Briar Campsite	●	07914 251970
south-west of Ipswich	Tomcat Farm Campsite (Camping and Caravanning Club Certificated Site)	●	01473 730913
Flatford	FSC Flatford Mill Hostel	▲	01206 297110
Henny Street	Henny Riverside Camping	●	
Little Cornard	Willowmere Caravan and Camping Park	●	01787 310422
Bures Green	Little Ropers Woodland Camping	●	07908 185393
west of Nayland	Rushbanks Farm Caravan and Camping Site	●	
Ardleigh	Ardleigh Caravan and Camping Park	●	01206 231134

Accommodation

Web/Email	Comments/Location
www.thesunnyfield.co.uk	north-west of Folkestone
www.romneymeadowscaravanandcamping.co.uk	
www.heronspark.com	
www.orcacampsiterye.co.uk	between Dungeness and Rye
https://hareandhoundsrye.co.uk	
www.idenwoodcamp.co.uk	
https://battlehillfarm.co.uk	
www.visitleevalley.org.uk/lee-valley-campsite-sewardstone	north of Chingford, beside the River Lea
www.yha.org.uk/hostel/yha-london-lee-valley	
www.sparrowscampsite.co.uk	8km north-east of the route beyond Braintree
www.debdenhouse.com/campsite-epping-forest.html	
https://strangersholidaypark.co.uk	west of Wrabness Nature Reserve
www.anglianwaterparks.co.uk/alton-water-park/camping	south of Alton Water
https://thebriarcampsite.co.uk	west of Alton Water, close to the midpoint
https://tomcatfarm.co.uk	
https://fsc.inn.fan	
www.hennyriversidecamping.co.uk	
https://willowmerecaravanpark.wordpress.com	
www.littleroperswoodlandcamping.co.uk	
https://rushbankscampsite.co.uk	close to the midpoint
www.ardleighcaravanandcampingpark.co.uk	south-west of Manningtree

Appendix A

Location	Name	Type	Tel
Route 11 - Three Ferries and a Power Station			

There is plenty to choose from here. Not a great area for wild camping, although options include Upper Hollesley Common, Rendlesham Forest, Tunstall Forest, Westleton Walks and Dunwich Forest.

Location	Name	Type	Tel
Shottisham	Shottisham Campsite	⛺	01394 411247
Sutton Heath	Holistic Woods Wild Campsite	⛺	07585 565376
Sutton Hoo	Sutton Hoo Holidays Campsite	⛺	01394 389013
Wickham Market	The Orchard Campsite	⛺	07818 034729
Blaxhall	YHA Blaxhall	⬆	03453719305
Leiston	Applefields Caravan and Camping Site	⛺	01728 833501
Westhall	Sunnyside Campsite	⛺	07582 818911
Route 12 – North Norfolk Ways			

Inland from the coast, north Norfolk is a quiet and remote place, and this is certainly part of its charm. However, it also means that campsites are thin on the ground. There are options for a camp before starting the ride near Diss, and a hostel in Sheringham at the end. If you can make an early-ish start on the first day, consider booking a pitch at the Four Acres Campsite. Wild camping possibilities include the Brecks, Roudham Heath, Hockham Heath and Dersingham Fen.

Location	Name	Type	Tel
Diss	Willows Caravan and Camping Park	⛺	01379 740271
Foulden	Everetts Farm Campsite	⛺	01366 328615
East Winch	Four Acres Campsite	⛺	07538 607130
Sandringham	Sandringham Camping and Caravanning Club Site	⛺	01485 542555
Dersingham	Pinecones Camping	⛺	01485 544224
Sheringham	YHA Sheringham	⬆	0345 371 9040

Accommodation

Web/Email	Comments/Location
www.shottishamcampsite.com	St Margaret's House, Hollesley Road
www.holisticwoods.co.uk	
www.orchardcampsite.co.uk	
www.yha.org.uk/hostel/yha-blaxhall	
	very friendly, well-run site
https://sunnysidecampsite.co.uk	near Brampton Station
http://willowscampingpark.co.uk	east of Diss, close to the start
www.facebook.com/everettsfarm.co.uk	west of Little Cressingham (end of Stage 3)
www.campingandcaravanningclub.co.uk	east of King's Lynn
www.campingandcaravanningclub.co.uk	
https://pinecones.co.uk	
www.yha.org.uk/hostel/yha-sheringham	

Appendix B
Bike shops

Entries are listed in route order.

Route 1 – From the Forest to the Sea

Boost Bike Hub
2–4 Brookley Road
Brockenhurst
SO42 7RR
01590 624204
www.boostbikehub.co.uk

New Forest Cycling
Ringwood Road
Burley
BH24 4AB
tel 01425 403584
www.forestleisurecycling.co.uk

Cycle Rescue
41 Christchurch Road
Ringwood
BH24 1DG
tel 01425 501227
www.cyclerescueringwood.co.uk

The Forge Cycleworks
The Furlong Shopping Centre
Ringwood
BH24 1AT
tel 01425 482797
www.forgecycles.co.uk

The Woods Cyclery (bike shop, hire and café)
56 High Street
Lyndhurst
SO43 7BG
tel 02380 282028
www.thewoodscyclery.co.uk

Figgures Cycles
Henderson Court
Lymington
SO41 9FQ
tel 01590 672268
www.figgurescycles.com

Route 2 – Ticket to Ryde

TAV Cycles
140 High Street
Ryde
PO33 2RE
tel 01983 812989
www.tavcycles.co.uk

Wight Mountain
31 Orchard Street
Newport
PO30 1JZ
tel 01983 520530
www.wight-mountain.co.uk

Al's Bikes
Senator Trading Estate
Sandown
PO36 8EH
tel 07962 373277
www.facebook.com/alsbikes

Route 3 – A Tower, a Temple and a Punch Bowl

The Spokesman Bicycle Workshop

Bike shops

Home Farm
Shere Road
Albury
GU5 9BL
tel 01483 351466
www.spokesmanbicyclerepairs.com

Cogs Workshop
43 South Street
Dorking
RH4 2JX
tel 01306 735364
www.cogsworkshop.com

Dorking Bicycle Repairs
14B Cotmandene
Dorking
RH4 2BT
tel 07583 055870

Nirvana Cycles
5 Guildford Road
Westcott
Dorking
RH4 3NR
tel 01306 740300
www.nirvanacycles.com

Beyond Bikes
82B Smithbrook Kilns
Cranleigh
GU6 8JJ
tel 01483 267676
www.beyond-bikes.co.uk

MB Cyclery
19–21 West Street
Haslemere
GU27 2AB
tel 01428 648424
www.mbcyclery.co.uk

Liphook Cycles
16 The Square
Liphook
GU30 7AH
tel 01428 727858
www.liphookcycles.com

Route 4 – The Chilterns Off-Road Cycleway

The Bicycle Workshop
Rookwood Cottage
Great Missenden
HP16 0QS
tel 07973 530914
www.bicycleworkshopgreatmissenden.co.uk

Saturday Bike Clinic at the Gate pub
Bryant's Bottom Road
Great Missenden
HP16 0JS
tel 07739 614579
www.cycletechuk.co.uk/saturday-bicycle-clinic

E-Bike Barn
Conway Farm
Henley-on-Thames
RG9 4QZ
tel 01491 628711
www.e-bikebarn.com

Rides On Air Cycles
48–50 St Mary's Street
Wallingford
OX10 0EY
tel 01491 836289
https://ridesonair.com

Appendix B

Route 5 – Come on Pilgrim

The Velo Barn
Betsoms Farm
Westerham
TN16 2DS
tel 01959 546159
www.thevelobarn.co.uk

The Bike Warehouse
53–55 High Street
Sevenoaks
TN13 1JF
tel 01732 464997
www.thebikewarehouse.net

Kemsing Bikes
20 West End
Kemsing
TN15 6PX
tel 07927 775268
www.kemsingbikes.com

Route 6 – High Weald Drifter

On Your Bike
Felbridge Forge
East Grinstead
RH19 2RQ
tel 01342 777700
www.onyourbike.com

Bikegoo
Lexden Lodge Industrial Estate
Crowborough
TN6 2NQ
tel 01892 668800
www.bikegoo.co.uk

Route 7 – Battle Cruiser

Hastings Cycles
St Andrews Market
Hastings
TN34 1SJ
tel 01424 444013
www.hastingsbikes.co.uk

Ebike Repairs
204 Cooden Drive
Bexhill
TN39 3AH
tel 07429 425651
www.ebikerepairs.co.uk

Eastbourne Cycles
Pevensey Bay
Eastbourne
BN24 6EG
tel 01323 660150
www.eastbournecycles.com

Route 8 – The Cantii Way

Gabs Bicycle Servicing and Repairs
8 Kingfisher Place
Chartham
Canterbury
CT4 7DJ
tel 07794 623629
https://gabsbikes.wixsite.com/home

Kent Cycles
81b Castle Street
Canterbury
CT1 2QD
tel 01227 941308
www.kentcycles.uk

Bike shops

Cycles UK
St George's Lane
Canterbury
CT1 2SY
tel 01227 457956
www.cyclesuk.com

Herberts Cycles
103–105 High Street
Whitstable
CT5 1AY
tel 01227 272072
www.herbertscycles.co.uk

Magic Spanner Bikes
48 Queens Road
Whitstable
CT5 2JF
tel 07929 358465
www.magicspannerbikes.co.uk

Kudos Cycles
St Augustine's Business Park
Whitstable
CT5 2QJ
tel 01227 792792
www.kudoscycles.com

Cycle Fixit (Herne Bay)
81a Sea Street
Herne Bay
CT6 8QG
tel 01227 749649
www.hythecycles.co.uk

The Bike Shed
71 Canterbury Road
Margate
CT9 5AS
tel 01843 228866

SP Cycles
98 Albion Road
Broadstairs
CT10 2UT
tel 01843 865769
www.spcycles.com

Harbour Bikes
20 Military Road
Ramsgate
CT11 9LG
tel 07807 727909

Locks of Sandwich Cycles
28 King Street
Sandwich
CT13 9BT
tel 01304 617161
www.locksofsandwichcycles.co.uk

Atman Cycle Shop
9 Galliard Street
Sandwich
CT13 9BG
tel 01304 611621
www.atman.uk.com

Renhams Cycles
17 Grace Hill
Folkestone
CT20 1HA
tel 01303 241884
www.renhamscycles.co.uk

Activ Cycles Folkestone
145 Sandgate Road
Folkestone
CT20 2DA
tel 01303 240110
www.activcycles.co.uk

Appendix B

Cycle Fixit (Hythe)
141 High Street
Hythe
CT21 5JL
tel 01303 239612
www.hythecycles.co.uk

Rye Bay E-Bikes
Rye Industrial Park
Rye
TN31 7TE
tel 01797 229351
www.ryebay-ebike.co.uk

Homewood Cycles
Ellingham Industrial Estate
Ashford
TN23 6LZ
tel 01233 621675
https://homewoodcycles.co.uk

ReVelo Sports
Tavis House Business Centre
Ashford
TN24 0YY
tel 07476 842735
https://revelo.cc

Route 9 – The Only Way

Spokes
Stondon Massey
Brentwood
CM15 0EQ
tel 01992 577702
https://spokesbikes.co.uk

Chelmer Cycles
6–7 New Writtle Street
Chelmsford
CM2 0RR
tel 01245 287600
www.chelmercycles.co.uk

CycleLife
5 Rayne Road
Braintree
CM7 2QA
tel 01376 320707

Mike Barnard of Dunmow
10 Hoblongs Industrial Estate
Dunmow
CM6 1JA
tel 01371 873441
www.mikebarnardcycles.co.uk

Giant Loughton
235 High Road
Loughton
IG10 1AD
tel 0208 508 1384
www.giant-loughton.co.uk/gb

Route 10 – Stour Valley Villages

Alan's Bicycle Workshop
Steele House
Harwich
CO12 3PN
tel 07565 148910
www.alansbicycleworkshop.co.uk

Alton Water Cycle Hire
Holbrook Road
Ipswich
IP9 2RY
tel 01473 328408alton water cu
www.anglianwaterparks.co.uk

Bike shops

The Bike Doctor
The Garage
Heath Road
East Bergholt
CO7 6RL
tel 01206 298646

Route 11 – Three Ferries and a Power Station

Elmy Cycles
86–88 St Helen's Street
Ipswich
IP4 2LB
tel 01473 255247
www.elmycycles.co.uk

Sax Velo
6 Brook Farm Road
Saxmundham
IP17 1XT
tel 07484 805507
www.saxvelo.co.uk

Southwold Cycle Hire
Ferry Road
Southwold
IP18 6ND
tel 07946 338097
www.southwoldcyclehire.co.uk

Route 12 – North Norfolk Ways

Velomont Ltd
11 Victoria Road
Diss
IP22 4HE
tel 07728 474885
www.velomont.co.uk

The Cycle Shack
1 Chapel Street
Diss
IP22 4AN
tel 01379 641212
www.thecycleshack.co.uk

Madgetts Cycles Ltd
8 Shelfanger Road
Diss
IP22 4EH
tel 01379 650419
www.madgettscycles.com

Thetford Men's Shed – The Bike Shed
Exeter Way
Thetford
IP24 1EE
tel 07795 977699
www.keystonetrust.org.uk/projects/thetford-mens-shed

Anglian Bicycles
19 Tower Place
King's Lynn
PE30 5DF
tel 01553 763572

South Creake Cycle Centre
5 The Bungalow
The Common
South Creake, Fakenham
NR21 9JA
tel 01328 823036

Black Bikes
28 Beeston Road
Sheringham
NR26 8EH
tel 01263 822255

Appendix C
Recommended kit lists

Essential kit list

This is a suggestion of what you'll need if you are depending on local facilities for food, and using a campsite.

Clothes
- Padded shorts
- Off-road cycling shoes, trainers or trail shoes
- Two pairs of socks
- Long-sleeved top
- Short-sleeved top
- Waterproof jacket
- Helmet

Repair kit
- Two inner tubes for your tyres
- Tyre levers
- Multitool
- Chain tool and spare link
- Puncture repair kit or tubeless repair kit
- Pump

Camping equipment
- Tent or bivvy bag
- Sleeping bag
- Sleeping mat
- Inflatable pillow
- Head torch

Other
- Water bottle(s)
- First aid kit (including antiseptic wipes and plasters)
- Mobile phone (to provide alternative means of navigation)
- Lights (to see by and be seen by)
- Spare battery for lights
- Power pack to charge lights and phone
- Electrolytes
- Toilet roll
- Shovel

Recommended kit lists

- Map
- Compass
- Micro-rucksack

Extended list

As well as the items on the essential list, this is a suggestion of what you'll need if you are going out of season or being fully self-supported (not using local facilities and campsites).

Clothes
- Waterproof gloves
- Waterproof socks (eg Sealskinz®)
- Warm hat
- Arm warmers
- Thermal leggings
- Down jacket/Synthetic down jacket
- Full-length padded leggings
- Snood

Repair kit
- Spare chain
- Spare tyre
- CO2 gas canisters and dispenser
- Oil
- Rag

Other
- Cycling computer
- Backup power pack
- Tarp and hammock set up
- Gas stove
- Pot
- Mug
- Coffee equipment/Coffee
- Food for the duration
- Water filter
- Camping knife/tool (eg Leatherman®)
- Flint lighter (matches can get wet)
- Long spork
- Dry bags
- Cash

Download the GPX files

All the routes in this guide are available for download from:

www.cicerone.co.uk/1237/GPX

as standard format GPX files. You should be able to load them into most online GPX systems and mobile devices, whether GPS or smartphone. You may need to convert the file into your preferred format using a conversion programme such as gpsvisualizer.com or one of the many other such websites and programmes.

When you follow this link, you will be asked for your email address and where you purchased the guidebook, and have the option to subscribe to the Cicerone e-newsletter.

www.cicerone.co.uk

LISTING OF CICERONE GUIDES

BRITISH ISLES CHALLENGES, COLLECTIONS AND ACTIVITIES
Great Walks on the England Coast Path
Map and Compass
The Big Rounds
The Book of the Bivvy
The Book of the Bothy
The Mountains of England and Wales:
　Vol 1 Wales
　Vol 2 England
The National Trails
Walking the End to End Trail
Cycling Land's End to John o' Groats

SHORT WALKS SERIES
15 Short Walks Hadrian's Wall
15 Short Walks in the Lake District: Keswick, Borrowdale and Buttermere
15 Short Walks in the Lake District: Windermere Ambleside and Grasmere
15 Short Walks Lake District: Coniston and Langdale
15 Short Walks in Arnside and Silverdale
15 Short Walks in the Ribble Valley
15 Short Walks in Nidderdale
15 Short Walks in Northumberland: Wooler, Rothbury, Alnwick and the coast
15 Short Walks in the Yorkshire Dales: Grassington, Skipton, Malham and Ilkley
15 Short Walks in the Peak District: Bakewell and the White Peak
15 Short Walks on the Malvern Hills
15 Short Walks in Cornwall: Falmouth and the Lizard
15 Short Walks in Cornwall: Land's End and Penzance
15 Short Walks in the South Downs: Brighton, Eastbourne and Arundel
15 Short Walks in the Surrey Hills
15 Short Walks on Dartmoor North: Okehampton and Chagford
15 Short Walks on Dartmoor South: Ivybridge and Princetown
15 Short Walks on Exmoor
15 Short Walks Winchester
15 Short Walks in Bannau Brycheiniog: Brecon Beacons
15 Short Walks in Pembrokeshire: Tenby and the south
15 Short Walks in Dumfries and Galloway
15 Short Walks in the Trossachs: Callander and Aberfoyle
15 Short Walks on the Isle of Mull
15 Short Walks on the Orkney Islands
15 Short Walks on the Shetland Islands

SCOTLAND
Ben Nevis and Glen Coe
Cycling in the Hebrides
Cycling the North Coast 500
Great Mountain Days in Scotland
Mountain Biking in Southern and Central Scotland
Mountain Biking in West and North West Scotland
Not the West Highland Way: A Mountain High Way Scotland
Scotland's Best Small Mountains
Scotland's Mountain Ridges
Scottish Wild Country Backpacking
Skye's Cuillin Ridge Traverse
The Borders Abbeys Way
The Great Glen Way
The Great Glen Way Map Booklet
The Hebridean Way
The Hebrides
The Isle of Mull
The Isle of Skye
The Skye Trail
The Southern Upland Way
The West Highland Way
The West Highland Way Map Booklet
Walking Ben Lawers, Rannoch and Atholl
Walking in the Cairngorms
Walking in the Pentland Hills
Walking in the Scottish Borders
Walking in the Southern Uplands
Walking in Torridon, Fisherfield, Fannichs and An Teallach
Walking Loch Lomond and the Trossachs
Walking on Arran
Walking on Harris and Lewis
Walking on Jura, Islay and Colonsay
Walking on Mull, Coll and Tiree
Walking on Rum and the Small Isles
Walking on the Orkney and Shetland Isles
Walking on Uist and Barra
Walking the Cape Wrath Trail
Walking the Corbetts
　Vol 1 South of the Great Glen
　Vol 2 North of the Great Glen
Walking the Fife Pilgrim Way
Walking the Galloway Hills
Walking the John o' Groats Trail
Walking the Munros
　Vol 1 Southern, Central and Western Highlands
　Vol 2 Northern Highlands and the Cairngorms
Winter Climbs in the Cairngorms
Winter Climbs: Ben Nevis and Glen Coe

NORTHERN ENGLAND ROUTES
Cycling the Reivers Route
Cycling the Way of the Roses
Hadrian's Cycleway
Hadrian's Wall Path
Hadrian's Wall Path Map Booklet
The Coast to Coast Cycle Route
The Coast to Coast Map Booklet
The Coast to Coast Walk
Walking the Dales Way
The Dales Way Map Booklet
Walking the Pennine Way
Pennine Way Map Booklet

LAKE DISTRICT
Bikepacking in the Lake District
Cycling in the Lake District
Great Mountain Days in the Lake District
Joss Naylor's Lakes, Meres and Waters of the Lake District
Lake District Winter Climbs
Lake District:
　High Level and Fell Walks
　Low Level and Lake Walks
Mountain Biking in the Lake District
Outdoor Adventures with Children — Lake District
Scrambles in the Lake District —
　North
　South
Trail and Fell Running in the Lake District
Walking The Cumbria Way
Walking the Lake District Fells —
　Borrowdale
　Buttermere
　Coniston
　Keswick
　Langdale
　Mardale and the Far East
　Patterdale
　Wasdale
Walking the Tour of the Lake District

NORTH-WEST ENGLAND AND THE ISLE OF MAN
Cycling the Pennine Bridleway
Isle of Man Coastal Path
The Lancashire Cycleway
The Lune Valley and Howgills
Walking in Cumbria's Eden Valley
Walking in Lancashire
Walking in the Forest of Bowland and Pendle
Walking on the Isle of Man
Walking on the West Pennine Moors
Walking the Ribble Way
Walks in Silverdale and Arnside

NORTH-EAST ENGLAND, YORKSHIRE DALES AND PENNINES

Cycling in the Yorkshire Dales
Great Mountain Days in the Pennines
Mountain Biking in the Yorkshire Dales
The Cleveland Way and the Yorkshire Wolds Way
The Cleveland Way Map Booklet
The North York Moors
Trail and Fell Running in the Yorkshire Dales
Walking in County Durham
Walking in Northumberland
Walking in the North Pennines
Walking in the Yorkshire Dales:
   North and East
   South and West
Walking St Cuthbert's Way
Walking St Oswald's Way and Northumberland Coast Path

DERBYSHIRE, PEAK DISTRICT AND MIDLANDS

Cycling in the Peak District
Dark Peak Walks
Scrambles in the Dark Peak
Walking in Derbyshire
Walking in the Peak District -
   White Peak East
   White Peak West

WALES AND WELSH BORDERS

Cycle Touring in Wales
Cycling Lon Las Cymru
Great Mountain Days in Snowdonia
Hillwalking in Shropshire
Mountain Walking in Snowdonia
Offa's Dyke Path
Offa's Dyke Map Booklet
Scrambles in Snowdonia
Snowdonia: 30 Low-level and Easy Walks — North, South
The Cambrian Way
The Pembrokeshire Coast Path
The Pembrokeshire Coast Path Map Booklet
The Snowdonia Way
The Wye Valley Walk
Walking Glyndwr's Way
Walking in Carmarthenshire
Walking in Pembrokeshire
Walking in the Brecon Beacons
Walking in the Wye Valley
Walking on Gower
Walking the Severn Way
Walking the Shropshire Way
Walking the Wales Coast Path

SOUTHERN ENGLAND

20 Classic Sportive Rides
   in South East England
   in South West England
Cycling in the Cotswolds
Mountain Biking on the North Downs
Mountain Biking on the South Downs
The North Downs Way
The North Downs Way Map Booklet
The South Downs Way
The South Downs Way Map Booklet
The Cotswold Way
The Cotswold Way Map Booklet
The Ridgeway National Trail
The Ridgeway Map Booklet
The Thames Path
The Thames Path Map Booklet
The Two Moors Way
Two Moors Way Map Booklet
Walking the South West Coast Path
South West Coast Path Map Booklet
   Vol 1: Minehead to St Ives
   Vol 2: St Ives to Plymouth
   Vol 2: St Ives to Plymouth
   Vol 3: Plymouth to Poole
Suffolk Coast and Heath Walks
The Kennet and Avon Canal
The Lea Valley Walk
The Peddars Way and Norfolk Coast Path
The Pilgrims' Way
Walking Hampshire's Test Way
Walking in Essex
Walking in Kent
Walking in London
Walking in Norfolk
Walking in the Chilterns
Walking in the Cotswolds
Walking in the Isles of Scilly
Walking in the New Forest
Walking in the North Wessex Downs
Walking on Dartmoor
Walking on Guernsey
Walking on Jersey
Walking on the Isle of Wight
Walking the Dartmoor Way
Walking the Jurassic Coast
Walking the Sarsen Way
Walks in the South Downs National Park

ALPS CROSS-BORDER ROUTES

100 Hut Walks in the Alps
Alpine Ski Mountaineering Vol 1 — Western Alps
The Karnischer Hohenweg
The Tour of the Bernina
Trail Running — Chamonix and the Mont Blanc region
Trekking Chamonix to Zermatt
Trekking in the Alps
Trekking in the Silvretta and Ratikon Alps
Trekking Munich to Venice
Trekking the Tour du Mont Blanc
Tour du Mont Blanc Map Booklet
Walking in the Alps

FRANCE, BELGIUM, AND LUXEMBOURG

Camino de Santiago — Via Podiensis
Chamonix Mountain Adventures
Cycling London to Paris
Cycling the Canal de la Garonne
Cycling the Canal du Midi
Mont Blanc Walks
Mountain Adventures in the Maurienne
Short Treks on Corsica
The GR5 Trail
The GR5 Trail —
   Vosges and Jura
   Benelux and Lorraine
The Moselle Cycle Route
Trekking in the Vanoise
Trekking the Cathar Way
Trekking the GR10
Trekking the GR20 Corsica
Trekking the Robert Louis Stevenson Trail
Via Ferratas of the French Alps
Walking in Provence — East
Walking in Provence — West
Walking in the Auvergne
Walking in the Brianconnais
Walking in the Dordogne
Walking in the Haute Savoie: North
Walking in the Haute Savoie: South
Walking on Corsica
Walking the Brittany Coast Path
Walking in the Ardennes

PYRENEES AND FRANCE/SPAIN CROSS-BORDER ROUTES

Shorter Treks in the Pyrenees
The Pyrenean Haute Route
The Pyrenees
Trekking the Cami dels Bons Homes
Trekking the GR11 Trail
Walks and Climbs in the Pyrenees

SPAIN AND PORTUGAL

Camino de Santiago: Camino Frances
Coastal Walks in Andalucia
Costa Blanca Mountain Adventures
Cycling the Camino de Santiago
Mountain Walking in Mallorca
Mountain Walking in Southern Catalunya
Spain's Sendero Historico: The GR1
The Andalucian Coast to Coast Walk
The Camino del Norte and Camino Primitivo
The Camino Ingles and Ruta do Mar
The Mountains Around Nerja
The Mountains of Ronda and Grazalema
The Sierras of Extremadura
Trekking in Mallorca
Trekking in the Canary Islands
Trekking the GR7 in Andalucia
Walking and Trekking in the Sierra Nevada
Walking in Andalucia
Walking in Catalunya —
   Barcelona
   Girona Pyrenees
Walking in the Picos de Europa
Walking La Via de la Plata and Camino Sanabres
Walking on Gran Canaria
Walking on La Gomera and El Hierro

Walking on La Palma
Walking on Lanzarote and Fuerteventura
Walking on Tenerife
Walking on the Costa Blanca
Walking the Camino dos Faros
Portugal's Rota Vicentina
The Camino Portugues
Walking in Portugal
Walking in the Algarve
Walking on Madeira
Walking on the Azores

SWITZERLAND
Switzerland's Jura Crest Trail
The Swiss Alps
Tour of the Jungfrau Region
Trekking the Swiss Via Alpina
Walking in Arolla and Zinal
Walking in the Bernese Oberland — Jungfrau region
Walking in the Engadine — Switzerland
Walking in Ticino
Walking in Zermatt and Saas-Fee

GERMANY
Hiking and Cycling in the Black Forest
The Danube Cycleway Vol 1
The Rhine Cycle Route
The Westweg
Walking in the Bavarian Alps

POLAND, SLOVAKIA, ROMANIA, HUNGARY AND BULGARIA
The Danube Cycleway Vol 2
The High Tatras
The Mountains of Romania

SCANDINAVIA, ICELAND AND GREENLAND
Hiking in Norway —
  North
  South
Trekking the Kungsleden
Trekking in Greenland — The Arctic Circle Trail
Walking and Trekking in Iceland

SLOVENIA, CROATIA, SERBIA, MONTENEGRO AND ALBANIA
Hiking Slovenia's Juliana Trail
Mountain Biking in Slovenia
The Islands of Croatia
The Julian Alps of Slovenia
The Mountains of Montenegro
The Peaks of the Balkans Trail
The Peaks of the Balkans Trail
The Slovene Mountain Trail
Walking in Slovenia: The Karavanke
Walks and Treks in Croatia

ITALY
Alta Via
  1 — Trekking in the Dolomites
  2 — Trekking in the Dolomites

Day Walks in the Dolomites
Italy's Grande Traversata delle Alpi
Italy's Sibillini National Park
Ski Touring and Snowshoeing in the Dolomites
The Way of St Francis: Via di Francesco
Trekking Gran Paradiso: Alta Via 2
Trekking in the Apennines
Trekking the Giants' Trail: Alta Via 1 through the Italian Pennine Alps
Via Ferratas of the Italian Dolomites:
  Vol 1
  Vol 2
Walking in Abruzzo
Walking in Italy's Cinque Terre
Walking in Italy's Stelvio National Park
Walking in Sicily
Walking in the Aosta Valley
Walking in the Dolomites
Walking in Tuscany
Walking in Umbria
Walking Lake Como and Maggiore
Walking Lake Garda and Iseo
Walking on the Amalfi Coast
Walking the Via Francigena Pilgrim Route
  Part 1
  Part 2
  Part 3
  Part 4
Walks and Treks in the Maritime Alps

IRELAND
The Wild Atlantic Way and Western Ireland
Walking the Kerry Way
Walking the Wicklow Way

EUROPEAN CYCLING
Cycling the Route des Grandes Alpes
Cycling the Ruta Via de la Plata
The Elbe Cycle Route
The River Loire Cycle Route
The River Rhone Cycle Route

INTERNATIONAL CHALLENGES, COLLECTIONS AND ACTIVITIES
Europe's High Points
Pocket First Aid and Wilderness Medicine

AUSTRIA
Innsbruck Mountain Adventures
Trekking Austria's Adlerweg
Trekking in Austria's Hohe Tauern
Trekking in Austria's Stubai Alps
Trekking in Austria's Zillertal Alps
Walking in Austria
Walking in the Salzkammergut: the Austrian Lake District

MEDITERRANEAN
The High Mountains of Crete
Trekking in Greece
Walking and Trekking in Zagori
Walking and Trekking on Corfu

Walking on the Greek Islands — the Cyclades
Walking in Cyprus
Walking on Malta

HIMALAYA
8000 metres
Everest: A Trekker's Guide
Trekking in the Karakoram

NORTH AMERICA
Hiking and Cycling the California Missions Trail
Hiking the Pacific Crest Trail
The John Muir Trail

SOUTH AMERICA
Aconcagua and the Southern Andes
Hiking and Biking Peru's Inca Trails
Trekking in Torres del Paine

AFRICA
Climbing Toubkal
Kilimanjaro
Walking in the Drakensberg
Walks and Scrambles in the Moroccan Anti-Atlas

NEW ZEALANDAND AND AUSTRALIA
Hiking the Overland Track

CHINA, JAPAN AND ASIA
Annapurna
Hiking and Trekking in the Japan Alps and Mount Fuji
Hiking in Hong Kong
Japan's Kumano Kodo Pilgrimage
Japan's Kumano Kodo Pilgrimage
Trekking in Bhutan
Trekking in Ladakh
Trekking in Tajikistan
Trekking in the Himalaya

TECHNIQUES
Fastpacking
The Mountain Hut Book

MINI GUIDES
Alpine Flowers
Navigation

MOUNTAIN LITERATURE
A Walk in the Clouds
Abode of the Gods
Fifty Years of Adventure
The Pennine Way — the Path, the People, the Journey
Unjustifiable Risk?

For full information on all our guides, books and eBooks, visit our website:
www.cicerone.co.uk

CICERONE

Trust Cicerone to guide your next adventure, wherever it may be around the world...

Discover guides for hiking, mountain walking, backpacking, trekking, trail running, cycling and mountain biking, ski touring, climbing and scrambling in Britain, Europe and worldwide.

Connect with Cicerone online and find inspiration.

- buy books and ebooks
- articles, advice and trip reports
- GPX files and updates
- regular newsletter

cicerone.co.uk